D0585126

CURRENT PERSPECTIVES IN ORGANIZATION DEVELOPMENT

J. JENNINGS PARTIN
Editor

Zenith Radio Corporation

ADDISON-WESLEY PUBLISHING COMPANY
Reading, Massachusetts
Menlo Park, California • London • Don Mills, Ontario

74-08588

PREFACE

Anyone who writes on the topic of organization development (OD) should do so knowing that he will immediately have cause to evaluate his degree of self-esteem. There are valid opposing views for practically every point one might make on the subject. Through this dialectic, however, OD is emerging as a significant participant in organizational life.

The purpose of this book is to contribute to OD literature by reporting what is going on at the grass-roots level of OD. To date there exists an impressive array of literature by prominent authorities from the academic community and practitioners from predominantly high-technology companies. One might get the impression that very little of note is occurring elsewhere. This book is something of a personal journal describing OD as it is practiced in a number of organizational settings, many of them reporting for the first time.

The intended audience is not the experienced OD practitioner. It is rather those for whom organization development is relatively unknown. Our purpose is to provide the reader with a perspective about what OD is and to describe how it is done in a variety of organizational settings from both the public and the private sector of our society. Hopefully, it will enable the reader to grasp a better understanding of how OD is done in an organization similar to his own. This knowledge is potentially useful for himself as well as for the others he might wish to share it with.

We anticipate that many readers will find that there are already some OD-type activities going on within their organizations. This information may suggest how these activities might be better coordinated to achieve greater objectives by working in concert with one another with the facilitation of a change agent within the organization.

The authors speak for themselves only — not their organizations or the industries and tax-supported organizations they belong to. No attempt was made to represent every industry or public institution that has ongoing OD programs. The intent was rather to fill an existing void and hope that others would fill in additional gaps.

It is presently impossible to write a comprehensive book on OD. There are too many diverse viewpoints. Instead, the authors attempted to describe some typical programs they have been involved with and supply enough program designs to enable the reader to understand how the activities were conducted. In most

cases references were made to major sources that will provide in-depth information on the concept used. We hope that the information included is sufficient and
that enough interest can be aroused to encourage others to make their beginnings
in OD. It is our opinion that the degree of sophistication is not great enough to
prohibit anyone with effective interpersonal skills and a realistic sense of how
people work together in organizations from being an effective agent for change.
There are a number of existing programs to develop his skills as an OD practitioner
so that he, too, can join the ranks at the grass-roots level. This book is a report on
how some people just like him got started and how they accomplished their work.

Chicago, Illinois   J. J. P.
July 1973

CONTENTS

1 ORGANIZATION DEVELOPMENT: A PERSPECTIVE
J. Jennings Partin

Why Organization Development   3
Characteristics of Organization Development   5
Major Issues in Organization Development 15
Change Agent Skills and Knowledge 20

Appendix 1.1 Role Description for an OD Group 25

2 ORGANIZATION DEVELOPMENT IN AN ALUMINUM AND
CHEMICAL SETTING
Donald L. Koppes

Diagnosing and Setting the Contract 30
The Workshop 35
Results 42

Appendix 2.1 Team Building Workshop Design 44
Appendix 2.2 Analysis of Interventions in this Chapter 44

3 ORGANIZATION DEVELOPMENT IN A PHARMACEUTICAL SETTING
Stokes B. Carrigan

Introduction 48
What is OD? 48
The Beginning 49
The SK&F Management Course 50
The First Spark 51
OD in the Complex Organization 57
Management Course Alumni Meeting 58
The First Big Step 59
Pharmaceutical Sales Department 63
Our Demotion Intervention 65
Observations 66

4   ORGANIZATION DEVELOPMENT IN AN AIRLINE SETTING
Kent F. Wampler

The Presenting Problem — A Definition   70
Programs Take Shape   71
A Significant First Project   73
The Search for a Viable Intervention   75
The Transition Over a Five-Year Period   77
A Critique of the Five-Year Effort   79
Some Remarks about the Future of OD   81

Appendix 4.1 Managerial Learning Laboratory   82
Appendix 4.2 Job Enrichment   84
Appendix 4.3 Team Development   85

5   ORGANIZATION DEVELOPMENT IN AN AEROSPACE SETTING
Michael Hill

Program Development   100
Management Concepts and Skills   109
Concluding Remarks   110

Appendix 5.1   111
Appendix 5.2   112
Appendix 5.3   113

6   ORGANIZATION DEVELOPMENT IN A BANK SETTING
Theodore Scott

Introductory Comments   116
Part 1 — The Development of OD in Banks   117
Part 2 — Where Are We Today in OD?   118
Part 3 — Some Thoughts on the Future of OD   123

7   ORGANIZATION DEVELOPMENT IN AN INSURANCE SETTING
James C. Faltot

Getting Started   134
Appendix 7.1   144

8   ORGANIZATION DEVELOPMENT IN A UTILITY SETTING
Kathleen L. Wakefield

Establishing a Role   150
Case Study — Engineering Department   152
Case Study — Personnel Department   155

Appendix 8.1 162
Appendix 8.2 166
Appendix 8.3 168
Appendix 8.4 170
Appendix 8.5 172
Appendix 8.6 174

9   ORGANIZATION DEVELOPMENT IN A FEDERAL GOVERNMENT SETTING
John Farrell

Region 2 of the Bureau of Reclamation 180
Impact of Job Corps Program 181
Introduction to Organization Development 182
In-House Trainer Training Program 182
Team Building 184
Team Leader Training 185
Role of the Organization Development Specialist 185
Problems Which Arose as a Result of the OD Effort 186
Reflections on Organization Development in a Public Agency 190

10   ORGANIZATION DEVELOPMENT IN A STATE MENTAL HEALTH SETTING
Arthur M. Freedman

1 How Does the Internal OD Consultant Find Out What Is
  Going on in the (Mental Health) System? From Which Source(s)? 195
2 Who Is the OD Consultant's Client? 199
3 What Change Agent Intervention Styles Can an Internal OD
  Consultant in a (Mental Health) System Adopt and Use? 202
4 How Is a Consultant to Know Whether his Activities Have
  Been Effective? 205
Epilogue 209

11   ORGANIZATION DEVELOPMENT IN A CITY GOVERNMENT SETTING
Joel M. Cohen

Program Origins and Development 212
Appendix 11.1 216

12   ORGANIZATION DEVELOPMENT IN A PUBLIC SCHOOL SETTING
A. Walden Ends and David J. Mullen

Theoretical Underpinnings 226

Appendix 12.1 School Program Bonanza Game   239
Appendix 12.2 School Organizational Development Questionnaire   242

13 ORGANIZATION DEVELOPMENT IN A STUDENT ORGANIZATION SETTING
Henry I. Feir

Considerations for Viewing Students and Student Organizations   250
An OD Model for Student Organizations   253
Some Examples of Specific OD Efforts   256
Some Final Comments   264

Appendix 13.1 Introspection-Fantasy   265
Appendix 13.2 Adjective Construct   265
Appendix 13.3 Sharing and Feedback   266
Appendix 13.4 Structured Exercises   266
Appendix 13.5 Pyramid   267

14 ORGANIZATION DEVELOPMENT: SOME EMERGING PERSPECTIVES
J. Jennings Partin

Characteristics of the Preceding Cases   271

GENERAL OD BIBLIOGRAPHY   277

ORGANIZATION DEVELOPMENT:
A PERSPECTIVE

Organization Development:
A Perspective

J. JENNINGS PARTIN

The term organization development (OD) is being used increasingly but with different meanings for different people. It is necessary to define the term in order to discuss it meaningfully in practically every group. This is so because no single definition has caught hold in spite of the attempts made by the pioneers of the OD movement.

There are at least two schools of thought on what OD is and what it is not. One school, the System-Process school, sees OD as a process by which organizations can understand their relationships with their environment and can make intelligent decisions about what the organization should be in order to operate effectively in the light of what is known about the organization-environment interface. Proponents of this view perceive an organization as a system which can be identified, changed, and developed in ways that best achieve its goals and objectives. The best organization, therefore, is one that maintains optimal efficiency over time through developing a self-correcting, self-renewing system that effectively utilizes the resources of the organization to achieve its ends. It is an optimal integration of the needs and wants of organization members with the goals and objectives of the organization.

The second school, Program-Procedure, although not necessarily disagreeing with the first, tends to view OD as the effective implementation of policies, procedures, and programs expressed by the management of the organization. Typically, the personnel organization is the group within the organization that is responsible for these OD activities. Organization development is thus construed to mean anything that develops the organization. This would include recruitment, training, career development, management development, organization planning, compensation, and other personnel activities that contribute to the overall growth and enhancement of the organization.

J. Jennings Partin is Corporate Manager of Organization and Management Development for Zenith Radio Corporation, Chicago, Illinois. He previously held positions in training, management development, and organization development with RCA and the Indiana Department of Mental Health. He was also a public school teacher and an instructor in psychology for Indiana University. He holds a B.A. in Education from Arkansas Polytechnic College, a B.D. in Theology from the Southern Baptist Theological Seminary, and an M.A. and Ph.D. in Education from Indiana University.

The Program-Procedure school is the older in that it is derived from long-established functions performed by personnel organizations. The System-Process school has developed since insights from the behavioral sciences (primarily psychology and sociology) have been applied to management. The two are not necessarily incompatible but they are often found to be in conflict. This happens for a number of reasons. On the one hand, behavioral scientists are often unfamiliar with life inside the organization and the terms and concepts they use sound foreign to that setting. On the other hand, experienced personnel people often find it hard to translate behavioral science findings into appropriate meanings in a work setting.

Frequently, these two schools of thought, when brought together, find that they each can benefit from the insights of the other. This book is an attempt to show how these two schools of thought can be welded together into a pragmatic OD approach that gets results. The chapters that follow are, in effect, case histories of OD practitioners who have combined often esoteric, abstract OD theories with extensive experience within organizations. This is a grass-roots story of OD as it is practiced by people who live with the trappings and limitations of organizational traditions but have found ways to innovate and apply behavioral science insights for the improvement of the total organization.

It is the purpose of the book to ask basic questions such as — Why OD? How does it begin? Who should do it? How is it done? The purpose of this chapter is to provide some of the theoretical underpinnings of OD theory as it is often expressed. Hopefully, the novice to OD will be able to relate this to his experience and have a relevant perspective for understanding and evaluating the experiences each contributor describes. Each contributor explains how he views OD, how he became involved in the experience he reports, what he did, and what the results of it were. Our hope is that OD will be viewed as a viable approach for humanizing the organization and increasing its effectiveness, doing so with a sound theory base that successfully integrates behavioral science insights with the traditional wisdom of people who have learned a lot about people and organizations by having lived a long time in an organization.

WHY ORGANIZATION DEVELOPMENT

Organization development is now a rather popular term. The American Society for Training and Development (A.S.T.D.) has a special OD division *(Organization Dev. Div., P.O. Box 5307, Madison, Wisconsin, 53705)*. The National Training Laboratories (N.T.L.) has an OD network *(N.T.L. Institute for Applied Behavioral Science, P.O. Box 9155, Arlington, Virginia, 22209)*. Numerous organizations have personnel referred to as OD consultants, OD practitioners, and OD specialists. An even greater number of people in traditional training and development functions, personnel generalists, and specialists within personnel organizations are doing organization development. Many of them have traditional personnel responsibilities with some assigned responsibility for OD. Fewer people are full-time OD consultants.

There is an increasing number of people who have full-time OD jobs (defined in a variety of ways). Why the growth? It is in part the result of a gap not closed by management training and development programs, manpower planning programs, and the other standard personnel programs. It is caused also by a growing recognition that the behavioral sciences have a role to play in making modern management effective.

Typical personnel departments are responsible for such things as (1) recruiting and employment, (2) compensation and benefits, (3) training and development, (4) labor relations, (5) counseling and (6) employee safety and health. These are staff activities that involve personnel departments with every member of the organization. Contacts throughout the organization regarding these established programs have made it possible for some personnel generalists to get involved in other OD-type activities. Gaps have been identified which regular personnel programs have not concentrated on. This has made it possible for OD activities to become a legitimate part of personnel responsibilities.*

In general, existing OD programs within personnel departments are concerned with total organization effectiveness, however that might be defined. Typical personnel activities also contribute to organization effectiveness but they are often viewed as management control functions. They tend to maintain the system that management wants. An emerging role for OD focuses on concerns that traditional personnel programs deal with only in part. OD practitioners typically work with intact work groups (e.g., family groups) as well as selected members of various departments (e.g., cousin groups). Programs of this type look at such things as (1) task accomplishment (e.g., how the group functions as a group, decision-making patterns, how work is actually done), (2) interpersonal relations (e.g., how the group gets along, how members affect one another by their behavior, relationship between personal behavior and members doing their jobs), (3) intergroup relations (e.g., work flow across functional lines, impact of practices in one work unit on other units), and (4) total system performance (e.g., ascertaining the effectiveness of the total organization in accomplishing its goals, exploring methods of improvement, resolving system problems). The emerging role of the OD practitioner is one of filling some of the missing parts of the personnel function by dealing with process problems of groups at various levels of the organization.

The OD function has evolved differently in every organization that has one. Its practitioners have varying charters (if they even exist) and go about their work in their own unique ways. They commonly function to make explicit what has been implicit all along. They ask questions about what a group's goals are, help the group's members identify what they are doing, and determine whether any changes are warranted. This is a helping relationship which is in contrast to the controlling function most personnel departments are perceived to exercise. It is a broad-gauged human resource development function that helps individuals achieve their own goals as well as assisting the organization to better achieve its ends.

---

*See Appendix 1.1

CHARACTERISTICS OF ORGANIZATION DEVELOPMENT

Thus far OD has been described as gaining entry into organizations essentially via the back door. In many cases people became involved in OD projects accidentally. Increasingly, OD functions are being identified by an enlightened management that sees a legitimate role for someone in the organization to study its process. They recognize the validity of a body of behavioral science knowledge relevant to the daily activities of the organization. Although OD projects have often occurred because of some fortuitous circumstance (being the right person at the right place at the right time), there exists an increasingly scientific body of knowledge that can provide guidance on how to go about doing OD.

There are diverse opinions about the aims of OD as well as approaches to doing it. What follows is an attempt to generalize the characteristics of OD as it is commonly practiced today and to comment on the issues that are raised. The succeeding chapters then are illustrative of the varying ways OD is done in differing organizational settings from a variety of viewpoints.

1. The Target is the Total Organization.*

The total organization is the major unit of which the OD activity is a part. This could be the corporation, the operating division, or a local unit of a larger organization. The assumption is that the entire system should be considered, insofar as possible, when diagnosing any needs that would lead to change programs. The organization is a system or pattern of relationships. Changes in one part of the system directly or indirectly affect the constituent parts. Total system change programs can therefore obtain optimal collaboration, mutual reinforcement, synergism, and efficiency.

The OD literature often refers to cultural change within the organization. This denotes a thoroughgoing change that filters throughout every unit of the organization. It means that the attitudes and behaviors of the total group (culture or system) must be changed consistently throughout or else the prevailing forces will influence the initiated changes to return to the norm or status quo.

2. The Goal is Improved Organizational Effectiveness.

Organization effectiveness must be defined in every case. This proves to be a difficult job in most instances. There is a plethora of individual performance rating systems and productivity measures on goods and services produced but comparatively few assessment instruments that adequately measure organizational effectiveness. Typically, this involves looking at such things as (1) organization structure, (2) job design, (3) work climate, and (4) the decision-making, problem-solving patterns of the organization.

A study of the *organization structure* looks at such things as the functions performed, reporting relationships, and span of control. It necessitates a system-

---

*The Characteristics of OD outline were presented at the Philadelphia OD Network Meeting, November 23, 1970 by Peter Friederich, Miles Kumnick, Jennings Partin, John Robb, and Marvin Weisbord.

atic analysis of the performance and relationships of each member of the organization under study with every other member of the work unit. There are several approaches to doing this. An OD approach would require appropriate participation of each member of the organization in identifying the elements of the system and utilizing their inputs in deciding what the ideal structure should be. This is in contrast to the application of some *a priori* span of control principle that is used to make arbitrary decisions about what the structure ought to be. The optimal organization is one in which each member fills a role uniquely suited to him and integral to the work of the group.

A second area of investigation for possible organization improvement is the *design of the jobs* performed. This takes into account such things as responsibilities and authorities, distribution of work within the unit, and work flow. In recent years there has been an increasing interest in the feelings and attitudes of workers as these affect job performance. It is thought that what a person thinks about his job affects how he goes about his job (i.e., morale, productivity). Behavioral science findings have led to a concept of job enrichment which is a process of enhancing, enlarging, or redesigning jobs to obtain increased commitment and motivation to one's work.[1] This has been particularly effective at lower-level, entry-level jobs. More recently it has been applied to higher-level, management jobs. The results to date indicate that concern for the worker (i.e., taking into account his attitudes, feelings) has increased productivity as well as job satisfaction.

A third possible area for increased organizational effectiveness is the *work climate*. The structure of the organization and the design of the jobs performed exist in a cultural matrix. The kind of work climate that exists has an influence on the way in which the organization performs. OD theorists have data which suggest that openness, trust, and acceptance have positive influences on the way things are done. On the other hand, defensiveness, suspicion, and hostility often foster bizarre behavioral patterns that affect the work of an organization.

A careful study of communication within the organization (i.e., its patterns, openness/closedness, effectiveness in achieving objectives) often reveals symptoms that affect job performance. This is associated with interpersonal relationships between supervisors, subordinates, and peers. OD programs designed to improve communication can exercise a profound change on the perceptions people have regarding themselves and others. An OD program of this type would attempt to map out the realities of the work climate and help the group to identify and achieve realistic alternatives for the betterment of all concerned.

A fourth area of inquiry for possible improved organizational effectiveness is in the *patterns of decision making and problem solving*. Organizations often have habitual patterns or norms of making decisions and solving problems. OD theory posits the principle that problems and decisions can be best dealt with whenever all appropriate resources are brought to bear on the issue. Some problems can best be handled by experts or supervisors. Others can best be dealt with by employing the collective insights of all who share in the concern. The latter approach has the advantage not only of obtaining the best inputs of the group but of fostering the support of those who participate in the problem-solving and decision-making process. Behavioral science research suggests that enlightened management should make intelligent decisions about how to utilize its human resources in deciding, planning, and implementing so that it facilitates individual growth and development toward an employee's potential (as viewed by himself as well as the organization's plans for his future).

3. Strategies, Methodologies and Interventions are Based on the Behavioral Sciences and Other Socio-technical Disciplines.

OD as a theoretical body of knowledge has its roots in the psychological and sociological research that has been done regarding human behavior. From psychology it profited from the insights of personality theory, counseling theory, group dynamics (e.g., leadership, decision making, power, and influence), behavioral measurement, and experience-based learning concepts. From sociology it borrowed such concepts as norms, normative change, organizational culture, and social systems. The combination of these two disciplines (psychology dealing with the microsystem, sociology dealing with the macrosystem) and others (e.g., cultural anthropology, engineering concepts, computer models) contribute to an eclectic body of knowledge often called the behavioral sciences.

OD theory is the amalgamation of learnings from a variety of sources selected on the basis of their relevance to organizations. Still in its infancy as a science, OD suffers from the lack of agreement as to what it is, how it is done, what its objectives are. Untold meetings have been held and books written to (1) define OD, (2) propose a methodology for doing it, and (3) determine its objectives, goals and values. The intent of this book is not to better define or redefine OD but to say that there are enough knowns for the OD practitioner to proceed in his organization while continuing to pursue answers that may not yet exist to the elusive questions concerning OD.

An OD *strategy* is a long-term plan for implementing and maintaining the change program being considered. The strategy takes into account all of the relevant known data about the organization and applies it in a systematic sequence designed to achieve the objectives of the program and reinforce the behaviors as required to maintain the changes that have been initiated.

The *methodologies* employed are the set of techniques or systematic procedures employed that enable the participants to achieve their objectives under the guidance or with the assistance of the OD practitioner (i.e., change agent, consultant). These methods are largely utilized in group settings with the target group (i.e., client system). The appropriate method is usually one of the following (or a variation) selected on the basis of the needs or requirements determined by a preliminary diagnostic study of the situation:[2]*

1. Training or education: procedures involving direct teaching or experience-based learning. Such technologies as lectures, exercises, simulations, and T-groups are examples.

2. Process consultation: watching and aiding ongoing processes and coaching to improve them.[3]

---

*Reprinted with permission from R. Schmuck and M. Miles, *Organization Development in Schools*, Palo Alto, Cal., National Press, 1971.

3. Confrontation: bringing together units of the organization (persons, roles, or groups) which have previously been in poor communication; usually accompanied by supporting data.[4]

4. Data feedback: systematic collection of information, which is then reported back to the appropriate organizational units as a base for diagnosis, problem solving, and planning.[5]

5. Problem solving: meetings essentially focusing on problem identification, diagnosis, and solution intervention and implementation.[6]

6. Plan making: activity focused primarily on planning and goal setting to replot the organization's future.

7. OD task force establishment: setting up ad hoc problem-solving groups or internal teams of specialists to ensure that the organization solves problems and carries out plans continuously.[7]

8. Techno-structural activity: action which has as its prime focus the alteration of the organization's structure, work-flow, and means of accomplishing tasks.[8]

These methodologies when deliberately planned and implemented by a change agent are *interventions* into the system. An intervention is an ongoing entry into a relationship with the client group for the purpose of helping them help themselves. There are three basic requirements which should be met to the satisfaction of the change agent before any intervention is initiated.[9]

1. He must possess valid information about the client system.

2. The client system must maintain its ability to make free, informed choices regarding its activities throughout the process.

3. The client system must be committed to any decisions for changes made.

The strategies, methodologies, and interventions of the OD practitioner differentiate his role from the standard roles performed by others in the organization. That is not to say that line managers cannot act as change agents. It simply means that usually the OD person is the specialist in the organization who uses these tools daily in his work. He is an expert on group process and applies his skills in working with various groups throughout the organization to facilitate their growth and development. This is in contrast to traditional management consulting which usually leaves the client dependent on the consultant beyond the initial consultation. An OD approach tries to enable the client to acquire the skills of the OD consultant insofar as they are useful to the client.

4. Examines the Relationship of Management Practices, Individual Feelings, and Behavior in Relationship to Outcomes.

OD is concerned with the outcomes or end results of organizational processes. Its practitioners ask questions like: What are we really doing, what are our goals, where will we end up if we continue as we are? Those questions cannot be correctly answered without considering interrelationships within the system. Management exercises a degree of power and influence over the course and direction the organization is moving in. The feelings of the individuals comprising the organization also have a definite effect on how management decisions are implemented. The observable patterns of behavior throughout the organization are indexes of the relative health or sickness of the organization. All of these interacting factors can be observed and analyzed in order to determine the effectiveness of the total organization in accomplishing its goals.

The existing management philosophy and its resultant practices have a definite impact on the way an organization functions. Douglas McGregor dealt at length with two theories of management (Theory X, Theory Y) which have significant implications for how an organization is managed and the concommitant responses of organization members to the styles.[10]

Theory X, as he described it, emphasizes management control and direction of the organization's activities. It places prime responsibility on management to organize and direct the human, material, and financial resources of the organization toward its objectives. It assumes that people are passive and resistant to organization needs and must, therefore, be persuaded, rewarded, or punished as required. People according to this view, lack initiative, are self-centered, and resist change.

Theory Y, according to McGregor, takes a softer approach toward managing. Management is still responsible for directing the activities of the organization but it makes some different assumptions about how this is to be done. It sees people not necessarily as being passive and resistant to change except as they are conditioned this way by their experience in organizations. They have a capacity for growth that can be cultivated and utilized for their own good as well as for the organization's benefit. It is the organization's responsibility to establish the conditions whereby workers can achieve their own goals and direct their own efforts toward realizing their own objectives while they pursue organization objectives.

Rensis Likert, another management theorist, describes organizations in terms of systems of management behaviors. System 1 is an exploitive-authoritative approach. System 2 is authoritative with benevolence. System 3 views management as consulting subordinates on matters managers choose to solicit employees about. System 4 emphasizes participative management. According to these descriptions, most organizations would register on the authoritative end of the continuum with varying degrees of participation. Organizations would likely have representatives of all four systems working together.

There is a sharp contrast between Systems 1 or 2 and System 4. Management in systems 1 or 2 exerts considerable pressure to see that organization members conform to the prescribed behaviors required to accomplish organization objectives. System 4 managers, pursuing the same objectives, would encourage a supportive working climate that is intended to cultivate and activate internal motivational factors within subordinates. The effects of these contrasting styles of management on workers result in different attitudes and behaviors in the group. The authoritative systems characteristically have less group loyalty, feel pressured, are less motivated, and do not perform well in the long run. The participative system encourages and obtains high group loyalty, greater cooperation, higher motivation to produce, and maintains higher performance standards over time.

Impressive data have been gathered which indicate that management practices (whether they deny or affirm internal motivational factors) have an influence
on the attitudes, behavior, and performance of members of the organization.
McGregor, Likert, and a host of other theorists have provided OD practitioners
with a conceptual base for understanding organizations that, when utilized, provide
useful insights for setting targets for organization change programs. Even a simple
systems model (input-process-output), as described in much OD literature, gives
the practitioner a basis for analyzing an organization in such a way that the relationship between management practices, individual feelings, and behaviors can be
assessed and identified as a potential area for an OD project.

5. A Continuing, Long-term Effort.

Planned organization change is a complicated, lengthy process. The time required
varies with the nature of the proposed change, the size of the organization, and the
climate of the target group. Typically, change occurs more slowly the larger the
group and the more resistant its members are to dealing with threatening areas under
study. Smaller groups that are more open to new ideas can change more readily.
The time required can only be known after thorough diagnosis of the situation and
careful consideration of the strategy most likely to obtain the desired results.

There are a number of organizational change models that vary in their complexity. The best model is one that is appropriate to the situation and can be effectively utilized by the change agent. Most models owe their derivation to the
pioneering efforts of Kurt Lewin and those others who viewed change as occurring
in an environmental field of interacting elements.

A popular change model is the one expressed by Edgar Schein who described
the mechanism of change in terms unfreezing, changing, and refreezing.[12] It is a
process of influencing the forces at work in a given situation toward desired ends.

The Process of Influence and the Mechanisms
Underlying Each Stage[13] *

Stage 1. Unfreezing: Creating Motivation to change

Mechanisms:

  a) Lack of confirmation or disconfirmation

  b) Induction of guilt-anxiety

  c) Creation of psychological safety by reduction of threat or removal of barriers

Stage 2. Changing: Developing New Responses Based on New Information

Mechanisms:

  a) Cognitive redefinition through

  1) Identification: information from a single source

  2) Scanning: information from multiple sources

---

*Reprinted with permission from Bennis, Schein, Steele, and Berlew, eds., *Interpersonal Dyna-
mics* (Homewood, Ill., The Dorsey Press, 1964) p. 363.

Stage 3. Refreezing: Stabilizing and Integrating the Changes

Mechanisms:

a) Integrating new responses into personality
b) Integrating new responses into significant ongoing relationships through re-confirmation

This change model looks at the past, present, and future of the situation to be changed. It requires a close study of the organization's past history, antecedent factors that have a relationship to the present. It also necessitates a look at those forces that work to support or restrain the desired condition. The refreezing process includes all those activities that maintain the behaviors which indicate that the change has been accomplished.

One technique that has been used in conjunction with this change model is called force-field analysis.[14] In brief, the procedure is as follows:

1. Identify the problem you want to work on.
2. What are the driving and restraining forces that affect the problem? (list)
3. Identify the 2 or 3 most significant forces that drive or restrain the problem situation.
4. List possible action steps that would reduce the effect of the restraining forces and increase the power of the driving forces.
5. Review the feasibility of each proposed action step and decide which ones to implement.
6. Identify the resources (people, material, finances) available for carrying out each action step.
7. Develop a comprehensive action plan, sequence activities, assign responsibilities for implementation.
8. Implement as planned.
9. Evaluate.

This approach to change assumes that there are a variety of forces at work in every situation. Organization change occurs via a series of stages that are planned and implemented by the change agent.

One model that demonstrates the long term, continuing process of change that affects the power structure of an organization is described by Larry Greiner[15] (Fig. 1.1).

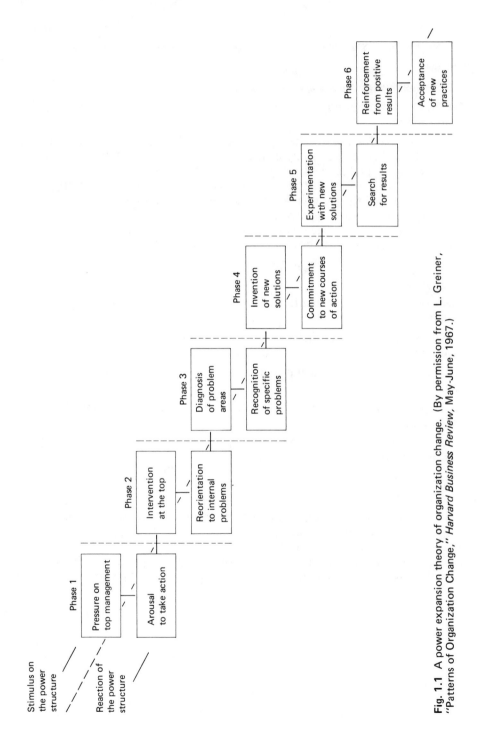

Fig. 1.1 A power expansion theory of organization change. (By permission from L. Greiner, "Patterns of Organization Change," *Harvard Business Review*, May-June, 1967.)

One can readily see that organization change programs involve a series of steps each associated with some kind of contact with the target group. The type of change anticipated, the size of the group, the amount of time available for the project and other constraints dissuade short-term change efforts. In general, OD projects involve months and years. Significant OD projects (aiming at behavioral changes) require two or three years of multiple interventions to maintain the changes initiated. Consequently, it requires the sustained attention of one or more people in the organization to make certain the changes, once implemented, continue to achieve the desired results.

6. Based on Explicit Human Values

Values are one of the most difficult problems that OD practitioners deal with. Every organization has its own values (as manifested in its behaviors), its members have theirs (often in conflict with those of the organization), and so does the OD practitioner. Every change effort should consider the values it is dealing with — those of the organization as a whole, the values of the management, those of the client group, and the values underlying the change program. Values determine our perceptions of reality as it exists as well as influence our perceptions of our objectives (organizational and individual).

The value changes that are evident in society in general are also visible in the varying organizations comprising that society. The OD literature, although not in uniform agreement, deals with the questions of values as these apply to change efforts. Richard Beckhard describes some values that probably would be endorsed by a great majority of OD practitioners.[16]

1. Man is and *should* be more independent/autonomous.

2. Man has and *should* have *choices* in his work and in his leisure.

3. Security needs should be met. Man should be striving to meet higher order needs for self worth and for realizing his own potential.

4. If man's individual needs are in conflict with organization requirements, the man then perhaps *should* choose to meet his own needs rather than submerge them in the organization requirements.

5. The organization should so organize work that tasks are meaningful and stimulating, and thus provide intrinsic rewards plus adequate extrinsic (money) rewards.

6. The power previously vested in bosses is and should be reduced. With choices in work and leisure, managers should manage by influence (appropriate behavior), rather than through force or the giving or withholding of financial rewards.

The matter of values is where most OD practitioners experience great personal stress. Standard personnel programs are intended to establish and maintain the views of the management. Traditionally, they allow for very little deviation from the prescribed policies and procedures of the organization. OD values tend to encourage openness and confront differences with a view toward resolving them in ways beneficial to individuals as well as the organization. If the OD practitioner always sides with the management view (if they are different), his efforts may be interpreted as another attempt to achieve conformity, this time using applied behavioral science to achieve it in ways more subtle than the enforcement of an unalterable rule.

Values then provide a continuing source of role conflict for the OD practitioner who attempts to live according to OD values (generally intended to humanize the organization, emphasizing openness, collaboration, and seeing value in constructive conflict) while being expected by management to use his influence to help the organization work harmoniously toward its objectives. This is especially difficult in Theory X, System 1 organizations that emphasize control of the organization and compromise only if forced to do so. The task then becomes one of raising the question of values at appropriate points so that client groups make known their choices on the matter rather than live with traditions that are no longer in the best interests of the organization (if its values are markedly different from those of its members). The OD practitioner is constantly faced with the problem of being a change agent for his client without compromising his integrity to the point that he sells himself to any group regardless of the demands made of him.

7. The Assigned Task of One or More Persons in the Organization

Organizations have a variety of ways for describing their functions and relationships (e.g., organization charts, job descriptions, mission statements, responsibilities and authorities). It is not necessary that an organization have a full-time OD practitioner designated and promulgated as such throughout the organization. In many cases, OD functions are performed on a part-time basis by personnel people or line managers. Every organization must decide what form is best for it according to the *talents* it possesses for doing OD, the *value* it places on it, and the *needs* it may have.

The best OD programs are not necessarily those which are run by a staff of OD specialists who work full-time on their projects. Much can be said for equipping line managers and others to do OD at every level of the organization as called for. There is an advantage, however, in having at least one person in the organization (at the location or in the functional division) who helps coordinate OD efforts so that concerns for the total system are considered in every change program. The whole support for OD could be undermined if there were no collaboration or consistency of approach to OD. Moreover, the results of such mishandling might contribute to general confusion rather than increased organizational effectiveness. The requirements of a total organization change program are such that those responsible for change projects at any level should consider the impact these will have on the entire system.

My experience suggests that every organization of a thousand people should have at least one person designated as the chief change agent or coordinator. Depending on the scope of the OD program, others could be trained and utilized or other full-time staff added to meet the organization's needs. A small cadre of trained OD practitioners (four to six) can function effectively in a large organization (with a potential client group numbering in the thousands) if they select strategic change programs and use members of the client organization to actually implement the change programs. If the program's effectiveness depends solely on the change agent's work, this is a sign that there has been inefficient use of the OD person's time, there is not enough ownership of the program, and that the program cannot be implemented adequately. His influence can increase greatly to the extent that he can involve the client group in implementing their own change programs while working with them closely enough to see that things go as planned.

Numerous OD programs got started because some person attended an NTL lab, read something on the subject, or otherwise began performing his job with an OD perspective (according to its values and concepts). Today change agents, working according to OD theory, can be found in practically every organization function. As OD becomes recognized as a legitimate function, it is best done explicitly as the assigned responsibility of someone in the organization. That is not to say that an OD program exists only if it is done by someone who calls himself an OD practitioner and his work OD. Many organizations have little regard for the behavioral sciences (often for good reason) and for them any label signifying OD would kill the effort from the start. This is another factor to consider in evaluating the readiness of an organization for doing OD. Hopefully, the results of OD programs and the development of more valid theory will enable OD practitioners to operate more openly because organizations will value their services and OD values as being essential to the well-being of the organization.

Summary

Thus far we have dealt with why OD evolved, its concern for organization effectiveness, and a general classification of the characteristics of OD programs. It is simply one perspective of how OD occurs in organization and how OD programs can be identified, if not specifically labeled as such. Many programs and individual efforts strive toward OD objectives without possessing every characteristic of OD programs that were described. However, these characteristics are useful in identifying those efforts within an organization and the persons responsible for them who constitute a potential OD team.

Every organization is changing. Every organization has someone or some group that plans for change (however inadequately). These characteristics of OD are useful for analyzing what change efforts are now under way and who is responsible for them. Once identified, the various programs and change agents could be coordinated in such a way that an embryonic OD program can be cultivated and managed to accomplish greater objectives than can individual programs working in isolation, without knowledge or concern for the others.

MAJOR ISSUES IN ORGANIZATION DEVELOPMENT

There are still many issues about which OD theorists and practitioners have not reached agreement. OD has its roots in diverse disciplines and has evolved differently in many organizational contexts. As in any movement of this type there are schools of thought and cults that speak a common language but have difficulty communicating with those having differing perceptions. There is no end to these variances although there is an increasing consensus among the different groups. The following is a list of major issues that are debated in the literature and are subjects discussed at professional meetings.

1. Where Do You Begin OD?

It was once the predominant view that OD should begin at the top of an organization and filter down to lower levels. An OD consultant (whether internal or external) would try to gain entry with top management because that is where the greatest power and influence for change resided. If the goal were to be total systems change, what better place to begin than at the top? This approach led many organizations to conduct diagnostic studies with top management, even to take them as a group to some off-site meetings, and attempt to accomplish the anticipated changes in the top management team. The next stage was to work with the next level of management and so on down through the organization.

This approach (no matter how attractive from a theoretical viewpoint) has not always worked. It is difficult to maintain the effort over an extensive period of time because of many restraining forces. There are many instances where programs thus conceived did not receive continuing support from the top, unanticipated demands on the organization made the programs obsolete, or changes in top management personnel made it impossible to continue.

A more pragmatic view is one in which proponents say that OD should begin wherever there is a need and an opportunity. This is especially attractive when (at the early stages of an OD program) there is a need for clients. It gives the OD practitioner visibility in the organization and, if he is successful, opportunities to work with other client groups, perhaps in more strategic positions. Where this approach has been successfully followed, there invariably has come a time when the OD person has had to make judgments about the use of his time and a more systematic program has evolved according to priorities.

It is simply impractical for most OD practitioners to refuse involvement with anyone who is not a member of top management. Typically, other good opportunities occur as spin-offs from admittedly low-priority, low-payoff projects. On the other hand, it will eventually be frustrating to the more pragmatic practitioner (who takes clients as he can at lower organization levels) to find that his programs are adversely affected by the prevailing powers emanating from the top of the organization. An astute OD change agent will consider the long-range effects of his efforts every time he is approached by or approaches a potential client. Some of the best OD projects do have top management support but there have been cases where the tail has wagged the dog. The task is to get to know the organization well enough so that every OD undertaking fits into a master plan that will eventually permeate the organization with the enlightened support it requires.

2. Who is Responsible for Initiating Change?

This issue is a matter clarifying the role of the client group and that of the change agent. Ideally, the client group should be able to diagnose its own problems and solve them. Some organizations realize they have problems but either (1) don't know how to solve them or (2) go about solving them in inappropriate ways. There is an advantage to having an outsider assist the group in problem identification, problem solving, and implementing action plans. This becomes unhealthy if it fosters a dependency on the outside facilitator that prohibits the organization from taking appropriate action as quickly as it recognizes a need. An effective OD consultant will help clarify both his role and his client's from the start. It is usually best that the client organization view the change program as belonging to them, as being their responsibility to implement, and as being something that they control throughout. The consultant helps them help themselves but does so in a developmental way designed to increase their ability to function independently of his interventions. A mature change agent will profit in the long run by enabling his clients to get credit for the things they do. The results of his efforts will speak for themselves as he gains credibility in the organization.

3. Who is the Client?

On the surface, this seems to be an easy question to answer. However, numerous OD projects have failed or faltered because this was not clear. Is it the manager of the client group or the group itself? If it is only the manager of the group, the task is to obtain the commitment of the target group to the program. If the entire group is the client and the manager is functioning as another member of the group, the group may be more committed but this may pose problems for the manager if the group wants to go in directions that he doesn't support. Will he then pull rank on them or is he, too, open to change? If the total group is the client or a representative team is acting for the rest there are varying implications in gathering data, defining the problem, and taking action to resolve the problems as identified.

4. How Do You Know What Changes are Needed?

The term "data-based intervention" is frequently used to describe OD activities which follow a diagnostic study to determine the nature and extent of the problem under consideration. Rarely are "felt" needs those which, after a careful examination, are the ones that are dealt with first. What is usually felt are symptoms of larger problems of significance to the system. Diagnostic studies no matter how sophisticated make assumptions and have biases that affect the definition of the problem. However, an effective analysis of the problem is usually more valid and can be defended easier than acting on hunches or feelings alone.

The task is to come up with a definition of the problem that can be identified as accurately as possible, measured to the extent possible, and evaluated later to ascertain the effects the OD program had on the extent of the problem. How this is done has an effect on what problems are identified, how support is obtained from the client group, and what approaches are valid for accomplishing the desired change.

5. How Does Change Occur?

Numerous debates have been held and continue as to whether individuals change or groups change. Both types occur. The particular methodology employed may be directed primarily toward one type rather than another. Training and education interventions are usually directed toward individual change. Classroom-type learning is generally directed toward changing individual perceptions or individual skills which are to be employed to accomplish organizational objectives. Team-building, process consultation, task forces, and other group activities typically have greater impact on organizational behavioral changes.

At this point behavioral scientists are not in agreement as to which has the greater payoff for long-term change objectives. OD is concerned with individuals and groups. Change occurs in both. It is not necessary to have a position either way. It is helpful to have a conceptual model that helps the practitioner understand what he is doing and to be able to communicate it to others. However, like so many other aspects of OD, if one had to wait for definitive answers before acting, many of the accomplished results OD has to its credit never would have happened. The practitioner therefore should be as well versed as possible in learning theory as it applies to individuals and groups and he should learn how to apply it wherever it has relevance to situational requirements.

6. What Approaches Should Be Used?

In the early days of OD a lot of people felt that sensitivity training was the best way to change an organization. More recently, that view has come under serious fire because it did not accomplish its claims. The technique is not invalid under all circumstances but other methods have dealt with the same issues without some of the risks involved.

Today the buzz word is team-building. This term is used in so many different ways that it usually has to be defined whenever used. However defined, the current emphasis is on working with teams or groups. This bias toward group work has led many in the OD community to have aversions toward anything that smacks of atomistic, isolated change methodologies (i.e., training, education). To these adherents "training" is a bad word because it is typically directed toward unintegrated slices of the organization. Groups are the thing!

The answer is not in having a position in favor of one method or another. Any number of interventions can work even in the same situation. The objective is to use a variety of approaches (as appropriate) and use whichever one seems to be most helpful at any point in time. At present there is no one best way to intervene in any situation. Unfortunately, it is possible to attend numerous "professional" meetings and get the idea that the frontrunners in OD are doing one particular thing so that must be the best way to do OD. Very often, however, OD practitioners have personal reasons for choosing one approach over another and have a tendency to use their choice simply because they favor it. The most effective OD practitioner is apt to be one who possesses a variety of skills in working with individuals and groups and uses whichever one (or combination) is suited to the unique situation he is dealing with at the moment. Whatever approach he uses should be within his area of competence, acceptable to the client group, and have sufficient conceptual validity to obtain the desired outcomes.

7. How Do You Measure the Effects of OD Projects?

Like many other areas of behavioral science, there is still much to be done here. There are currently many measuring instruments available on the market. To the novice, it might appear that these have the same amount of reliability and validity as other standardized instruments long used for psychological assessment. Many of them are indicative if perhaps not definitive. They are often used to measure somewhat global, gross indexes of change. However, they should not be used by someone unfamiliar with behavioral measurement who neither understands how the instruments were constructed nor can interpret the results accurately.

All of which is to say that it is still difficult, if not practically impossible, to accurately measure the effects of many OD programs. That is not to say that evaluation shouldn't be done or that the measured effects are invalid. It does mean that every OD practitioner must utilize his best skills in designing and implementing an evaluation of his programs.

The fact that so little now exists and that what does has such limited usage should not imply that nothing of value can be done. In many organizations simply to inquire what objectives are is the first step toward determining how any proposed project might be evaluated. Many organizations have highly sophisticated methods for assessing certain aspects of their performance but have very little knowledge of how to measure a group's effectiveness or even that of the total organization.

An effective evaluation program begins by getting the client group to agree on what the objectives of the project are. The next stage is to determine what constitutes valid data on the extent the objectives can be changed or modified. The next phase consists of determining how and when the data can be gathered. This may require that an instrument be designed especially for the project. If there are to be assessments taken before the change program and after it, the times must be decided on.

Evaluation of OD programs is still very far from attaining the accuracy of the physical sciences. Consequently, it would often undermine the future of an OD activity if it attempted to guarantee certain results. At present there are still too many uncontrolled variables and inadequate measuring devices to make any such claims. The task then becomes one of justifying the value of an OD program on the basis of identifiable results while pressing on toward more valid evaluation measures.

8. What is the Role of the OD Practitioner?

This is perhaps the most difficult question to answer of all the major issues in OD. The field itself suffers from a diversity of opinion as to its nature and purpose. This prohibits it from being considered a discipline. Its role varies considerably from organization to organization. OD practitioners come from a wide variety of backgrounds. Individual differences in practitioners and the organizations they serve make it difficult to state what the OD function should be. The role established depends on the people involved and what the situation needs or allows.

It is perhaps easiest to talk about the skills the OD practitioner needs. If OD is essentially the application of the behavioral sciences to organizational needs, then it follows that an OD practitioner needs to be thoroughly grounded in the behavioral sciences. N.T.L., perhaps the greatest single contributor to the development of OD as a legitimate organizational function, has suggested in its literature that a change agent needs the following skills: [17]

CHANGE AGENT SKILLS AND KNOWLEDGE*

Skill Area 1

Assessment by the change agent of his personal motivations and his relationship to the "changee."

Some skills and understandings needed for this aspect of change follow.

Understanding his own motivation in seeing a need for this change and wanting to bring about a change

Understanding and working in terms of a philosophy and ethics of change

Predicting the relation of one possible change to other possible changes or to those that might come later

Determining the possible units of change:
  What seems to be needed
  What is possible to him (or them)

Determining the size, character, structural makeup of group of changees

Determining the barriers, the resistance, the degree of readiness to change

Determining the resources available for overcoming barriers and resistance

Knowing how to determine his own strategic role in the light of the situation and his abilities.

Skill Area 2

Helping changees become aware of the need for change and for the diagnostic process.

Some skills and understandings needed for this aspect of change follow.

Determining the level of sensitivity the changees have to the need for change

Determining the methods which changees believe should be used in change

Creating awareness of the need for considering change and diagnosis through shock, permissiveness, demonstration, research, guilt, "bandwagon," and so on

---

*By permission from the *Reading Book,* 1972 edition, of the NTL Institute for Applied Behavioral Science, associated with the National Education Association.

Raising the level of aspiration of the changee and making aspirations realistic

Creating a perception of the potentialities for change expectations

Creating expectations to use a step-wise plan and to have patience in its use

Creating perception of possible sources of help in this change

Creating a feeling of responsibility to engage in this change by active participation

Skill Area 3

Diagnosis by changer and changee in collaboration concerning the situation, behavior, understanding, feeling, or performance to be modified.

Some skills and understandings needed for this aspect of change follow.

Making catharsis possible and acceptable when indicated as a starting point

Skill in use of diagnostic instruments appropriate to the problem: surveys, maps, score cards, observation, and others

Diagnosis in terms of causes rather than "goods" or "bads"

Skill in helping changees to examine own motivations

Examination of the relation of one change to other changes possible in that situation and helping changees to understand these relationships

Clarifying interrelationship or roles between changer and changee

Skill in dealing wisely with changee's ideology, myths, traditions, values.

Skill Area 4

Deciding upon the problem; involving others in this decision; planning and implementing action.

Some skills and understandings needed for this aspect of change follow.

Techniques in arriving at a group decision

Examining the consequences of certain possible decisions

Making a step-wise plan

Doing anticipatory practice in carrying out a plan

Providing for replanning and assessment at later stages

Providing administrative organization

Eliciting and eliminating alternatives.

Skill Area 5

Carrying out the plan successfully and productively.

Some skills and understandings needed for this aspect of change follow.

Building and maintaining the morale of the changees as they try the change

Deciding upon the amount of action to be made before pausing for an assessment of process and progress being used

Understanding the effects of stress on changee's beliefs and behavior

Defining objectives in a manner that leads to easy definition of methods

Creating a perception of the need for relating methods to the goal in mind.

Skill Area 6

Evaluation and assessment of changee's progress, methods of working, and human relations.

Some skills and understandings needed for this aspect of change follow.

Diagnosis of causes when group action becomes inefficient, through the use of measuring instruments, interviews, interaction awareness panel

Use of score cards, rating scales, and other measures.

Skill Area 7

Insuring continuity, spread, maintenance, and transfer.

Some skills and understandings needed for this aspect of change follow.

Creating perception of responsibility for participation in many persons

Developing indicated degree of general support for change

Developing appreciation by others of work of participants who need support.

In short, the OD practitioner needs to be knowledgeable of people (individual behavior) and organizations (organizational behavior). How he applies this knowledge is a function of his skill and his role in the organization. The problems of establishing a role vary depending on whether it is a new role for a person previously performing a traditional role (e.g., a personnel generalist performing one of the traditional functions) or if the person and the role are new to the organization (e.g., a person hired from outside the organization to perform the role, with OD credentials). In the first case, there is a tendency to discredit the person because of the "prophet-without-honor-in-his-own-country" syndrome. In the second case, he may be viewed with suspicion because (1) he is a newcomer to the organization and (2) fear that he is some kind of "shrink."

In either event, he must establish his credibility in the organization. This can be done in a variety of ways. In general, the first attempt should be a low-risk venture with a high probability of success. To the extent possible, the project should be one that will give visibility to the OD practitioner. In a new OD activity the problem of getting clients is a serious one. It usually involves some "selling" of oneself and OD concepts. This is preceded by an analysis by the would-be OD practitioner of existing problems in which he feels he could be a help. The next step is gaining entry into the client group to discuss the possibility of his participation in a matter that "hurts" the client group enough that the members want to do something about it. In selecting potential clients, it is of strategic importance to select an individual or group with influence in the organization. A success here usually brings other clients to the OD person's door for similar help. Once having established a sufficient amount of credibility, one can begin thinking of a long-term change effort involving the total organization or a substantial part of it. More often than not, the role of OD is established after a number of small but significant successes that give the OD practitioner a hearing with strategic groups in the organization.

This is often speeded up by the inauguration of a large scale program involving outside OD consultants with sufficient credentials to lend prestige to the program as well as the OD function. The selection of outside consultants should be done carefully to ensure that (1) there is a compatibility between the internal and the external consultant, (2) the skills of the outside person are appropriate to the needs of the organization, and (3) that the outside consultant doesn't "feather his own nest" at the expense of the internal consultant and the organization. Ethical outside consultants recognize their responsibilities both to the internal consultant and to provide the services as requested without fostering an unhealthy dependence on them for the purpose of gaining future business.

Basic to the establishment of any OD function is the perception the organization has of the OD practitioner as a person. One's personal characteristics and skills can vary greatly but one must be able to be perceived as being helpful (i.e., have appropriate OD skills and convey a genuine interest in helping the client). If one is perceived as being an advocate of unpopular ideas, one may never get opportunities to work with many clients. In the early stages it is perhaps best to maintain a low profile. As one's power base increases greater risks can be taken. It remains for the OD practitioner to know his own values as well as those of the organization he serves. If there is a conflict, these must be negotiated. If not, there are at least two options. He can quit or he will be asked to leave. Both happen frequently.

The nature of OD work is such that persons with a good deal of self-confidence (if not misplaced) can function effectively in many different settings. It is often a lonely job that requires a person to find intrinsic satisfaction in working with people. Success is often long in coming because of the nature of the work itself. Establishing an OD role is still an art not a science. Perhaps it will always be that way. This issue, like all the others in OD, if it is to be resolved, is more dependent on the person's acting as he judges necessary rather than relying on a supporting body of knowledge that makes all things clear.

Summary and Conclusions

The evolution of OD has not been a series of cumulative successes culminating in a refined discipline. Its origins were somewhat diffuse contributing to a diversity of practices in organizations where it existed. That is not to say that it isn't becoming more systematic and developing greater agreement among its practitioners. In keeping with OD theory, conflict and differences can be healthy and constructive.

Some generalizations can be made, however.

1. OD is grounded in the behavioral sciences.
2. It is typically found in personnel functions.
3. OD practitioners come from diverse backgrounds.
4. It is possible to identify OD activities according to a system of classification that indicates change programs (actual and potential).
5. The role of OD and its practitioners will vary depending on the person and the organization.
6. Although there are still many unknowns and unresolved issues, there is sufficient knowledge to conduct OD activities with confidence in the theoretical concepts and the value of the results.

The growth in the number of practitioners and the increase in OD literature are manifestations of its increased popularity. There are charges (many of them valid) that OD is a fad and will soon pass. However, I think this is more a reference to the individual practitioner and his effectiveness in helping the organization than an evaluation of the validity of OD concepts. In cases where organizations discontinued OD functions (often for avowed budgetary reasons), I think a careful investigation of what the OD activity was doing for or to the organization is warranted. The human needs of organizations (whether they be in management or among rank and file members) are such that there is sufficient work to be done that is meaningful to individuals and organizations. Standard people-oriented programs do not meet all of these needs. The following chapters are examples of how OD can be done in such a way that its worth is recognized by the organization and provides convincing evidence that it is not merely a fad. OD is here to stay but it must continually earn its right for recognition alongside traditional organizational functions which also had to compete for berths as legitimate contributors toward organization objectives.

APPENDIX 1.1 ROLE DESCRIPTION FOR AN OD GROUP

Organization Planning and Systems Development

1. Charter – To help develop a fully functioning organization whose goals and objectives are achieved through optimal use of its human and material resources.

Organization planning and systems development are primarily the responsibility of operating management. The role of the organization and systems group is to provide technical assistance to management for achieving its goals and objectives. This group serves as an internal consultant to line management on a variety of issues regarding (1) organization structuring, (2) management system design, (3) performance evaluation, and (4) problems that often involve interfacing groups.

2. Goals

1. To develop a fully functioning organization that optimizes its human and material resources in accomplishing its specific goals and objectives.

2. To develop a work climate built on openness, trust, and respect for individual members.

3. To develop a proactive organization that anticipates problems (where possible) before they occur and plans for them as soon as it is realistically possible to do so.

4. To affix appropriate authorities and responsibilities for organization members and facilitate the development of a work climate that encourages individual initiative and personal fulfillment.

5. To create, develop, and maintain effective management systems that are designed to facilitate optimal organization performance.

3. Responsibilities and Authorities

1. Assist management in diagnosing organization or system problems and implementing plans to overcome them.

2. Conducting studies to ascertain optimal organization structure or management system design.

3. Develop and implement plans for initiating and maintaining organization or management system changes.

4. At management's direction, assess the effectiveness of designated corporate-wide or divisional programs with respect to their stated goals and objectives.

5. Identify and develop plans for increasing management effectiveness and improving work relationships.

6. Participate in the design or re-design of organizations or management systems.

7. Coordinate the implementation of newly established functions.

4. *Approach*

A. *To provide* an internal consulting resource to management.
    1. To identify barriers to effective organization performance.
    2. To analyze conditions which impact the organization and affect its performance.
    3. To propose action plans which can resolve organization problems through effective problem-solving and decision-making.
    4. To assist management in designing and implementing plans to resolve problems.

B. *To assist* client organizations in
    1. Identifying and clarifying goals and objectives.
    2. Identifying barriers to achieving goals and objectives.
    3. Analyzing possible causes of continuing organizational problems.
    4. Developing effective problem-solving mechanisms.
    5. Designing and implementing plans to overcome problems identified.

5. *Typical Activities*

A. *Organization*
    −analyzing functions (who does what)
    −organization structuring
    −identifying authorities and responsibilities
    −job design and redesign

B. *Systems*
    −mapping out the present system
    −identifying dysfunctions caused by duplication, omissions, inefficiencies
    −planning for attaining system improvement

C. *Planning*
    −identifying short-term and long-term goals and objectives
    −anticipating problems
    −developing plans to maximize organizational effectiveness
    −improving communication, feedback
    −enhancing problem-solving capabilities at lowest possible level

D. *Applied Research*
    −analyzing policies, procedures and practices of the client organization
    −assessing organization effectiveness as it relates to its external environment, interfacing organizations, members' perceptions
    −identifying or clarifying goals and objectives
    −developing standards of performance

—examining management practices
   -hiring
   -promotion
   -grievance handling
   -etc.
—evaluate ongoing programs
   -operating plans
   -manpower plans
      -succession planning
      -minority programs
      -high-potential programs
      -professional development

6. Procedures

1. Ascertain the objectives of the project to be undertaken with the client.

2. Gather data that clarify the extent of the problems that relate to the project objectives.

3. Present preliminary findings to the client for further clarification and/or direction.

4. Propose a specific plan of action that will
   —clearly identify the problem
   —identify a feasible problem-solving model
   —implement proposed solutions
   —evaluate outcomes

5. Conclude the project when satisfactory results have been achieved.

7. Specific Competencies

1. Problem-identification
   —intrapersonal
   —interpersonal
   —interorganizational

2. Data-gathering
   —from surveys
   —from interviews
   —from existing historical data
   —etc.

3. Data-feedback
   —clarification of felt problems
   —climate analysis
   —management systems performance

4. Design problem-solving models
   —appropriate to the situation
   —collaborative
   —participative (as appropriate)

5. Develop action plans
   —specific to the task
   —supported by the client
   —within target dates
6. Evaluate outcomes
   —consultant's actions
   —effectiveness of the project's design
   —establish criteria for evaluating effectiveness of action plans

FOOTNOTES

1. Ford, Robert N., *Motivation Through the Work Itself*, New York, American Management Assoc., 1969.

2. Schmuck, Richard A., and Matthew B. Miles, *Organization Development in Schools*, Palo Alto, Cal., National Press, 1971.

3. Schein, Edgar H., *Process Consultation: Its Role in Organization Development*, Reading, Mass., Addison-Wesley, 1969.

4. Beckhard, Richard, "The Confrontation Meeting," *Harvard Business Review*, March-April, 1967.

5. Burke, W. Warner, and Harvey A. Hornstein, *The Social Technology of Organization Development*, Fairfax, Va., NTL Learning Resources Corporation, Inc., 1972.

6. Davis, Sheldon A., "An Organic Problem-Solving Method of Organizational Change," *Journal of Applied Behavioral Science*, Vol. 3, No. 1, 1967.

7. Luke, Robert A. Jr., *Temporary Task Forces: A Humanistic Problem-Solving Structure*, unpublished manuscript presented at NTL New Technology in OD Conference, New York, 1971.

8. Burke and Hornstein, *op. cit.*

9. Argyris, Chris, *Intervention Theory and Method: A Behavioral Science View*, Reading, Mass.: Addison-Wesley, 1970.

10. McGregor, Douglas M., *The Human Side of Enterprise*, New York, McGraw-Hill, 1961.

11. Likert, Rensis, *The Human Organization: Its Management and Value*, New York, McGraw-Hill, 1967.

12. Bennis, Warren G., Kenneth D. Benne, and Robert Chin (eds.), "The Mechanism of Change," in Edgar H. Schein *The Planning of Change*, New York, Holt, Rinehart, and Winston, 1969.

13. Ibid., p. 98

14. *A Problem-Solving Program for Defining a Problem and Planning Action*, Washington, D.C., NTL Institute for Applied Behavioral Science, 1969.

15. Dalton, Gene, Paul Lawrence, and Lawrence Greiner, *Organizational Change and Development*, Homewood, Ill., Irwin-Dorsey, 1970.

16. Beckhard, Richard. *op. cit.*

17. This material is taken from the *Reading Book*, 1972 edition, of the NTL Institute of Applied Behavioral Science, associated with the National Education Association.

ORGANIZATION DEVELOPMENT
IN AN ALUMINUM AND CHEMICAL SETTING

What happens when a company acquires a new facility? One of the first things is that there are problems in developing the new management team and integrating its members into the style of management practiced by the acquiring company. The following case is a team-building effort in which the OD consultant assisted the group in problem identification, problem solving, and action planning.

The consultant worked with the plant manager and his immediate subordinates in an off-site meeting that focused on group data gathered from interviews with each member of the team. The trainer used a variety of interventions — process, theory inputs (e.g., Johari Window), and exercises (e.g., fishbowl, NASA game). The results of this experience indicate that there is now increased collaboration, improved interpersonal relationships, and definite plans to improve the work climate of the organization.

Organization Development in an Aluminum and Chemical Setting

DONALD L. KOPPES

One of the potential interventions in organization change and development which we have found to be effective in initiating a change effort is "team building". (Fig. 2.1) We define this term rather broadly and use it as a means to bring about change in both interpersonal and group processes and as a means to provide managerial training in such areas as problem solving, decision making, priority identification and action planning.

My purpose in this chapter is to provide the reader with a case study of a team building session as it occurred in one of Kaiser's manufacturing facilities and for which I was the trainer.

DIAGNOSING AND SETTING THE CONTRACT

I was invited to visit the facility by the plant manager who was interested in getting some help in seeing how he could increase the effectiveness and productivity of his organization. He had done quite a bit of reading on organization development and had also heard of some of the work we had done in other Kaiser plants. Although he had previous experience as a plant manager he was new to this assignment and saw it as perhaps being an opportune time to begin an organization development effort.

We agreed that during my visit I would collect information about the organization both from him and by interviewing each of his subordinates. When this was finished he and I would get back together and mutually attempt to "diagnose" the organization and determine what direction he should follow. At that time we would determine what, if any, contract we should work out between us.

From my discussions with the manager the following evolved: The plant was purchased from another company about two years ago. Since the beginning of ownership of the plant the management had been plagued with technological problems in running the operations. This seems to be fairly under control now,

Donald L. Koppes is Corporate Manager of Employee Relations for Kaiser Aluminum and Chemical Corporation, Oakland, California. He previously held management positions in Industrial and Labor Relations with Kaiser and U.S. Steel. He holds a B.A. degree in Economics from Bucknell University.

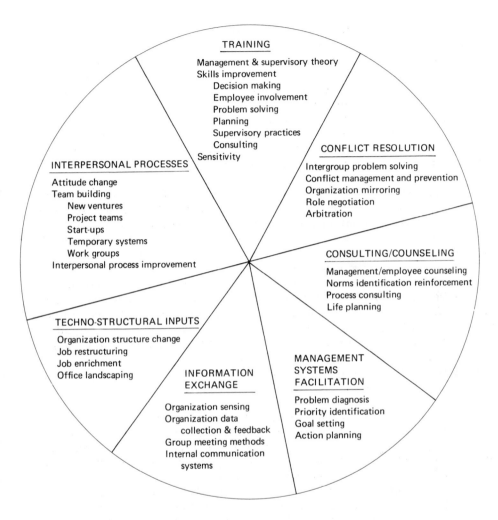

Fig. 2.1 Potential Interventions in Organization Change and Development

but the capital investment required to straighten these problems out considerably exceeded the original forecast.

The current manager was the third man to supervise the operation since Kaiser's purchase of the facility and his style of management was perceived as being considerably different from his predecessors. In addition, he had no previous experience in this particular manufacturing process, a fact that seemed to cause some uneasiness among his subordinates.

His predecessor, who had managed the facility for the majority of the two-year period, had a management style which was fairly authoritarian. He was used

to getting very much involved in all phases of the operation and personally directing many phases of the work. He generally made most of the decisions and instituted corrective action as he saw fit. He freely told people what to do and
how to do it. During the start up and "shake down" phase of the operation and
having to work through and solve the many technological problems, this was
seen as the most effective management style.

By contrast the new manager's style leaned more towards a participative
type of management. He was anxious to have his subordinates assume responsibility and make their own decisions. At the same time he certainly planned to give
direction and hold people accountable for their actions.

He viewed his management group as young, aggressive and competent. He
saw them having some trouble adapting to his management style and generally not
really believing that the freedom they seemed to have was "for real." Also, since
they were not used to making many decisions on their own, they seemed to lack
some of the necessary skills in this area. He felt that he was not yet accepted by
the group and had not yet gained their full confidence. He saw several issues that
needed to be worked on before he and his other managers could realize their full
potential and increase the effectiveness of the organization. Among these were:
The need to build skills in the areas of problem solving and decision making? do
more and better long range planning? get people to look more at the organization
as a whole rather than just being concerned for the area of their specialty; find
ways to more effectively handle plant maintenance and reduce down time; improve
interpersonal skills; and manage competitiveness and improve collaboration. Additionally, he was anxious to establish and continuously reestablish the ground rules
of having "openness" and "leveling" in his meetings and discussions with his
people.

He also wanted to talk in some detail about one of his subordinates, the
plant superintendent, who troubled him. He and the superintendent — an extremely capable, bright young man — had difficulty relating to and accepting one
another. Some strong signals were coming through which started me thinking that
there might be quite a confrontation in the making.

We concluded the meeting and planned my next step which was to spend some
time with each of his subordinates. There were twelve men, and I planned to
spend about an hour with each of them and this was scheduled over the next two
days. The manager also asked if I would be interested in attending a staff meeting
that afternoon to see how they functioned as a group. I told him I would like very
much to sit in and feed back to him by observations.

I began each interview by explaining that my goals were three-fold. Primarily, I wanted to get acquainted with them and they with me. (There was a fairly
universally expressed feeling of apprehension prior to my visit about having to sit
down with me to have their "head shrunk!") Second was to see how they generally viewed the organization as to the manager's style, problems they faced, etc.,
and thirdly, what they thought of working together on doing some team building.

The group was quite diverse and actually took in three levels of supervision
(Fig. 2.2.). The men ranged in age from the mid-twenties to the late forties and

had a wide range of business and industrial experience. Most saw the new manager's style as very welcome but a little uncomfortable. Their discomfort stemmed largely from trying to find some new direction and in testing what their new parameters really were. Generally, however, they all seemed quite open and receptive to meeting together to do some constructive work.

The afternoon staff meeting provided me with some additional insights as to how the organization functioned and what some of the interpersonal issues might be. The basic objective of the meeting was to look at current operating problems and review the previous months' cost performance. The meeting was not very old before the manager and his plant superintendent got into it. Apparently, the manager had previously asked the superintendent to get some particular equipment installed and the deadline had not been met. It was clear that the superintendent had not agreed with the manager's decision and instruction to get the equipment installed, and he proceeded to offer several reasons why it hadn't been done. It was also clear that he had not openly expressed his disagreement at the time the instruction was given. I could sense considerable tenseness in the group as the dialogue between the two got stronger. Finally, the manager told the superintendent that in his opinion the work hadn't gotten done because the superintendent hadn't cared about getting it done and may not have even intended on doing it in the first place — and as far as he was concerned this was not acceptable. The superintendent did not respond and the meeting got on to other subjects.

After the meeting the manager discussed what had transpired between him and the superintendent. I asked him how effective he felt his "attacking" his superintendent was in a meeting such as that. He stated he had tried other ways without results. He felt that this way was effective and seemed to get results, yet he was still a long way from where he would like to be with this man. He further said that he had "gotten into it" with his superintendent like this on other matters within the last several days. I asked if he felt the superintendent viewed this as effective behavior and a way to get things straightened out between them. He felt that he did but that he had not actually checked out this assumption, and he agreed that he should do this.

I resumed my interviews the next day and continued to gather information which indicated that people felt a need for and were anxious to work on team-building issues. Expressed needs were to improve their working relationships with each other and with the plant manager; to improve their communication skills; to get into positions where they were controlling the operation rather than be controlled by it; etc. Then it became time to sit down with the superintendent. I was anxious to get his views, although my anticipation was that they would be quite negative.

We seemed to establish a good rapport fairly quickly and he talked quite openly. I soon learned that my assumptions about his being negative were wrong, but he did have a great concern for the way things were going — not well at all — and for his relationships with the manager. I said that I was concerned about the interaction between him and the manager in the staff meeting and asked him if he saw it as being effective. He said he felt it was not effective at all and that it had been

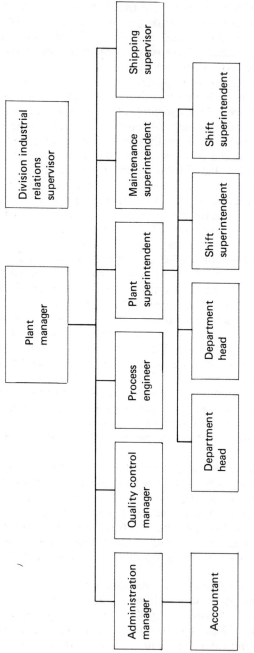

Figure 2.2

going on for several days. He also felt that this conflict was having quite a disruptive effect on other members of the group and that rather than function as a team, people were being forced to choose between opposing forces. He felt there was a strong need to develop a more cohesive and collaborative management effort and the sooner the better.

When I concluded the last interview I got back with the manager and we reviewed the information I had collected. I said that it was my perception that both he and his subordinates felt a strong need to begin a planned change effort directed toward accomplishing their goals and objectives. I said that holding an off-site team building session would be the most appropriate way to initiate his organization development work and I felt I could help him and the group accomplish their objectives. He agreed that this seemed to be the appropriate way to go.

We then talked about our "client-consultant" relationship. I explained that I felt it was essential that we view our relationship as that of peers and that we keep the communications and feed back channels between us completely open. I also stated that we should each maintain the freedom to cancel "the contract" if we weren't finding it productive or as meeting our objectives.

This was acceptable to the manager so we agreed to a mutually satisfactory time beginning the session on a Thursday evening and lasting through noon Sunday. One difficult question still concerned him: How to staff the plant to manage the operation while these key people were away? I suggested he give this problem to his staff and the responsibility for working it out. During the next two weeks all the arrangements were finalized.

THE WORKSHOP

I returned to the plant two days before the session was to begin in order to do some final planning and to meet with the group as a whole. The purpose of the meeting was to define my role as being there to help them accomplish whatever objectives they might set for themselves. I explained that I would be tuned in more to the way they were working on issues rather than the issues themselves. I stated the kind of issues that had come up from our earlier discussions and the things which could get worked on. I tried to stress that they must assume the ownership* of the meeting and its outcomes and that I felt an obligation to them to maximize the productiveness in any way I could.

I suggested that as homework they come prepared to verbalize their expectations about what they would work on during the session and what they would like to see as outcomes. I tried to get out any questions they might have had and they either had none, which I doubted, or chose not to ask them, which I suspected. I started feeling that people were wondering what they were getting into and I began to have my own anxieties about how well things would go.

Note: We view the matter of "ownership" as being critical to any organization development effort. The organization must feel a strong sense of responsibility for any change effort and must be internally committed to carrying it on. If it is viewed as a "program" which has been given to them by some external source, it will not survive — even if they initially think it is a good thing to do.

The facility which the manager had chosen provided an excellent setting for our workshop. It was about 150 miles from the plant — far enough for people to disassociate themselves from their plant and home life activities. The fourteen of us were all comfortably housed in the same building which had ample space for meetings. Dining and recreational facilities were within walking distance.

After dinner we began our first meeting.* I said that I thought a good place to start would be for each of us to share our expectations for what work would get done during the next few days and what were the desired outcomes. This could be a first step in setting our agenda.† To get things started, I began by sharing my own. I stated that I expected us to do a lot of work but that we would have fun doing it. I saw this as a rather unique opportunity in that it gave us an opportunity to really step back and look at how we work and find ways of increasing our effectiveness. I said that I expected to be looking at the "ground rules" or norms by which this group functioned and would try to get these verbalized. It was my hope that we would establish norms of openness, expressing feelings, giving and receiving feedback, testing assumptions, etc.

Next, the manager told the group what his expectations and desired outcomes were. This was the same list as he had expressed to me during our first meeting together. Next, a department head began talking about how he saw things now as compared to how they used to be. From there, the group began a general discussion about the business, current problems, etc. In other words, they talked about things they were comfortable talking about — but with no apparent concern for getting anything done. When someone began discussing a particular problem and then finished his statement as to what he thought the problem was, someone else would begin talking about some other problem in a different subject area.

After this had gone on for about thirty minutes, I intervened and asked the group to take a look at what they were doing and see if they could say what it was. After an instant's pause, they picked up where they had been stopped by my interruption. This went on for another fifteen minutes when I interrupted again by saying that I wanted to give them an observation of what I had been seeing going on for the last forty-five minutes. They listened to this politely for the two or three minutes that it took and again, picked up where they left off. They continued to talk about history — rehashing what had been done in a given situation — and often with differences of opinion. As time wore on, however, some of them began to question just what was being accomplished. I came in again and tried to bring them back to where the evening began. I also restated the importance of setting an agenda so that we could maximize the utilization of our time. I suggested that they break down into three small groups and in this manner, try to list on paper the problems they wanted to work on. I suggested they form in groups any way they wanted to as long as they were fairly equally divided in terms of numbers. They all agreed to go along with this suggestion.

My attention focused on how they went about picking their groups. The

---

*Appendix 2.1

†Appendix 2.2, Part 1, Operating Hints

first formed quickly and included the manager and the superintendent. The second was a little slower in forming and the third was made up of those not included in the first two — and apparently for no other reason. I felt it might generate some useful data if I could test out their feelings about the formation exercise.

The groups seemed to work quite well and at the end of an hour, felt they had accomplished their task. I asked them how much longer they wanted to work that night, and the consensus was that they were about ready to quit. I asked them to work about five more minutes because I wanted to test out how they felt about their group formation and how effectively they worked. I then asked them to answer the following questions by rating on a scale of from 1 to 10. The questions were:

1. Did you end up with the people you wanted most to be with — ranking from "not at all" to "completely."

2. How much did you initiate the formation of your group — ranking from "not at all" to "a great deal."

3. The degree to which your group worked effectively — ranking from "not effective" to "greatly effective."

4. The way in which the groups ended up being constructed resulted in the _____ composition — (rank from "poorest" to "best").
     (fill in)

I immediately posted their scores on a sheet of newsprint so that they could analyze and use the data as they saw fit. The data showed that essentially two-thirds of the men were happy with the way the group they worked with was formed and their degree of effectiveness. The other third ranked things more negatively. I suggested they analyze this for themselves as to what it meant and asked if it was typical in any way of how they organized to perform tasks, and if they weren't satisfied, what could they do to change it. I stated that we would be working in groups at other times over the next few days and they should try out ways to change in order to have positive feelings about organization and effectiveness. One last thing we decided upon was the time schedule we would follow for the next two and one-half days. The schedule looked like this:

8:30 - 12:00		work
12:00 - 1:00		lunch
1:00 - 4:00		work
4:00 - 7:00		break and dinner
7:00 - 10:00		work

We would follow this Friday and Saturday and shoot to wrap up Sunday at noon. With that, we called it a night — although a lot of "work" continued as people stayed up and worked informally.

On Friday morning, the group tried to pick up where they had left off the night before. They again met in the same groups and made several changes to their lists. It seemed that they were not really satisfied with some of the generalities they had listed and wanted to better define their objectives.

Once they finished, I asked them to select a representative from their group. I then had these three get in a fish bowl setting – the three of them in the middle with the rest of the group sitting around them in an outer circle.

Along side of the three in the center, I placed an empty chair. The task for the inner group was to review the respective group lists and by combining these to agree on a single listing in terms of the priorities by which they wanted to work. Those in the outer circle could make whatever inputs they wanted to, but only by occupying the empty chair. I suggested to the inner group that they might first want to decide how they would work together and how they would make decisions. They did not verbalize this, but rather began to work and left the ground rules unsaid as to how they would work and make decisions.

They had a little difficulty getting started but once they warmed up, they worked very well. The outer circle took advantage of the empty chair and supplied inputs which were generally quite helpful. In about thirty minutes, they completed their listing of ten items in order of priority. We then took about ten minutes to "process" the exercise to see what the learning experience was. I asked the inner group to express how they felt about the roles they were playing both as representatives of their original group and as members of the current group. I also asked them how well they thought they performed their task. The outer group was asked to look at their feelings about being represented and about why they really did or didn't use the empty chair.

Our next activity was to take the priority one issue – what are our respective roles in terms of authority, responsibility, accountability and how do they interrelate – and decide how to work on it.* We began well enough by looking at alternate ways of attacking the issue. Suggestions were made such as doing it individually, or breaking down into groups. However, as alternatives were presented, they were dropped and the discussion would ramble on.

After this had gone on for awhile, I asked them to stop and reflect upon what they were doing. They all pretty much agreed they were spinning their wheels. They then made the decision to break down in groups to work on the issue and then get back together to look at and conclude what they had done. The manager suggested that the groups might function with more latitude if he stayed out and defined his role separately and then got back into it when the total group met. He said he recognized that both his presence or absence could be seen as an influencing factor. The group said it might be better to proceed without his presence since they would like to see how their "independent" assumptions about their roles matched his.

The group met after lunch and got into quite a productive session. Each man described what he perceived as his areas of authority and responsibility and then got feedback from the other members. There were often cases where people perceived themselves in ways that others had not. It also tied in quite well with other items on their "list of problems" such as need to improve communications, how to better know and use each other as resources, need to build helping and consulting skills; and how to reduce interdepartmental rivalries. It also seemed to

---

*Appendix 2.2, Part 2, Operating Hints

provide them with a good vehicle for working on the group's, and particularly the superintendent's, relationship with the manager.

My one concern was that there was a small number of people who were not really participating or getting involved and I made a note to check this out at the appropriate time. The session continued up to the afternoon break.

During the break, I tried to come up with a design for the evening session that would build upon the afternoon session and continue to support and develop the giving of helpful feedback to one another. I decided to build a design based on an intervention strategy developed by Roger Harrison.[1]

At the beginning of the evening session, I said that I thought they had accomplished a lot that afternoon and that it might be appropriate this evening to try to tie things together. I said that I had an exercise which they could work on which would cause them to look at their interaction on the job and provide them with a means for increasing their effectiveness. (As it turned out, I should have told them more, because I had more in mind as I'll soon explain.) Their response was affirmative, so I proceeded to explain the task.

I asked them to think about each of the other men in the room in terms of their interaction or their association with them as it affected them in terms of their doing their own jobs. I then asked them to answer three questions using a separate piece of paper for each man. The questions were: (1) List the things that if that person did *more of* or *did better*, it would increase your job effectiveness. (2) List those things that you wish that person *to continue doing* just as he has been which will continue to increase your job effectiveness. (3) List those things which if that person *did less of* or *stopped doing* it would increase your job effectiveness. I said they could do this anonymously. Once they completed this, each was to collect the papers which were addressed to him and list the information, by category, on a single, large piece of newsprint. I urged them to be as specific as they could and really think in terms of increasing their effectiveness in doing their jobs. They spent nearly two hours on this phase of the exercise.

When they finished, I asked them to put their sheets on the wall so that we could more easily share what we had. I then asked each member to ask questions about items on his list to clarify any comments that weren't clear. In doing this, they were to stick strictly to gaining more information and were not allowed to get into any pro and con or defensive type discussion.

As they got into their lists, the information flowed quite freely and openly. When someone would comment "I'm not sure what this means," the response would be "I put that in and what I meant was . . . ." This went on for about an hour. When they finished their discussion, I asked how they felt about what they had done. They all seemed to indicate that they found it quite helpful. I then explained that what they had done in sharing this information showed a lot of ways in which their effectiveness as managers could be considerably increased. However, the sharing of this information alone wouldn't do it — that it did not constitute change. We needed to carry it one step further, to negotiate with one another on a *quid pro quo* basis. The way to do this was to look at one another's lists and identify those specific things that they would like others to change. Next, they would negotiate with another individual and set a "contract" on the items they each agreed to change. This contract would be in writing. I then proceeded to give examples of what I meant.

Well, I blew it. They did not see that as a necessary or an appropriate thing to do. And, though I knew better, I began to argue why it was. One of the men in particular, who seemed to have the backing of the group, took me on. We "debated" for several minutes before someone suggested that since it was getting late to leave it where it was for now and see how we wanted to pick it up in the morning. Everyone agreed.

Later, in reflecting back as to why we did not conclude the exercise at that time, several things came to mind. Much of this came to me in a later feedback session with the group. These were — It was late in the evening and the fatigue factor was quite high; since I had not laid out the total model for them before we began, it seemed that I was trying to trick them into doing something they might not want to do; and there was a question as to whose needs were being met — theirs or mine.

The next morning they began discussing where they had left off the night before. They decided to "own up" to their inputs on everyone's list by initialing the items they had written. They next agreed to take the data back to the plant with them and work out the issues by a specific date.

We then got back to the "problem list" and took up the next item which was to work on building problem solving and decision making skills. I gave them a theory presentation and outlined a technique called "Force Field Analysis."[2] They then practiced this technique by applying it to another problem on their list having to do with machine maintenance and production down time. They did most of their work in small groups for the rest of the morning.

As we began after lunch, I was still concerned with a lack of participation by a few members of the group. I was also concerned with the need for a lot more work to be done and not having a whole lot of time to do it. As we were getting ready to start, several people asked me "How do you think things are going?" I said I thought it was more important as to how they felt about their progress and where they were right now. We checked this out by using a simple instrument. I drew a scale from 0% to 100% on a piece of newsprint. I then asked them to take a piece of paper and answer the following question using a percentage number: "Of the things you had hoped would be accomplished in this session, how much has been accomplished so far?" I then drew a second line and asked them in the same manner to answer the question: "How much do you feel you have personally contributed to the session so far?" I then asked them to either hand me their papers so I could transfer the data to the chart or just call off their numbers. They chose to call off their numbers.

The marks for the first question ranged between 50% and 70% and we discussed what that meant to us. The marks ranged all over the scale for the second question and a good discussion followed. Some who had marked low openly expressed their need for wanting to contribute more but either had a reluctance to do so, or questioned their ability to influence. The other members dealt with this quite effectively by being encouraging and stating their desire to listen and give support. The time spent on this seemed to give everyone a "shot in the arm", and we gave our attention back to the list.

What remained was: Building skills in communications, decision making and interpersonal relations. I commented that a good way of building some skills in these areas was by some experimental learning and said that I had some ideas on how to do this if they would like to try them. They were anxious to do so.

I then formed groups of six and eight (and included myself in the eight group). Each group then split and formed a fish bowl with an inner and outer group, which were then given specific tasks to perform and a time limit in which to perform them. The task for the inner groups was to "move closer together as human beings, to get to know one another better." The task for the outer group was to observe an inside member on two dimensions: (1) What he does that helps the group accomplish its task, and (2) what he does that hinders or gets in the way of the group accomplishing its task. When time was up (about ten minutes) the partners paired up and the observer gave "feedback" regarding his observations. Inner and outer groups changed seats and the inner groups were given the task to "share something personally significant about yourself." The observer group had the same observation task as before. Pairings were again made and the feedback given.

We then got back together as a single group and I attempted to help them see the experience they had just gone through in terms of the Johari Window[3] (Fig. 2.3).* I used the model to help them look at their behavior during this exercise as well as their experiences of the last two days. I illustrated that as they became more frank and open with others they reduced the hidden quadrant. Too, as others became more open and willing to feed back their perceptions to them, they reduced their blind quadrant. We also spent some time talking about what the "norms" were that governed the way each group functioned.

	Known to self	Unknown to self
Known to others	Public area	Blind area
Unknown to others	Hidden area	Unknown area

Fig. 2.3 Johari Window. (By permission from J. Luft, *Of Human Interaction*, Palo Alto, Cal., National Press Books, 1969.)

When we finished this, we again moved back to the list to see where we were and what we should work on next. We finalized some action plans as to who was going to do what and by when. They decided that they would like to spend the evening working on decision making skills and to continue to work on building their interpersonal skills.

After dinner, I ran through a short theory presentation on effective feedback outlining what it was and wasn't, and how to both give it and receive it.

---

*Appendix 2.2, Part 3

Following this, we divided into two groups and ran through Jay Hall's "NASA game,"* an exercise in consensus decision making, and it worked extremely well with this group.

When we had finished discussing the NASA exercise several people asked me how I saw things now. Again, I turned the question back to them and had them complete an instrument that would produce some data. I first asked them to rate their opinion of the session on a scale of 1 to 10, with 1 being "unworthwhile" and 10 being "completely worthwhile." I then asked them to list the items which they saw as most and least effective. I said that this would be good feedback for me.

The rating on 1 — 10 came out a pretty solid 9+ and the list of effective items was considerably longer than those seen as ineffective. The interesting thing here was that several people saw the "role negotiation" as least effective; yet, as they talked about this, it became apparent that more and more people saw this as an important vehicle for developing the ability to level with each other and produce valid feedback. They also saw those issues as something they could work on in an ongoing way "back home." Their perceptions of my behavior during that exercise was that I was pressing too hard and this caused them to react in a defensive way. At that time, they just did not want to get into the kind of confrontation I was urging.

At this stage, several people expressed the feeling of having finished their group agenda. Getting closure to a session of this type is a critical phase. It is our experience that it is best to have no unfinished business. I don't mean by this that every problem that is raised must be solved for obviously this is impossible and should not even be an objective. What I mean by no unfinished business is that when the session is concluded, the group has a specific plan of action for what it is going to do when it returns to the plant. Our strategy is to have the group form a plan of action for each item with which they have dealt. This should be in writing, showing names of people involved, what is going to be done and by when, and show who is responsible. Often, these action plans will show the need to receive inputs from sources outside the group and these also must be identified.

So that was the task we took on next. When we finished, we decided that Sunday morning would be a time when people could work on any of their own agenda items. Mine were to sleep late and fly back to California!

RESULTS

What I've described above does not include all the activities that go on during a team building session of this kind. People do as much work on issues outside the structure of the time schedule as they do within it, particularly on their interpersonal relations. I saw as a significant gain for the participants their identification of the barriers that separated them interpersonally and as it affected their ability to manage. They took a big step forward to break down these barriers and have continued to move forward ever since. This has been no more evident than in the

---

*Appendix 2.2, Part 4

situation involving the manager and the plant superintendent. They have openly confronted the issues between them and have built a solid and productive relationship, and I feel they have both increased their effectiveness as a result.

Other results from this particular team building session have been: a significant attitude change in the group which has resulted in a more collaborative approach to problem solving, acceptance of and confidence in the manager, better communications flow throughout the system and more effective utilization of meeting time; the commencement of a "job enrichment" effort to provide more meaningful work for hourly workers, directed at increasing their motivation to work more productively; the beginning phase of a preventative maintenance program to reduce operating down time; and a training program to increase the skills and competence of hourly maintenance workers.

Summary

As in the instant case, team building has been an effective way to initiate an organization development effort within Kaiser Aluminum. It often identifies and leads to the appropriate use of other intervention strategies such as training, intergroup problem solving and techno-structural changes (see Fig. 2.1).

APPENDIX 2.1 TEAM BUILDING WORKSHOP DESIGN*

1st Evening

6:30 - 7:30	Dinner
7:30 - 10:30	Share expectations and begin the "unfreezing" process. Attempt to start setting agenda for the workshop.

2nd Day

8:30 - 11:00	Setting agenda and establishing priorities
11:00 - 12:00	Problem solving
12:00 - 1:00	Lunch
1:00 - 4:00	Problem solving
4:00 - 7:00	Break and dinner
7:00 - 10:00	Role negotiation exercise

3rd Day

8:30 - 12:00	Problem solving
12:00 - 1:00	Lunch
1:00 - 4:00	Communications micro lab and Johari Window
4:00 - 7:00	Break and dinner
7:00 - 10:00	Decision-making theory - NASA Exercise

4th Day

8:30 - 12:00	Action planning
	Critique

APPENDIX 2.2 ANALYSIS OF INTERVENTIONS IN THIS CHAPTER

1. Agenda Setting — Multiple Group Membership

Working in subgroups, the participants are instructed to identify the problems and/or issues that they would like to see get worked on during the session. Next, the group is to list the items in terms of priority as to which gets worked on first, second, etc. The groups reform as a total group and spokesmen from each subgroup meet together in a "fishbowl" setting. The group arranges itself in concentric circles with the representatives seated in the inner circle, or fishbowl. An empty chair is also placed in the inner circle.

The task for the inner group is to come up with a single list in priority order. The outside group may make inputs only by occupying the empty chair.

Uses

This can be a good method to get a group to focus on issues and develop their own agenda for the workshop. Also presents a valid way of looking at their

---

*While this is the basic design that evolved during this particular team building session, it is important to recognize that every group is unique. The design must be based on the data that is generated both before and during the workshop.

multiple-group membership roles back at the plant. For example, in the exercise they maintain membership in their subgroup along with their membership in the fishbowl group — much like their roles as a member of a department in the plant and a member of the manager's staff.

Operating Hints

When giving the subgroups their assignment to identify issues and problems it is sometimes helpful to limit the number of items. For example, you might say, "Identify the five most pressing problems that you see as standing in the way of your being more effective as a group or plant." Also, when listing items they should identify those which the members of the particular workshop have complete authority, power, ability, etc. to solve as opposed to those which need input from persons who are not present. They should try to stick to issues which they can solve.

2. Role Negotiation

There are many ways this intervention can be used and adapted to fit a given situation. As it was discussed in this chapter it was used as a vehicle for group members to give and receive feedback on three dimensions — things one should do more or better, things one should continue, things one should do less of or stop doing. If time is pressing or the situation calls for it only one or two dimensions may be more appropriate.

Also the actual "negotiation" can be done in a variety of ways. Essentially the exercise is designed for people to express what they want from each other which then should lay the foundation for the "quid pro quo" negotiation. Often times it is more beneficial for the individuals who have issues with each other to publicly commit to working these out — but the actual work time and place is left up to them.

Uses

A good way to test and open up communications between individuals in a management group.
Part of team building.
Sets up good way to check behavioral change on an on-going basis—useful data to take back "home" and continue to work on.

Operating Hints

The focus should be strictly on issues that affect one's job effectiveness.

Keep the groundrule that as individuals seek clarity on their individual lists, that they refrain from defending or arguing. However, they should feel free to test to see how many others agree with the feedback.

Limitations

Can consume considerable time.

3. Communications Exercise and Johari Window

This intervention is pretty well described in the chapter. For additional informa-
tion see J. William Pfeiffer and John E. Jones (eds.), A Handbook of Structured
Experiences for Human Relations Training, Vol. I, pp 66-70, University Associates
Press: Iowa City, Iowa, 1969.

Uses

An effective technique for getting managers to really look at each other as human
beings.

NASA Exercise

This exercise calls for everyone to visualize themselves as members of a space crew
that has crash-landed on the moon. Their mission is to rendezvous with a mother
ship some 200 miles away, but the rough landing has ruined the ship and destroyed
all the equipment on board, except for 15 items. The task is individually to rank
the 15 items in order of importance for survival. After this, they were to meet in
their groups and receive a set of instructions for reaching group consensus. Their
task as a group, then, was to come up with a *single* listing of the 15 items in order
of their importance for survival. The exercise can be a lot of fun and at the same
time, produce a great deal of learning. For more information see Pfeiffer and
Jones book cited in 3 above.

SUGGESTED READING LIST

1. Harrison, Roger, *Role Negotiation: A Tough Minded Approach to Team
   Development,* Copyright 1971 by Roger Harrison. For a comprehensive
   explication of this approach, see *Social Technology of Organization Development,* edited by W. W. Burke and H. A. Hornstein, published by N.T.L.
   Learning Resources Corp., Fairfax, Va. 1972, pp. 84-96.

2. Fordyce, Jack K., and Raymond Weil, *Managing With People: A Manager's
   Handbook of Organization Development Methods,* Reading, Mass., Addison-
   Wesley, 1972.

3. Luft, J., "The Johari Window," *Hum. Rel. Tr. News,* 5, 1961, pp. 6-7. For
   the most comprehensive explication of the Johari Window, see *Of Human
   Interaction,* by Joseph Luft, published by National Press Books, Palo Alto,
   Calif., 1969.

4. Shein, Edgar, Warren Bennis, and Richard Beckhard (eds.), *Organization
   Development,* Reading, Mass., Addison-Wesley, 1969.

ORGANIZATION DEVELOPMENT
IN A PHARMACEUTICAL SETTING

We often talk about organization change without realizing that very often there must be a change in the individual who is to facilitate the change. The following case describes the growth of the person who was later to spearhead the change effort within his own organization. Very often the story of OD in an organization is the personal journal of the change agent who changed along with his organization. This chapter describes how outside consultants helped initiate a change program that affected the internal consultant as well as the client organization.

The author's experiences over a period of a few years show how OD evolved from a typical management development program with emphasis on content to a laboratory learning design emphasizing group process and interpersonal communication. This became the organization's first efforts to deal with in-depth interpersonal issues. This led them to experiment with intergroup problem-solving techniques and the use of assessment instruments to provide individual and group data.

Later a new company president and a reorganization provided an impetus for continuing effort of the type that had been started, although still viewed as a management development activity. By this time, the internal OD consultant had become convinced that a systems-wide change program was what was really needed. The author describes the difficulties he encountered in obtaining top management's commitment to this. As is often the case, a crisis in the organization provided an opportunity to conduct an OD program designed to resolve the impending problem — reduction-in-force and reorganization of the sales department. The techniques used were consulting pairs and instrumented interventions (e.g. Multiple Affect Adjective Check List [MAACL]) in an intergroup problem-solving meeting. These programs have enabled the participants to collaborate more effectively in problem solving and level with one another more. Experience-based learning techniques are accepted now as a means of helping managers to gain insights into the nature of the problems they experience in a changing environment.

Organization Development in a Pharmaceutical Setting

INTRODUCTION

The intent of this chapter is to describe, in a very personal way, how organization development was introduced into a complex, multinational company and some OD activities which then ensued. By sharing with the reader what we did, and what we might have done differently, I hope to respond, at least in part, to a whole range of questions that I have often heard raised at meetings or in discussions of various kinds about OD.

What is OD? How in the devil do you get an OD program started? Don't you have to start at the top? Is OD just sensitivity training? Are outside consultants necessary?

This is a personal case history, not an academic treatise. So people seeking definitive answers, if in fact there are any, will have to search elsewhere. What I plan to do is start with my views of what OD is, describe chronologically how we got started, and then select some of our major OD interventions and describe them briefly. We have attempted to research (measure) what we have done. As a consequence, more detailed descriptions of most of these interventions have been published elsewhere and will be duly noted. As I go along, and at the end, I will offer my views about what we did right and not so right.

WHAT IS OD?

In almost every company's annual report there usually appears some acknowledgement of the contributions of its employees and the fact that its human resources are, indeed, its most valued resources. Organization development is a way, perhaps the only way, to turn this statement from fiction into fact. Or to put it another way, organization development in its most elemental sense, seeks to improve the quality of life in organizations. It is both a philosophy and an evolving technology. As a philosophy, it holds to the belief that people, in fact, are O. K. and that institutions should serve them and not vice versa. As a process or tech-

Stokes Carrigan is Manager of Employee and Organization Development for Smith, Kline Corp., formerly Smith, Kline, and French Laboratories, Philadelphia, Pennsylvania. He has co-authored published articles on organization development efforts at Smith, Kline, and French. He holds a B.A. in History from Princeton University.

nology, it draws much of its sustenance from work being done in the applied behavioral sciences.

For me, the most critical thing is a company's own philosophy or values. Are they compatible with those of organization development? Does the company really give a damn about its people? Does it want to try and match their needs and goals with its own? In some instances, this may be unclear until it is tested but somewhere early in the game the question must be answered affirmatively for organization development to succeed. Some of the objectives that organization development strives for would include the following:

—work should be made as meaningful as possible
—people should be treated like adults not children
—people should be allowed, if not encouraged, to interact with all of themselves — their emotional selves as well as their rational selves
—they should be involved, as much as possible, in the decisions which will affect them
—trust and mutual respect should be fostered
—conflict which is inevitable should be confronted and managed
—collaboration in meeting work goals should be encouraged and destructive competition minimized.

How to accomplish this is the neat trick, and this is where the technology comes in. Many organizations are trying. I will describe the efforts of one.

THE BEGINNING

Because our entry into OD was a gradually emerging process, I feel it is important to sketch briefly the key factors which brought it about.

First and foremost, was my good fortune to meet and work closely with our two outside consultants, Dr. Arthur Blumberg, now at Syracuse University, and Dr. Robert Golembiewski from the University of Georgia. Without their help, their prodding, and their continuing support, neither I nor the company would have gotten very far in the realm of OD. I met Art first, shortly after I became Training Director in 1963. We hit it off from the start, and it was through his gentle persuasion that I finally decided to attend a sensitivity training lab.

This was the second key factor in the process and represents for me a critical point of personal change. Even if this sounds excessive, I must say that the sensitivity training lab (T-Group) that I attended was one of the most valuable learning experiences of my life. For quite awhile I resisted Art's urging to attend. I was present when Chris Argyris and George Odiorne held their now famous debate in March, 1964, in New York City. I also attended, that same year, a conference at the Sterling Forest Conference Center, where speakers included Jack Gibb, Robert Blake, Bob Kahn, and Goodwin Watson. None of these experiences, nor what I read, changed my negative feelings about T-Groups. For me, they represented some strange and mystical group experience that deliberately and unmercifully invaded a person's private self. No one, least of all responsible corporations, should be involved with them. Art finally convinced me that, in my role as Training Director, I should at least learn first-hand what they were all about.

I decided to attend a Management Work Conference run by the National Training Laboratories at Arden House in January, 1967. It was a fantastic experience, and I returned completely converted. If space permitted, I could elaborate at length on the things I learned about myself and others, about values and attitudes that I had been using as a crutch, about experimenting with the way people organize themselves to accomplish a task. The critical thing, as far as OD is concerned, is that I returned to work convinced that the behavioral sciences offered a way to get at and solve people and organizational problems — that people could change, and, through them, so could organizations.

THE SK&F MANAGEMENT COURSE

One of the first things I decided to do upon my return, and this was the third factor, was to engage SK&F managers in a T-Group experience. The vehicle would be the SK&F Management Course which had been a traditionally didactic approach to learning about manager behavior. Our first "cousin" lab * was scheduled for April, 1967 and Blumberg and Golembiewski would be the trainers. It would consist of 24 participants divided into two T-Groups. Art and Bob designed it with several goals in mind.[1]

First, it was imperative that trust be developed and tested at several levels of organization since the participants, in several instances, worked closely with each other, although none (by design) held a superior or subordinate relationship to another. They were expected to be cautious, to say the least. Also it was felt important to provide a number of theory inputs, not only to aid T-group development but also to help participants practice what they learned back on the job.

Second, participants should have an intense T-group experience and at the same time engage in a variety of situations similar to those encountered at work.

Third, trust should be developed within each T-group between the two groups, and also between cross-T-group "pair partners," who met each of the first three days. Trainers did not want to reinforce inter-unit strife which is too often an organizational reality.

Fourth, the design attempted to emphasize, through experiential learning, processes and cognitive insights that were easily transferrable to back home. Specific attention was paid to observation skills, feedback skills, and helping/consulting skills. The cognitive material emphasized feedback processes, felt to be critical for effective confronting.

During the week, participants met in individual T-groups for a majority of the time. But early in the week and particularly at the beginning, the two groups met together in a group-observing-group model. They also met in pairs, as well as in general sessions.

* As distinguished from stranger labs, which is what the name implies, cousin lab participants are members of the same organization and may work together, but no one reports directly to anyone else there.

The theory sessions focused on the Johari Window to encourage initial openness and levelling; the concept of degenerative and regenerative feedback cycles and six guidelines for effective feedback; and confrontation technique and its application to complex organizations. In later labs the force field analysis model for looking at change process was also introduced.

Measurement of change induced by the lab experience was done via a pre and post administration of a Problem Analysis Questionnaire[2], which indicated personal and interpersonal learning took place to a statistically significant degree.

Before the lab began, I went to my boss and told him what we planned to do. His quick approval, I'm convinced, stemmed more from my enthusiasm than from his knowledge or my explanation of what T-groups were all about. I next sent a memo to the participants in which I tried to describe T-groups, and followed this up with a meeting for the same purpose. No mention, I believe, was made to this group about voluntary attendance, however, I did screen, through the health benefits clerk and the plant physician, for anyone who might have a history of psychiatric problems.

I was very anxious about the success of the lab and quite concerned about how participants would react. Many of them were personal friends. We all had to go back to the organization and work together. And I was anything but certain about what the outcome would be. As it turned out, the outcome was excellent as measured by the Problem Analysis Questionnaire and a post-lab attitude survey. No one felt negative about his experience and many were extremely enthusiastic. I was encouraged to offer the "new" SK&F Management Course two more times in the fall of '67 and the spring of '68. During most of this period I had not contemplated organization development at all. The goal of the T-groups had been simply to give approximately 60 middle managers a chance to learn something about their own and others' behavior – to communicate straighter, to listen better, and to experience the power and delight of more open, trusting relationships with the hope that they would return home and be more effective managers.

THE FIRST SPARK

In early 1968, the national sales manager of one of our major divisions queried me about management training for his sales managers. His management group consisted of 13 regional managers reporting to two divisional managers, all of whom had risen from the "ranks" of a rapidly expanding sales force. In most instances, managers had been promoted on the basis of seniority, and their orientation was towards personal selling and not managing. The national sales manager felt strongly that the emphasis on selling versus managing had to be reversed, especially in view of the expected continued growth in sales and the introduction of new products. He, himself, had recently transferred from a sales organization in another division which was older, more highly structured, and had a long history of being autocratically managed.

When he took command his initial goal was to straighten things out and to impose on the newer organization the operating methods of its older brother. This strategy had not gone over too well. In addition, his own personal style and physical size made him a rather imposing figure. The net result was that his managers, almost to a man, were quite fearful of him.

I suggested that perhaps the same training that we had been offering to middle managers via the Management Course would be appropriate. Fortunately, his chief lieutenant had attended the fall lab a few months before and had spoken highly of it to him. He quickly agreed to make his 13 regional managers available. I was concerned, however, that unless he prepared himself for what I hoped would be a more confronting posture on the part of his men, a tentative beginning would be quickly wiped out at their first interface and their relationship made worse rather than better. I told him so and proposed that all three levels of sales management, starting with himself, undergo sensitivity training to be followed up with team building.

I told him that this would be the first time an organizational unit of some size in the company would undergo a training experience en masse, and I had great hopes for transference to the job because of the potential for positive reinforcement.

He agreed to send his two divisional managers to the Management Course coming up in March; to attend an NTL Key Executive conference himself, as soon as he could arrange it (which turned out to be in November '68); and to send his 13 regional managers to a "brother"* lab that we would design and run.

Gratifyingly, things began to happen as soon as the two divisional managers came back from the Management Course T-group. Both men, as reported with glee by the National Sales Manager, were more open and confrontive with him. This was no small achievement, since I observed and commented to him on subsequent occasions that his tendency to dominate and not to listen continued unabated.

The "brother" lab was scheduled for May, 1968, at Hilton Head, South Carolina. Bob Golembiewski and I would comprise the staff. A major difference in design from our previous labs was the arrangement to have the two divisional managers fly down for a final day confrontation, if the regional managers agreed to this. We also planned to measure whatever change took place[3] and the persistence of that change[4] with Likert's Profile of Organizational Characteristics (Form T).

The goals of the lab were several and were oriented almost entirely toward developing the organization in directions desired by its members. Personal growth was desirable, but peripheral to the main thrust. One of the overall aims, then, as seen by the trainers was to get the members in touch with the kind of organization they wanted to work in; to share their views with one another both horizontally and vertically; and to experiment with behaviors that would help to induce the kind of organization climate which would be congruent with their needs.

Since participation by the 13 regional managers was not voluntary, the trainers desired that the basic learning design meet two imperatives:

"Managers were encouraged to consider a change in the style of their interpersonal and intergroup relations, but they were continually alerted to the

---

*I use the term "brother" to describe a lab in which all the participants are peers, work in the same organizational unit, and have a common boss or "father" who is not present. If, and when, the father is present, the "brother" lab becomes a "family" lab.

constraints on what they and their immediate superiors could reasonably influence. Consequently the learning design featured a number of decision points explicitly intended to test commitment by various levels of management to the unfolding program. The consequence to be avoided was a feeling by any of the managers that they had been manipulated into a position they had found uncomfortable, but from which they could not gracefully escape. In positive terms, the overall objective was a feeling of psychological success among the managers; a sense of personally owning the change program as opposed to a sense of the program being imposed upon them."[3]

The approach taken was to work first on the relations of the regional managers — to experiment with confronting behaviors in a relatively low risk situation and, in the process, to induce a greater sense of unity and trust. For example, a common complaint expressed among the "brothers" early in the lab was a past failure to support each other when one of them stuck his neck out and battled with his superiors in a group setting. This was explored, and feelings of inadequacy and fear of retribution from above emerged as the primary causes rather than competitive retribution. Agreement was reached to support one another in the future, if they shared similar views. They refused, however, to give up their right to dissent.

This issue and others, such as feelings of aloneness, newness, educational inadequacy, domineering behavior were shared, and there was unavoidably a fair amount of emphasis on "there and then" behaviors. In fact, the general tone of this part of the program which went from Sunday evening through Wednesday evening had more of the flavor of team building than that of a traditional T-group with its heavy emphasis on "here and now" behavior.

At the outset the trainers explained the general outline of the design and stressed the fact that their divisional managers were waiting in Philadelphia on an "as needed basis." That is, if the thirteen regional managers decided they wanted to discuss any issues directly with their two immediate superiors, the divisional managers were prepared to come to Hilton Head and meet with them Thursday evening and Friday morning. It took some time for the decision to be made, but they finally said yes. Then, once having agreed to the meeting, they seemed to studiously avoid the fact that it was going to take place. The trainers intervened heavily on Thursday and reminded them that they only had that day to decide what issues they wanted to raise and how they were going to do it, that is, meet in separate divisions, the whole group together, present a laundry list on newsprint, or verbally describe their concerns one at a time. They finally buckled down and by that evening were ready to go.

The Thursday evening session was volatile. The issues essentially revolved around the National Sales Managers' perceived heavy-handed attempts to induce change and the divisional managers' failure to stand up to him and represent the regional managers adequately. Divisional managers' behavior was for the most part defensive, and the trainers had to intervene from time-to-time to calm things down. Following the formal evening session, an impromptu barbecue with jokes and storytelling helped considerably to reduce the tension. The climate the next morning was much calmer, and one of the regional managers started off with a review of the previous evening's process and how unproductive it had been.* This seemed to strike a responsive chord in all of them, and throughout the morning a successful effort was made to listen, to seek understanding, and to explore solutions. The primary agreement reached was that the divisional managers would go back and confront the national sales manager with their feelings and concerns and communicate his response at their next meeting.

An obvious question: Were we successful in achieving our goals? Based on subjective anecdotal reports, our own observations, and data gathered from four administrations of the Likert Questionnaire, we feel we were. The questionnaire was administered once before the lab and three times following. The fourth time was about a year and a half after the lab took place. The research has been described rather extensively elsewhere[3, 4] and there is not room to go into it here. However, one aspect of it bears reporting, by way of illustration. Reports of change in directions that we felt were consistent with the lab values we hoped to engender were positive between the first and second administrations on 47 of the 48 items, with 28 reaching the .05 level of significance or better. When comparing the fourth administration to the first, we found positive change still existed for 38 items, with nearly half of these reaching the .05 level.

As originally planned, the lab was intended to be the starting point for a continuing effort. A few months after the lab ended, I attended divisional meetings in Chicago and Atlantic City as a process consultant. This was my first attempt to perform this role, and I wasn't sure what I was going to do except try to keep them from copping out if the going got rough. With no basis for comparison, I was pleased with the way the meetings went, especially Chicago. The national sales manager attended this one. He wasn't hesitant to state his views or opinions and encouraged his managers to do the same. They did to his expressed delight, and afterwards he reported to me that the meeting was a great improvement over prior ones. This is another important measure of the success of OD, that is, client pleasure with the results.

There was more activity which I will briefly sketch as a conclusion to this phase of our OD work. In March, 1969, (a little later than we wanted) there was a two-day reinforcement session. Issues and concerns were solicited, and there were some hot ones, such as the division's credibility with their customers due to a significant change in selling strategy. Bob Golembiewski also took this opportunity to feed back to them the results of the first three administrations of the Likert questionnaire.

In May, 1970, as part of regular divisional sales conferences, they set aside an evening and a day, before the business part of the conference started, to do some OD work. In the evening, I met with the divisional manager and his regionals to

---

*Since this chapter is intended to have a "how to" or "how not to" flavor to it, I want to interject something I learned on this occasion. The Thursday night confrontation might have gone better, I suspect, if less "spirits" had been consumed by the managers and if the trainers had spent more time helping the divisional managers get ready. They were extremely anxious, and I think we should have dealt with that directly. We did attempt to preview the general themes of what the regional managers were going to present, but I feel we could have been more helpful by anticipating with them their feelings and various behavioral responses.

focus on their own relationships. The next day we tackled the age-old problem of relations between field and home office staff, which were seen by all to be a source of conflict. The home office staff comprising a sales trainer, a sales promotion man, an administrative manager, and the national sales manager had met with me previously on several occasions to work on their own relationship issues.

For the one day intergroup meeting, I used what has become, by now, a classic confrontation technique (Beckhard, 1967; Blake, Mouton, and Sloma, 1965; Golembiewski and Blumberg, 1967). The two groups, meeting separately for about an hour, were asked to write on sheets of newsprint phrases which would answer the following questions: "How do we see or describe the other group?" "How will they describe us?" and "How do we describe our relations with them?" Then they came together, posted their sheets side-by-side and began to cross-check their perceptions of one another. This usually generated enough business to work on for the rest of the day.

What resulted? The consensus was that greater understanding of each group's problems was achieved and a commitment, of sorts, was made to continue to seek this understanding before making unfavorable judgments about the other. Extracts from some memos that I found in my file will illustrate that such confrontations, where conflict issues are surfaced and worked through, can produce positive feelings. One of the divisional managers wrote to me, "The consensus was that your Team Building session was one of the most helpful experiences we've ever had. We are all delighted. The understanding and respect the groups gained for each other enhanced our solidarity and will accelerate the growth and development of each." (I only wish he had felt it was "theirs" rather than "my" team building session).

And one of the home office staffers writing to the field division managers said, ". . . It was just tremendous! Personally, it was the best thing that has ever happened to my relationship with you and your managers. I feel like I really got to know your men and that we have a selling team that's top notch . . . a team I'm proud to be associated with. It was a very worthwhile session and one I'll remember for a long time to come."

The work that was done with this particular sales group, the positive changes that have taken place in terms of a more open, confronting style of communications, and its continuing commitment to OD goals has satisfied me that an OD effort can be sustained in a functional subunit of a complex organization. You have to start at the top of the particular unit you are going to work with but not necessarily at the top of the larger organization. Admittedly, various members of the sales group have expressed, somewhat longingly, the desire to have the other home office groups with whom they interact "on board" with them. There is a good chance this will be one of our next major OD thrusts.

OD IN THE COMPLEX ORGANIZATION

The largest and most profitable division in our corporation is the pharmaceutical division. However, by the beginning of 1968 dark clouds were appearing on the horizon. The division was still turning in a handsome profit, but the growth curve for both sales and earnings had flattened to almost a true horizontal. The patent on 'Thorazine,' far and away its most successful product, was going to expire in 1970, and to quote an article which appeared in the October 26, 1968 issue of *Business Week*, "The company has not put out a major new prescription drug in four years — and new ethical products are the lifeblood of a fast-growing pharmaceutical producer with the supercharged profits to which SK&F has grown accustomed." There had been a shakeup at the top the year before, with Tom Rauch being named president and chief executive officer only 18 months after his predecessor had been given the job. One of Rauch's first acts had been to reorganize severely the R&D division. The winds of change were starting to blow at gale strength, and to say that "the natives were becoming quite restless" would be an understatement.

As Training Director, I had been given the assignment to prepare a program to meet one of the division's stated goals — "to develop a broader group of employees qualified for management positions through personnel development programs." As I struggled with this through the early winter and spring of 1968, and as I talked to many managers, particularly at the middle and lower levels, I became convinced that what was needed was not individual manager development but rather a massive, system-wide program to change the climate of the organization — to reduce the fears and anxieties which were eroding the trust and openness of communications between top management and the rest of the organization.

Armed with my gut feeling and a lot of moral support from Art Blumberg and Bob Golembiewski, I went to my boss at the eleventh hour and told him that I wanted to respond differently to the assignment I had been given — that I wanted the company to engage in an organization development program first and a management development program second. He didn't understand what I was talking about at first, but we had a lot going for us in the terms of mutual trust and respect. So he listened, questioned, questioned some more, and after three hours agreed with my plan to recommend OD.

MANAGEMENT COURSE ALUMNI MEETING

At the same time I was struggling with what kind of program to recommend, we had fortuitously scheduled a reunion of alumni from our three Management Course T-groups. I say fortuitously because the meeting provided the concrete data I had been lacking to give plausibility to my proposal. This, then, became the data feedback portion of my introduction strategy.

Fifty-three Philadelphia-based alumni were invited with only about a week's notice to a "T-group follow-up." Twenty-nine accepted, and a number who didn't, told me testily that they would have been able, had I given them more notice. We deliberately divided them into functional groups to see if the openness obtained in the T-groups would prevail in a mix of "strangers" who, nonetheless, had undergone a similar experience. We asked them to review their operating areas over the past year, share their concerns, and report back to the whole group. I promised them, before they started, that I would personally transmit the essence of what they said to the head of the pharmaceutical division.

We started the meeting at 4:00 p.m. and ended it at 10:00 p.m., and I realized I had my work cut out for me. They were quite open in venting their feelings of hostility, frustration, and anxiety over what was happening in the company. One of their biggest peeves was that they were being treated as children when they wanted to be treated as adults. They knew the company was headed for some troubled times, and they wanted to be leveled with and called upon to help. The fact that top management seemed to be trying to paint an unrealistically rosy picture made them suspicious. I wrote all this up in my proposal memo and, before submitting it, checked with a number of attendees regarding the accuracy of my reporting.

THE FIRST BIG STEP

The memo went to the top man of the division in early July, and I waited with baited breath to hear his response. Nothing happened. I sent a few information copies to people with whom I had discussed my plan, and they agreed that I had really "told it like it was." I was feeling pretty good about having taken a large risk and receiving acclaim for doing so. At the same time I had to admit to myself that the risk had not been that great. I had simply been a reporter in one sense and a proposer of positive action steps in another. I also had had a long association with the division head, and had had prior opportunities to test his readiness to receive unfavorable news. He was not a threatening person, and I had great respect for him. Several weeks later when we got together to review the proposal, I sensed that the gist of what I reported was already known by him.

What I had proposed to him was that we start on an organization development program as soon as possible, the overall goal of which would not be "to make everybody happy but to make the organization stronger, more viable, more flexible, and consequently better able to cope with crisis or change." I quoted from Beckhard's article in the *Journal of Applied Behavioral Sciences*, which describes his work with a medium-sized hotel concern[5], in order to show that OD was not just a pie-in-the-sky theory but had been used effectively to pursue specific organization improvement goals such as,

—improved communications among various parts of the organization
—change in management style from management by control to management by objectives
—improved operating efficiency
—increased problem-solving skills of the total management
—establishment of a systematic program of growth and development for management executives.

Our work with the sales managers of another division, which I have described above, was also cited to illustrate that we were already engaged in an OD program.
I recommended that as a start:

—we should engage behavioral science consultants (specifically Blumberg and Golembiewski) who could review organization theory as it related to SK&F; collect data through observation and interviews; advise us on things we could do to resolve some of our difficulties; and help implement these efforts

—he should do some background reading on the behavioral sciences and OD

—he and the three levels of management below him should attend sensitivity training labs

—I should investigate the services offered by the Institute for Social Research at the University of Michigan to see if they could help us measure organization climate and subsequent change, if any.

It was a long session, because he was not easily convinced that what I had proposed would do any good. My immediate boss was with me and he helped tremendously in our several efforts to clarify and explain. Finally, the division head said okay — he would take it to his operating committee, composed of his vice-presidents of marketing, manufacturing, R&D, and administration and finance. However, he wanted me to rewrite my proposal (which I had spent weeks on) and cast it in a more positive tone, because it would get a better reception from the V.P.'s. Inwardly, I bristled, but I didn't deal with my feelings openly. I felt we had a foot in the door, and I didn't want to lose this advantage. And so I fell back on a lot of rationalizations about why it was better to lose the battle and win the war. Nevertheless, I felt deep down that his request, which I perceived as an effort on his part to avoid confronting unpleasantries, was wrong, and that I had been compromised. I regret now that I didn't confront him openly and immediately.

So I rewrote my memo the way I had been told; made a number of generalizations about the age of change we were in; cited some internal and external examples; and suggested that

"a manager's ability to manage change and an organization's ability to cope with it will depend increasingly on more open communications, greater respect and trust on both an inter and intra-unit basis, and more focus on problem solving rather than defending status quo positions."

Again I recommended attending labs and hiring consultants, but this time I attached an article called "A Management 'Be In'" which describes briefly, but excellently, the action of a T-group, the kinds of learning that take place, the role of the trainer, and things for sponsoring organizations to consider before getting started, such as:

"It is not unusual for a participant to come to know himself and then to decide to leave his company because it is much too authoritarian and dogmatic. The values back home had best lend some support to the values in the T-group. Or watch out, baby, there's going to be an explosion."[6]

The memo was to be reviewed at a staff meeting the day after Labor Day. I expected to attend and spent part of my vacation, the week before, anticipating questions I would be asked and reading Warren Bennis' book, *Changing Organizations*, in preparation. The division head and his staff usually met alone and would call people into the meeting when their bit of business came up on the agenda. I never was called. I found out later from the V.P. of Administration and Finance, who, a short time before, had been made my boss's boss, that they accepted the recommendations as stated and did not feel the need for any additional input from me. As it turned out, the division head had already decided to proceed and merely wanted their agreement.

This was my second mistake. I should have insisted on attending to make certain they had a good understanding of what they were "buying" into. I was concerned that they did not have sufficient understanding and was later proved right.

Nevertheless, the four functional V.P.'s signed up for the NTL Key Executive Lab in November. The division head was supposed to attend an NTL President's Conference on Human Behavior the week before they went, but had to postpone until February because of work pressure. We, the OD consultants and I, had suggested that we hold an important checkpoint meeting as soon as the four returned to determine if they still wanted to proceed with the plan to train their directors and department heads. The V.P. of Administration and Finance said before they left that this wouldn't be necessary. They would have to catch up on a lot of work and besides, they had already committed to the plan. I said fine, if that's what they wanted, and this was my third mistake. The meeting was intended to be a critical decision point, and I should not have acquiesced.

As it turned out, we had the meeting anyway and at the time originally chosen, because they called me during the middle of their lab and asked for it. My clairvoyant consultants, Art and Bob, had kept their calendars clear, and so in November, 1968, for the first time, the outside consultants, my boss, and I finally got together with the five top managers to form an OD core group and discuss our long range OD plans.

The meeting had three objectives: first, to begin to develop the relationship between managers and consultants; second, to check out the V.P.'s concerns about continuing; and third, to present our four-phase plan. Relationship building was a continuing process, and we began by asking them about their experience at the lab. At my request, they had been put in different T-groups and, for the most part, were noncommital about discussing what had happened. They did feel they had benefited, but they didn't want their subordinates to undergo some of the things they had experienced. We explained how our "cousin" labs probably differed from the "stranger" lab they attended — that we were aware participants had to continue to work together, reminded them of that, and set ground rules about inappropriate subjects for discussion. This seemed to satisfy them, especially when they were reminded we had already run three successful labs. We then went on to review our plan which had three distinct phases and a possible fourth depending on the success of the first three (See Fig. 3.1).

Phase 1 involved basic training, via T-groups, for a broad clientele of managers and the building of internal change agent supports. The principal internal change agents were to be me and my assistant, Walter Mead, but we knew we would be spread pretty thin for Phase 2 unless we got some other people inside who could help us part time. Phase 2 would concentrate on developing team relations, cleaning up organizational garbage, and building trust in order to pave the way for Phase 3 which was to work on structural and procedural inhibitors to effective functioning and goal achievement. Through '69 and '70 this effort was to be concentrated at the top of the organization. After that we would spread out through the organization. All phases were intended to overlap, and we especially wanted to start building team relations while we continued with the basic T-group training.

Phase 1

Division Head				Mini-core			Presidents lab	Core
V.P.'s		Key exec. conf.		group conf.				group review
Directors and Department Heads					T-group 4	T-group 5		
Internal Change Agents		Preparation of skills, attitudes (Carrigan) (Mead)		Serve as co-trainees, attend outside labs, e.g., program for specialists in OD, consulting skills lab.				
Change-agent Supports		Selected individuals from T-groups 1 - 5				Skills development — OD seminar — Co-training opportunities		
Broad Clientele	T-groups 1 - 3							
Timing	Prior to Nov.	Nov. 10–16	Nov. * 19	Dec. 8–13	Jan. 26–31 1969	Feb. 2–8	Feb. * 12–15	

*Checkpoint

Fig. 3.1 Schema of an OD program for a complex organization (designed by Robert Golembiewski)

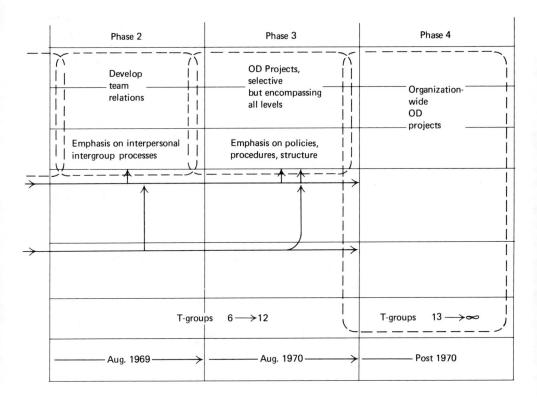

The meeting took several hours, and at the end, the V.P.'s had changed their thinking from not wanting to continue to agreeing to complete Phase 1. Several things contributed to the change of heart. First, we, the OD staff, had a chance to explain in detail for the first time, what we proposed to do and why, and the outside consultants established themselves as competent professionals by describing some of the work they had done. Second, I am convinced that my image with them began to change. I felt that after this meeting they saw me in a "professional" role and were more willing to listen to my suggestions. Third, and perhaps most important, the division head, who had not yet attended the President's Lab, admitted that he felt "out of it," and he was going to leave the decision to continue to the four V.P.'s. The decision process, thus, shifted from autocratic to participative, and I felt there was a heightened sense of ownership.

It will be impossible to describe in detail all the OD related events that took place during the following year, so I will summarize most of it and describe a few events at greater length.

In December '68 and January '69 all the directors and most of the department heads* in the pharmaceutical division attended a T-group. After the division head went to the President's Lab, the OD core group met again, and agreed to continue sensitivity training down to the first line-supervisory level. (At this juncture, we have run 17 "cousin" labs and six "brother" labs for the sales managers. The total number of managers who have attended a T-group is 373.)

In February '69, as soon as the division head returned from his lab, he and his four V.P.'s attended a two-day, off-site team building session. They held several of these, and, in addition, I served as process consultant at a number of their staff meetings. At about the same time, each of the functional V.P.'s met with his own immediate subordinates, the directors, for a similar two-day, off-site session. And in the case of marketing and R&D, team building/problem solving meetings were held with the V.P., directors, and department heads attending.

One of the issues that was troubling many at the top three levels was lack of definition of responsibility. The directors, caught between the department heads and the V.P.'s, especially wanted to work this issue. Thirteen of them met with the top five in an intergroup confrontation session, which started with their sharing and cross checking perceptions of the other group.

Other organizational units at lower levels got together on their own initiative, to work on intragroup issues. To sum it up, there was an enormous amount of OD activity, and I recall feeling pleased and yet concerned that it was getting away from us. I would learn about events after the fact and worry that an internal process consultant had not been invited to lend assistance and make sure it went "right," that is, to ensure that productive and not counter-productive levelling took place. (Recent feedback has revealed that, in some instances, my fears were well founded.)

---

*It was agreed that attendance at T-groups would be strictly voluntary and managers who were close to their retirement would not be invited. I now have regrets about the latter decision. Our focus was going to be on improving organizational relationships and building for the future. Older managers, in effect, were already being set aside, and I feel we could have helped them in this transition with a laboratory approach to retirement planning.

In July, 1969, my colleague, Wally Mead, interviewed the four V.P.'s and 21 other managers selected at random from among the directors and department heads. The purpose was to find out how they felt about sensitivity training and whether they perceived any positive changes in attitudes, behavior, and problem-solving efficiency resulting from it. What we got back was a tempered endorsement. Most felt that, as a result of T-groups, communications were more open, many one-to-one relationships had improved, and it had been personally rewarding. However, they were not as positive about team building or intergroup confrontation. These were seen as more risky, since managers were still unsure about the value of making issues and unpopular opinions public. We concluded that trust was still low, and we had not explained clearly what OD was trying to accomplish. To help rectify the latter point, we sent a copy of Warner Burke's article, "What Is Organization Development," to all our T-group alumni, and spent time at the end of subsequent T-groups, explaining OD and some of the things that were happening in the company.

PHARMACEUTICAL SALES DEPARTMENT

In terms of commitment to OD, measured by man hours devoted to it and the length of time of this involvement, the pharmaceutical sales department has been our best client. Our OD consulting relationship with pharmaceutical sales started in January '69 and is still continuing. At best, I can only briefly sketch the many events that have occurred in this period of time.

It all started when the national sales manager attended the January '69 Phase 1 T-group for department heads. Upon his return, he asked us to help him train his eight divisional managers and 42 regional managers. Based on some direct feedback that I had received, plus the opinion of others from personnel who had worked with the salesmen, morale in the field was very low, and the national sales manager was very much aware of this. He also knew about the work we had done with the sales managers from the other division the year before, and there was a history between the two sales forces of "keeping up with the Joneses." The major issue was lack of trust between managers in the field and the home office. The management style for years had been autocratic with almost all decisions (including the hiring of salesmen) being made in Philadelphia. The man who had been vice-president of sales for several years and only a few months before had been promoted to another job, had wanted to change management style to a more decentralized one. However, his methods of inducing change generated tremendous fear of him in the field. They were also afraid of the national sales manager because they perceived his behaviors to be punishing. Added to all this were the external changes affecting the pharmaceutical industry, and lack of communications about internal changes that were being contemplated and how these would affect their jobs. Anxiety levels were high.

The OD staff recommended that this sales organization follow the same design which had been carried out successfully with their "younger brother." The sales manager and the new vice-president of sales, who had attended the December '68 lab for directors, agreed, and they also agreed to measure our efforts with the

Likert Profile of Organizational Characteristics (Form S). The national sales manager wanted to get started quickly and turned over to us the time that had already been scheduled for spring sales meetings.

This whole effort, particularly the research findings, has been reported elsewhere[7], but it might be helpful to touch on some of the highlights. For one thing, the design differed from the pilot effort. "Brother" managers met on Saturday afternoon and T-grouped until Wednesday. Wednesday morning and afternoon was spent preparing the agenda for a confrontation with the next two higher levels of management — the national sales manager and the vice-president of sales with the divisional managers, and the respective divisional managers and the national sales manager with the regionals. The confrontation started Wednesday evening and continued through the next morning. A substantial number of one-on-one issues were worked, not only in the group setting but also outside. I vividly recall one bit of heavy business that the national sales manager and a regional manager resolved at a curbside conference during coffee break. On Friday, the divisional managers held a regular business meeting with their regionals, while the trainers served as process consultants.

Altogether we ran five of these sessions, starting with the division managers and then working with two divisions at a time on four occasions. Art Blumberg, Bob Golembiewski, Wally Mead, and I did the training, working two at a time in mixed pairs. Administrations of the Likert questionnaire were given to all the managers before any training started; after divisional manager training in March '69; after the first four divisions trained in May; after the second four divisions trained in July; during a reinforcement session in September; and finally, six weeks later. Change in a positive direction was noted but not nearly to the degree that was recorded in the pilot study the year before. Nevertheless, there was ample anecdotal evidence of change in the way interpersonal and intergroup problems were dealt with. When two California divisions and two divisions in the Northeast were merged, two days were set aside, in each instance, to work through the issues, such as dominant and subordinate group feelings, new reporting relationships, boss manager's style, etc. A number of one-on-one issues were resolved with third party consulting help. I remember one I was involved in where a divisional manager was on the verge of firing an excellent regional manager because of perceived insubordination. Both parties came to the home office, and we worked on it for half a day. Agreement on the key issues was achieved, and the boss subsequently rated the regional manager as one of the best in his division.

As our activity with the sales managers increased, more and more salesmen voiced a desire to get into the act, that is, to undergo a comparable learning experience. Sales management approved, and we began to make plans to do a three day, non-T-group, but lab oriented program for each division. However, before this extension of the OD effort got started, a marketing task force in the home office recommended that marketing spend be reduced by 25 percent. This meant a substantial layoff of salesmen and the potential layoff of 13 regional managers, some of whom had been managing for many years.

OUR DEMOTION INTERVENTION

During the deliberations about how to proceed with this unpleasant task, one of the thorny issues that had to be resolved was what to do about the 13 excess regional managers. This group was divided roughly in half between older, long-service managers and younger, newer managers. One option was to lay them all off; another was to lay off those who, it was suspected, might become malcontents and demote those who would be most likely to accept this action gracefully. A third one, which the OD staff pushed for, was to offer all of them a chance to leave with a generous severance allowance or accept a demotion to senior salesmen. Sales management chose the third after we proposed a plan to work with the demotees to ease the trauma, which we all felt would be severe.

The plan was that it would be mandated that any of the 13 who chose demotion would have to come together at a central location the week following the announcement of the layoffs to share their feelings, to develop coping strategies, and to interface with their new regional manager bosses. The intent of this intervention was "to confront the imaginings induced by the demotions with the sharing of resources in a community setting that hopefully would increase a demotee's sense of mastery over the consequences of his demotion."[8]

Eleven of the thirteen chose to take the demotion, and Wally Mead and I met with them in Chicago at the end of October, 1970. Because we wanted to measure the effect of this intervention in reducing levels of anxiety, depression and hostility, we asked them at the beginning of our meeting to fill out Zuckerman and Lubin's *Multiple Affect Adjective Check List*[9], designed to measure the state of these emotions in a subject at a given point in time. Mutely, but not suspiciously, they all complied. Wally and I were known to all of them, and throughout the experience, I never felt any hostility directed at us except by one person who felt the meeting constituted unwarranted "hand holding." At the outset we encouraged them to share their feelings about the demotions, how it was communicated, family reaction (one older manager said his wife was delighted because now he would not have to travel), future prospects for more layoffs, the company's concern for and value of them (someone offered that the meeting itself was evidence of this).

Because they all were scheduled to attend sales meetings the following week, we wanted them to begin looking ahead as soon as possible and not dwell overly long on what was past and could not be changed. We asked them to compile a list of relevant people with whom they would have to interact and discuss how they were going to handle these situations. The list included new bosses, doctors, competitive salesmen, wives, peers who, in some cases, would be former subordinates, friends, etc. The commonly shared feeling was that they should not avoid discussing what had happened but rather talk about it without embarrassment. And under no circumstances should they "bad-mouth" the company, which they felt some doctors, peers, and competitors would try to goad them into doing. A commonly shared theme was that they had made the choice to stay with the company, and having made that decision freely, their effort should be devoted to doing the best possible job.

That evening Wally and I met with their new bosses. Our first bit of business was to administer the MAACL. Then we explored how they were feeling, which could be summarized as "there but for the grace of God go I." Strategies for interfacing the next day were shared, and it was generally agreed that smothering the demotees with sympathy would not be especially helpful. Instead they should focus on helping them solve current or potential problems, such as moving to a new location, dismantling their office, organizing their territory, etc.

The next morning they met in pairs for several hours. I visited about half of them before time ran out and found the tone of the meetings to be universally positive. By design, I made certain to visit those pairs where the demotee was going to remain in the region he formerly managed. With them I posed the problem of salesmen maintaining their allegiance to their former manager and the potential conflict which might result. They agreed this was something to watch out for and should be dealt with immediately and openly should it arise.

At the end of the morning, they reassembled as a total group, and we asked them to fill out the MAACL again. That ended the intervention which had lasted a little less than 24 hours. When we scored the before and after administrations of the MAACL, we found that levels of anxiety, depression, and hostility were reduced in almost every instance. Specifically — of the 33 comparisons (11 demotees X 3 MAACL scales), 26 were reductions and three were no-change in scores. About 40 days later we asked them to fill out the MAACL again to see if the reductions persisted. Nine showed further reductions and two showed an increase on one of the scales but evenness or reductions on the others. Later interviews with demotees and several levels of their managers indicated that 10 of the 11 made the transition "in great shape" or "more than adequately" on a 20-point scale ranging down to "somewhat inadequate" and "critically inadequate."[10]

Our next major activity with the pharmaceutical sales force was to design and conduct a one and a half day learning experience for all the salesmen. Only rather than do it on a division by division basis as was originally planned before the layoffs, we did it with all 425 at one time, as part of a National Sales Meeting held in March, 1971. Extensive pre and post measurements were made and positive change was noted.[11] More importantly, without waiting for the data, it was obvious to most observers on the scene that the meeting caused an impressive turn around in negative morale. There is still a lot of work to be done with the sales force to help it adapt to changes in market, products, decision making responsibility, measurement, etc., but happily, sales management is aware of the needs and is willing to commit resources to meet them.

OBSERVATIONS

There are several brief comments that I would like to make, not necessarily in order of importance, but things that come to mind as I think about where we have been and where we are going with organization development.

First, I feel that for the internal change agent, it is extremely important to have outside consulting help. The outsider can bring a breadth of knowledge and experience to bear on problems that the insider more than likely will not have. In my case, for instance, Art and, especially, Bob have a tremendous knowledge of the literature that I have not had time to acquire. Also, we have found it expedient to have the outsider deal with certain line managers when special consulting help was required. But most importantly, the insider's role can be a lonely one, and it can be enormously valuable, if not essential, to have someone at hand who knows what you are talking about and can offer support and guidance.

Second, I do not feel you have to start at the very top of the organization, but you do have to start at the top of the subunit or functional area in which you are going to work. Having that boss not only believing, but also behaving in ways that are compatible with OD values, is extremely important for success. However, now that we have been at it for a while, and have the experiential data to show that it produces results, we plan to explain and/or demonstrate what OD is to our top management group. I think it is important that the internal OD staff know whether we can expect continued support or whether we should consider reallocating our resources and perhaps ourselves.

Third, to get OD started requires some careful nurturing, and this means having an adequate number of internal staff, either full or part time, to tend it. I did not push nearly as hard as I should have for internal help. My requests for this help were turned down for budget reasons or because there was other work to be done, and I acquiesced too readily. The result is that in several areas, we made a start but did not follow through. I now have a "turned on" group of four working with me and am very bullish about the future prospects for OD in the company.

Fourth, I want to make a strong pitch for sensitivity training labs, at least the kind that we have been running. OD is a lot more than just sending people off to labs and hoping that something good will happen as a result. But for us, T-groups were an essential part of our plan. They constituted the basic training without which, I am convinced, we could not have successfully changed existing programs or introduced new ones. For example, we now insist that all employees be allowed to read their formal performance appraisals, rather than merely being told what is in them. We are asking all our salaried employees to write down their career goals and list their development plans for achieving them, so that managers can better match personal goals with the organization's needs. And, we have just launched an assessment center program with comprehensive feedback as an essential ingredient.

Lastly, I want to share some anecdotal data on the effectiveness of our program. We had a very bright, promising manager who left our company several years ago for greener pastures and because of concern over the way the company was being managed. He returned at the end of 1970 to head one of our major divisions. In one of our recent discussions he mentioned the great improvement that had occurred in his absence in the quality of inter-group and inter-personal relationships. He felt this could only be attributed to our organization development efforts.

REFERENCES

1. Golembiewski, Robert T., and Arthur Blumberg, "Sensitivity Training in Cousin Groups: A Confrontation Design," *Training and Development Journal*, Vol. 23 (August 1969).

2. Oshry, Barry, and Roger Harrison, "Transfer From Here-and-Now to There-and-Then: Changes in Organizational Problem Diagnosis Stemming from T-Group Training," *Journal of Applied Behavioral Science*, Vol. 2 (June 1966).

3. Golembiewski, Robert T., and Stokes B. Carrigan, "Planned Change in Organization Style Based on Laboratory Approach," *Administrative Science Quarterly*, Vol. 15 (March 1970).

4. Golembiewski, Robert T., and Stokes B. Carrigan, "The Persistence of Laboratory-Induced Changes in Organization Styles," *Administrative Science Quarterly*, Vol. 15 (September 1970).

5. Beckhard, Richard, "An Organizational Improvement Program in a Decentralized Organization," *The Journal of Applied Behavioral Sciences,* Vol. 2 (March 1966).

6. Roberts, Ellis, and Charles Smith, "A Management 'Be In': T-Groups and Sensitivity Training – a Painful Way of Getting to Know Yourself," *Dare Magazine*, Vol. 5 (Summer 1967).

7. Golembiewski, Robert T., Robert Munzenrider, Arthur Blumberg, Stokes B. Carrigan, Walter R. Mead, "Changing Climate in a Complex Organization: Interactions Between a Learning Design and an Environment," *Academy of Management Journal,* Vol. 14 (December 1971).

8. Golembiewski, Robert T., Stokes B. Carrigan, Walter R. Mead, Robert Munzenrider, Arthur Blumberg, "Integrating Disrupted Work Relationships: An Action Design for a Critical Intervention," *Contemporary Organization Development: Conceptual Orientations and Interventions*, edited by W. Warner Burke, *NTL Institute for Applied Behavioral Science* (1972).

9. Zuckerman, M., and B. Lubin, *Multiple Affect Adjective Check Lists: Manual*, San Diego, Cal., Educational and Industrial Testing Service, 1965.

10. Golembiewski et al., *op. cit.*

11. Golembiewski, Robert T., Stokes B. Carrigan, Arthur Blumberg, Robert Munzenrider, "Team Building On A Mass Scale: Three Approaches to Measuring Effects," in manuscript.

4

ORGANIZATION DEVELOPMENT
IN AN AIRLINE SETTING

The following case describes how an OD function was identified in the corporate organization of a major airline. A person was recruited for the top spot and a staff was built up. It illustrates the problem of defining what OD is and establishing its role in the organization. The chapter deals with the differentiation that was made between standard management training programs and OD. A laboratory-type, experience-based program was developed for managers. The first major effort in OD was done with the stewardess college. This approach utilized consulting teams (using both internal and external consultants) who gathered data on the organization. The programs that followed were focused on job enrichment and team development. Later a program was conducted for customer service personnel on transactional analysis. The result was that the management and organization development activity had substantially changed its image but what had been gained/lost? The author has critiqued his five-year effort noting many of the shortcomings of OD programs in general. It provides a caution against becoming a "true believer" and failing to recognize some of the failures of OD (i.e. interpersonal, process problems, if solved, don't necessarily provide the whole cure for what ails the organization). He concludes by suggesting a legitimate role for OD throughout the organization and consequently a challenge for OD practitioners.

Organization Development in an Airline Setting

KENT F. WAMPLER

THE PRESENTING PROBLEM — A DEFINITION

In November 1972, a training officer with the state of California told me about the following incident. In mid year 1972 one of the training staff from the state and an outside consultant produced a videotape in which the two of them discussed attempts, successes, failures and potential of OD in the public service. The tape was viewed by a number of training staff groups in California. At the conclusion of one particular viewing a member of the audience reacted by pointing to an organization chart of his agency and stating: "I don't think what they are saying is relevant, because this is organization development!"

This incident was more confirming than surprising to me. Definitions of organization development have been and continue to be a problem.

The incident brought some related memories back to me. In 1966 I took a job as Manager, Organization Development with American Airlines, Inc. in New York. Prior to 1966 some internal bases had evolved for establishing a separate OD branch within the Training and Development organization. The Management Training branch had been experimenting with experience-based learning in centralized management development programs; a number of the corporate top management had attended the public Management Grid course; and the technical training staff for Sales and Services training had been moved from a line department and now reported to the Training and Development division in Personnel Services.

A position paper was written which described the function and duties of an organization development branch within Training and Development. I was recruited and hired for the position and an administrator from the management training branch was moved over to report to me.

The problem of definition of function arose in a number of ways. After I had been in the job for one month, pressures were exerted on my division head,

Kent F. Wampler is Executive Director of the Intergovernmental Management Institute, Oakland, California. He held previous positions in employee training, management and organization development with American Airlines and the State of California (Department of Public Works and Water Resources Agency). He was graduated from California State College, San Francisco, with a degree in industrial psychology. He has done graduate work in psychology at California State College, Sacramento.

70

the director of Training and Development, to change the function title of Organization Development. The pressures came from the Corporate Planning group which, along with other planning responsibilities, maintains the process of organization charting and updating of the formal organization schematics. The title Organization Development implied to the planning group that their function was being subverted. It was decided to change the functional title of Organization Development rather than run the risk of alienating the Corporate Planning Department. This event highlighted the difficulty of defining OD within the corporation.

A new designation was chosen — Employee Development Systems. This title resolved the problem with Corporate Planning; was broad enough to permit the branch to work the OD plans; and was a pretty fair representation of the duties and responsibilities within the new function. Outside of "pure OD" work, the function adopted a number of projects that were not defined as OD. These were maintaining a Management Candidate program; developing a new appraisal system; and providing staff for conducting the company's centralized training programs.

A second definition problem was distinguishing between the branch functions of Management Training and Employee Development Systems. The question of distinguishing between these two functions revolved around the issues of justification for existence of the functions, definition of responsibility, and rewards for performance. Aside from these organization system needs for defining the role of the two functions, between the functions, there was also a sense of different value systems and premises about how to create change. These last factors more than anything led to a lot of energy expended in differentiating between what Management Training was, and what it was to do, and what Employee Development Systems was, and what it was to do.

Table 4.1 implies the kind of polarity that developed in definition of functional responsibility and programs between the two branches.

PROGRAMS TAKE SHAPE

"Seeding" for OD Through Centralized Training

Just prior to and during the period of forming an OD organization branch, American Airlines had a significant centralized management training curriculum operating. Courses were conducted by the Training and Development staff at an executive training center in New York. An average of 700 managers each year attended one week programs titled:

- Basics of Supervision
- Basic Communications Skills
- Face to Face Communications
- Instructor Training
- Building Productive Work Teams
- Managerial Learning Laboratory

The Building Productive Work Teams course was particularly interesting from an OD standpoint because its design used interactive training techniques and

Table 4.1 Branch functions of management training and employee development systems

MANAGEMENT TRAINING		EMPLOYEE DEVELOPMENT SYSTEMS	
Functional emphasis	Program responsibility	Functional emphasis	Program responsibility
Centralized approach	Operate management training center	Provide field services	Administer management candidate program
Long term continuing	Conduct specialized courses	Short term project emphasis	Consulting services
Individual development	Administer tuition refund program	Team development	• Stewardess college
Classroom instruction	Clearing house for individual development resources	Development system	• Maintenance Department (GRID)
Concepts theory	Conduct course evaluation and follow up	Applied/ experiential	• Flight instructors
Heterogeneous groups		Homogeneous groups	• Airport supervisors
Horizontal groups		Vertical groups	Redesign management performance review system
Staff administered		Line administered	Conduct training and development staff development
			Develop OD research designs

many of the course concepts were borrowed from behavioral science sources. The Managerial Learning Laboratory had some of the same attributes, plus the course used a highly structured, week-long simulation exercise that allowed managers to gain practice in operating a hypothetical airline.

The Employee Development Systems (OD) group was asked to be responsible for the administration of the Building Productive Work Teams and the Managerial Learning Lab courses. The result, after a number of experiences in running the separate courses, was the welding of the two programs into a single course which continued to be designated as the Managerial Learning Laboratory (the content of which is given in Appendixes 4.1 through 4.3). The modifications resulting from the combining of the two courses could best be described as creating an "instrumented change laboratory." The course presented a structured approach through individual, group and intergroup exercises. Along with the basic structure, the participants had the opportunity to affect the process of the course through their own experiences, attitudes, and value systems. Through a period of five years, 1966 through 1971, the Managerial Learning Laboratory continued to be an important source of "seeding" for field OD projects initiated within the company. The course underwent modification as the technology of individual and organizational change and management concepts evolved. However, the behavioral model upon which the course was based has remained unchanged. This "Model of Managerial Behaviors" has served as a guide both for the centralized courses as well as for giving direction to the OD consulting process. The model in its simplest form is shown in Table 4.2.

For readers who want more detail on the Managerial Learning Laboratory* it is described in a research report published by the National Industrial Conference Board.[1]

At a later date, about 1970, the MLL course was redesignated the Management Development Laboratory (MDL) with the predominant change in the course being the addition of some strengthened "re-entry" designs built into the final day of the program. On the last day of the course a workshop on personal development and career planning was added, and a block of time was devoted to looking at OD and its potential application in the American Airlines organization.

A SIGNIFICANT FIRST PROJECT

A positive relationship had been developing between the administration and instructor staff at the AA Stewardess College in Fort Worth, Texas and the Training and Development staff in New York. In 1964 and 1965 Training and Development staff members worked with the Stewardess College to develop a study of instructional methodology used in training stewardesses. This study led to a series of instructor workshops to upgrade instructor skills and determine possibilities for curriculum modification.

Coinciding with the formation of an OD branch in Training and Development, in 1966 the company made a decision to invest in a major expansion of stewardess college facilities. "This . . . decision by top management to spend millions of dollars to increase the size of the stewardess college gave new impetus to the stewardess college curriculum study. It also confronted stewardess management, the college staff, and training and development with many practical questions. Assuming that a new instructional building was to be built, what kind of facility should it be? Should it contain traditional classrooms like the ones in the present building? Should the same kinds of training methods and equipment be used in the future? If not, what kinds of facilities and equipment should be designed into the planned building to make new approaches possible? Since the college was asked to submit its recommendations for the new facilities to the architect by the spring of 1967, these questions took on added urgency."[2]

The solution to the above issues and to developing the specifications for the new facility was found in a joint effort between the stewardess college staff, the OD group at American, and a team of outside consultants from Leadership Resources Inc. (LRI).

The approach taken was to develop a series of workshops in which LRI, American's OD group, and all levels of the stewardess college staff performed a

---

*See Appendix 4.1.

Learning Levels

Self-Awareness Level		Group Development Level		Intergroup Action Level	
From	Toward	From	Toward	From	Toward
Being closed	→ Being open	Surface discussions	→ Depth discussions	Competition with other groups	→ Collaboration with other groups
Denying feelings	→ Expressing feelings	Intra-group competitiveness	→ Intra-group collaboration	Win/lose conflict resolution	→ Win/win conflict resolution
Being defensive	→ Accepting feedback	Guarding information	→ Sharing information	Destructive inter-group relationships	→ Helping inter-group relationships
Conventional approach	→ Experimental approach	Denying feelings	→ Expressing feelings	One-sided problem-solving	→ Shared problem-solving
Suspicion of others	→ Trust of others	Undercutting other members	→ Supporting other members	Rejecting others' points of view	→ Accepting others' points of view
Being guarded	→ Being spontaneous	Being unaware of group process	→ Being aware of group process	Viewing other groups as enemies	→ Viewing other groups as colleagues
Avoiding conflict	→ Facing conflict	Using few group resources	→ Using all group resources	Suspicion of other groups	→ Trust of other groups
Being rigid	→ Being flexible	Win/lose conflict resolution	→ Win/win conflict resolution	Commitment limited to group goals	→ Commitment to total organization goals
Having a facade	→ Being sincere	Resistance or apathy to group goals	→ Commitment to group goals		
Shallowness of perception	→ Depth of perception	Self-enhancing behavior	→ Contribution to group action		
Distorted self-awareness	→ Accurate self-awareness				

Managerial Behaviors

Table 4.2 Managerial learning laboratory: course objectives expressed as directional movement at three levels of learning (From American Airlines Training and Development Division. Used by permission.)

diagnosis of past college practices and problems. This generating of substantive data was combined with sessions which were process oriented and enabled the college staff to work through some of the relationship issues between members that existed at the college.

The culmination of this work was the submission of a report recommending curriculum changes, new facilities specifications, and equipment and staffing changes.

The contents of this report proposed dramatic changes in the methodology of training conducted at the college and recommended on the supporting facilities required to make the changes possible.

Dedicated in 1970, the new stewardess college facility in Fort Worth represents tangible evidence that resources of an organization group can be effectively applied to complex organization development problems. I believe that without the interventions of the OD group and the outside behavioral science consultants the new stewardess college would have been substantially an expanded version of the old facilities. More important than the concrete, wood and metal, the new environmental change represents a different emphasis and direction in the approach taken to administration of the college organization and training of the stewardess students.

THE SEARCH FOR A VIABLE INTERVENTION

Excepting the Stewardess College project and a project within the Freight organization (which I will later describe) American used few outside consultant linkups to facilitate the OD process. Outside consultants were used primarily for purposes of Training and Development staff development, program design consultation, and were brought in briefly to provide exposure of the top management group to OD concepts.

The basic emphasis in the OD group was on building an internal staff consulting capability to work organization improvement without recourse to outside consultation.

Between the period of 1967 to 1970 the OD group conducted a good deal of experimentation with various concepts and models viewed as having a high potential to institute problem solving, change and personal growth in the managerial group. The predominant models and "inventors" that were applied were:

The Managerial Grid	Blake & Mouton
Interpersonal Relationships	Schutz
Communications	Luft
Needs Hierarchy	Maslow
Job Enrichment	Herzberg
Managerial Values	Argyris
Self Concept	Hayakawa
Rational Problem Solving	Kepner & Tregoe
Creative Problem Solving	Parnes
Managerial Beliefs	McGregor
Team Development	Morton

Leadership	Tannenbaum & Schmidt
Facilitative Learning	Rogers
Lateral Learning	Mead
Training Systems	Mager
Field Theory	Lewin
Conflict	Shepard
Human Resources	Likert
Achievement Motivation	McClellen
Self Renewal	Gardner
Management by Objectives	Drucker
Behavior Modification	Skinner
Interpersonal Transactions	Berne

Among this listing, the interventions which provided the greatest success in terms of acceptance by management, measurable impact where applied, and perpetuation of use (used extensively in a number of areas within the company) were Job Enrichment* and Team Development.† Job Enrichment projects undertaken were based directly on Herzberg's concepts and the experiences of Robert Fords' work with the concepts at A.T.&T. The Team Development design drew heavily from the Communications aspects of Carl Rogers' work and on the Communications theory developed by Joseph Luft. The process used in Team Development was one of data gathering from operational meetings of the client group; compilation and analysis of data; a series of offsite meetings in which data was fedback; group problem identification and analysis; action planning for change; and implementing changes. The design of an American Airlines Team Development project was published in the Training & Development Journal.[3]

Douglas H. Marr presently the Manager — Organization Development at American Airlines wrote a paper summarizing the experiences with Job Enrichment titled "What We Have Learned About Job Enrichment"[4] addressed in the summary are the issues of:

- Gaining entry into a job function
- Getting commitment and gaining authority from top management
- The need for a "contract" and criteria in a "contract"
- Defining the nature of a project - experimental vs permanent
- Selecting the job to be changed
- Measurement of project impact

Of the many interventions available these two, Job Enrichment and Team Development provided the most substantive results and received the most acceptance in the Organization Development effort.

What happened to other interventions that were attempted?

The Managerial Grid represented a high investment in terms of numbers of managers who attended public seminars in 1966 through 1969.

Although much seeding took place both in public seminars and in exploration of grid concepts in the company management programs Phase 2 of grid never

---

*Appendix 4.2.

†Appendix 4.3.

got established. It is my perception that the support and resources required to go through the long range, six-phase program were the major barriers to implementing grid OD. Management wanted something that could be treated as experimental (reducing the risk of "failure"), fast, and tangible.

During 1968 and 1969 the Freight organization undertook an OD project using an outside consultant. The consultant's services were supplemented with attendance of top management in key executive laboratories sponsored by National Training Laboratories (N.T.L.). Somehow the interventions of the Freight OD project never got linked into the priorities and operational issues in Freight, and although there is evidence that some individual growth and change resulted, the impact on the Freight function and system never came into clear focus.

In 1969 and 1970 organizational surveys were conducted using both the Likert instrument and a Climate & Performance survey designed within the company. The results of these surveys were used as interventions within a number of departments. The compiled survey data and programs of data feedback seemed to have little impact on working through issues and providing ownership for problems that would bring about committment to engage in efforts to change. It was all too easy for individual committment to get lost in the normative data.

In 1970 a program was developed which, through 1971 would be used to train about 4000 Customer Service personnel. This program known as T.A.C.T. (Transactional Analysis in Customer Treatment) was based on the theories of Eric Berne and the writings of Thomas Harris. Although Transactional Analysis was not being applied in an OD context in this program, evidence exists that the program has resulted in some meaningful individual change and some "unfreezing" between managers and employees exposed to the program. Transactional Analysis concepts seem to present a high potential intervention for Organization Development purposes.

THE TRANSITION OVER A FIVE-YEAR PERIOD

There were notable shifts in the goals and strategies of the Training and Development organization between 1966 when OD was introduced and at a period five years later in 1970. In 1966 the major thrust of the company's training effort was to gain acceptance for the function of an internal training capability. In 1967 the Training and Development goals called for a shift from emphasis on the "scientific" management approach to development to a behavioral science approach. In 1968 the goal was to integrate the individual development process with an organizational development process. In 1969 the theme was the legitimizing of OD as a process of management. And, in 1970 there was emphasis on the concept of the manager as a facilitator in his work group. The goals for 1970 implied that OD was leaving the experimental phase and entering a maintenance phase where the process could be carried out in and through the company's line management.

Table 4.3 conceptualizes this movement and shift in direction of the Management & Organization Development goals.

Table 4.3 Some Key Directions In Management and Organization Development

1966	1967	1968-1969	1970
Create emphasis on mgmt. as a profession within AA.	Build Behavioral Science focus at various mgmt. levels in AA.	Build support for OD and conduct follow up OD projects where acceptance exists.	Exemplify OD and Behavioral Science applications in Mgmt. Development curriculum (model the AA organization in Centralized Training).
Train as many managers as is possible by conducting formal Mgmt. Training.	Meet current and re-occurring Mgmt. Development needs within AA Mgmt.	Provide some type of formal Mgmt. Development for each level of AA Mgmt.	Build concept of development as integral part of getting work accomplished. Provide for individual development of mgmt. skills with local capability to implement.
Build acceptance for formal Mgmt. Training and for function of Training and Development.	Develop acceptance for Behavioral Science approach to Mgmt. among middle and lower level Mgmt.	Build transition between Mgmt. Development and Organization Development. Build committment with top Mgmt. and officer group for large scale OD approaches.	Support OD through providing resources for individual and work group development.

It has been my observation that there is a two to three-year lag between the expression of these annual goals and some sensing of results and movement approaching the goals. Around 1968 it was clear through indicators such as extent of participation in programs, interest expressed by upper management, and testimony, that the goals expressed in 1966 were well accomplished. Similarly, in 1970 much evidence could be pointed to which indicated that the 1968 goals were well on the way to being achieved. Taken in its total context this evolutionary direction in Management and Organization Development in the company seems natural, logical, and systematic. Taken in its parts there were many times during the five-year period when it seemed that little was changing or moving.

A CRITIQUE OF THE FIVE-YEAR EFFORT

In 1970 I outlined seven major issues of the OD approach that were chronic and significant. These criticisms were based upon the approach to OD that had been formulated in American Airlines and may not apply to strategies instituted by other practitioners in other organizations.

The first issue I identified was:

- OD limited to behavioral science approach may neglect other aspects of organizational/individual problem solving and growth — e.g., skill deficiencies, physical environment, work system, individual coaching (and/or therapy).

There are a couple of criticisms implied in this issue. One point is that not all problems exist in the relationship, certainly the relationships can be worked in order to facilitate correction of other problems, but the "true believer" in the behavioral sciences should recognize that he places parameters on the solutions to problems just as the industrial engineer or planning specialist does. My second point evolves from the first — that the OD practitioner should broaden his ability to sense and tackle organization improvement through a more interdisciplinary and eclectic approach than is now, in the main, being applied. In one particular instance — the rejection of individual development — OD has frequently been guilty of throwing out the baby with the bath water.

The second issue:

- OD is a long term change strategy — slow to evolve significant changes. Some circumstances may call for change which is fast and of temporary duration. OD is not equipped to institute power based change (or fight it when it occurs inappropriately).

I am not sure that OD must be synonymous with long range change. The long term change rationale for OD is probably a function of its staff-supported, process-oriented, nonoperationally based, character. On the other hand, I believe that power *can* corrupt the basic values of OD. I will leave this issue as a dilemma for both myself and the reader.

The third issue:

- The start at the middle approach creates disparities between management levels that either negate change or create new problems (which may not get worked through and be extremely dysfunctional while they exist).

American's approach has not been a neatly packaged "start at the top" OD process. The path of least resistance for OD interventions and projects has been middle management. If the choice were no OD or start in the middle I would still opt for starting in the middle. The most significant problems with beginning OD in the middle management group are the pressures placed on the middle manager to revert, or even more troublesome the widening of the disparity between what the manager perceives as the system and what he wants the system to be.

The fourth issue:

- OD as a subfunction of personnel suffers from the problem of offering mixed messages to client groups unless the personnel system as a whole is tuned into a common value base – e.g., while OD is advocating System 4, the employee relations group may be writing System 2 policy for the field to follow.

Perhaps OD should start at home. Certainly line management could not help but note a credibility gap between what OD as a function of personnel was advocating and what the personnel family was generating in policies and procedures for selection, compensation, and labor relations.

The fifth issue:

- We haven't learned to maintain an OD effort adequately. Each OD intervention results in discovery of more macro problems. The issue is how do we work the emerging issues building on the original OD base. The Stewardess College effort leading to identification of stewardess system problems is a good example.

It seemed that just as we were able to draw the skin around a problem and begin to focus on solutions a set of larger order problems would be defined. Every system that got involved in OD was a subsystem of some larger system. There was no independent system but a hierarchy of interdependent systems.

The sixth issue:

- OD can get institutionalized mighty fast – e.g., job enrichment, Likert data feedback. A problem is how to maintain a process consultation/action research model and yet offer a substantive process that management can understand and use.

I once had a company manager confront me with "When are you OD guys going to stop proposing this experimentation and spell out a systematic plan I can use?" I replied, "When are you managers going to allow us to do some experimentation so we can develop a systematic plan?" The packaged approach to OD ("Come in and plug in job enrichment") is most acceptable to management, yet, is fraught with the dangers of using the right tool for the wrong job. If American's experience is typical, as OD technology increases more and more practitioners seek the appropriate situation to apply a tool (or force the tool to fit) rather than invent a tool or select the appropriate tool among options.

The seventh issue:

- OD in its present form is a staff function. A problem is how to make OD a part of the responsibility of operational management – to build the diagnosis/intervention/evaluation model into the method of managing (this includes building in concern for human resources and process).

Success can be measured in many ways, from hard empirical approaches to pragmatic means. Some of the "softest" indicators of OD progress made me feel best. Like receiving a reprint on organization change from a line manager with a routing slip that said, "I thought you'd be interested in the attached." Or, there was my visit to an office of a high seniority line vice-president who had a reputation for being tough. One of his divisions had completed a team building project a few months before in which he was not directly involved. As I looked across his desk to the credenza behind him I noticed two things, a recent issue of the

Journal of Applied Behavioral Science and a copy of *The Human Side of Enterprise* by Douglas McGregor.

SOME REMARKS ABOUT THE FUTURE OF OD

I like to operate on the premise that the ultimate goal of the practitioner in the organization development function should be to work himself out of a job. Most, if not all, of the models for a "fully functioning" individual or organization involve the capability to be self-renewing. This means the line manager replaces the staff man as facilitator. It also means that organization members have the capabilities to sense dysfunction and to affect changes to correct it. The issue of how to maintain an OD effort (an issue which has so little experience to bring to bear), is tied up with the strategy question of how to obtain a line manager-facilitator talent in the organization. Contemporary behavioral and organizational models applied in OD demonstrate, through measurement and observation, that there is a disparity between what is and what might be in our organizations. This same disparity implies that the extrinsic rewards for the manager who takes on the role of facilitator are probably few. More likely there are punishments and forces that drive out the facilitator role. Rensis Likert's concepts of human resources accounting hold out the potential for building the extrinsic factors into an organization that would legitimize the role of manager-facilitator. MBA and other degree curriculums are recognizing the human factors side of the management business and building a consideration of behavioral sciences into the degree requirements.

That part of managing an organization that we refer to as organization behavior, human resources management, or behavioral science has certainly been legitimized as part of management's repertoire of functions. Perhaps OD as we now know it is the necessary agent of intervention that can bridge the gap between what is known in the field of research and model building and what the newer generation of managers would like to apply, and what is unknown and unapplied among the bulk of managers in today's organization. All of this is to say that OD practitioners, present and future, have their work cut out for them.

APPENDIX 4.1 MANAGERIAL LEARNING LABORATORY*

The Assumptions

1. Effective problem solving requires a large quantity of questions to be asked — particularly in the information gathering and problem identification phase. (Most managers ask too few questions.)

2. In problem solving, it is important for a manager to differentiate between what he knows and what he assumes.

3. Problem solving is more effective when a manager achieves a balance between convergent thinking and divergent thinking.

4. Most managers are more skillful at and use more convergent thinking than they use divergent thinking.

5. Being more aware of and open about his own feelings and the feelings of others improves a manager's problem solving. (In fact, it is often the unexpressed feelings which created problems which go unrecognized.)

6. Most managers are uncomfortable with their own and others' feelings and emotions (both positive and negative).

7. As a manager becomes more open about himself on both the feeling and cognitive levels, he also becomes a more effective problem solver.

8. Receiving feedback from others concerning his problem-solving skills, effectiveness, and ineffectiveness is essential if a manager is to learn how to

The Terminal Behavior Objectives

Managers will ask a large number of questions before attempting to generate alternatives or to solve problems.

Managers will specify in writing what assumptions they have made concerning the problem being discussed.

Managers will compare these assumptions with known facts to determine if they are reasonable assumptions.

Managers will use "creative questions" when speculating on alternatives.

Managers will develop a minimum of five alternatives for every problem or subproblem being worked on.

Managers will report their own feelings more frequently during group interaction directed at the last problem exercise in the program than they reported on the first problem exercise of the program.

Managers will rate themselves and be rated by others as having *smaller* "hidden areas" at the end of the program than at the beginning of the program.

At the end of the program, a manager will give more inputs to other managers concerning their performance effectiveness and ineffectiveness than

---

*All Managerial Learning Laboratory materials (Appendixes 4.1 through 4.3) used by permission of American Airlines, Inc., Training and Development Division.

become more effective. Managers can learn from each other.

he did at the beginning of the program.

By the end of the program, managers will also provide time for a feedback-generalization period during group problem solving.

9. Most managers strive for problem closure (deciding what the problem is and how it should be solved) sooner than is both necessary and effective.

By the end of the program, managers will remain in the "question-asking" (information-gathering) and "listing problems" (problem-identification) stages of problem solving longer before jumping into the speculation phase than they did at the beginning of the program (determined by problem-solving tape analysis).

10. Most managers are poor listeners. This impairs their problem-solving effectiveness.

At the end of the program, managers will be able to reflect on demand more accurately what the last speaker has said than they were able to at the beginning of the program.

11. Managers can be helped to learn to be more effective in both group and individual problem solving.

By the end of the program, managers will see problems as being more positive than at the beginning of the program.

Course Objectives

A. Work Team Productivity Increasing productivity through:

Awareness of the intellectual, emotional, interpersonal and communication factors that affect the team working process

Awareness of individual problem solving ability as a member of a work group

Defining group goals and controlling the forces that block group accomplishment

Using the resources of the group members in goal setting, decision making, implementation, and evaluation

Ability to deal with interpersonal and intergroup interaction and conflict

B. Self and Group Awareness

Examining the effects of various managerial styles in working with other people

Gaining insight into personal effectiveness as a leader and a member of a work group

Studying the effect of different kinds of team leadership and organization on performance

Exploring the relationship between individual and group achievement

Practicing setting work goals, achieving production under pressure and evaluating team effectiveness

Learning what managers do that strengthens or weakens commitment to work goals and personal growth and improvement

APPENDIX 4.2 JOB ENRICHMENT

Job Enrichment Workshop

1. State purpose of workshop — To determine the potential of using a concept of "Job Enrichment" to revise the content of work and improve productivity, morale, and attitudes.

2. Ask group to contribute to two listings: The first — the things in their jobs over the last year that made them feel good, that "turned them on" to their jobs. The second — the things in their jobs that made them feel bad, that "turned them off" about their jobs.

3. Introduce and show the film "Motivation through Job Enrichment" (Bureau of National Affairs) with Dr. Frederick Herzberg.

4. Discuss the elements in the film and relate the "motivators" and "hygiene factors" to the lists developed in item 2. (This gives the concepts face validity.)

5. Introduce and show the film "The Treasury Case" (American Telephone and Telegraph). Stop the film at the point where the jobs are described but prior to the suggestions for adding enriching factors, and ask the group to suggest and list the things they would do to enrich the jobs. After the group is satisfied that their listing is complete, show the remainder of the film. At the film's conclusion, compare the participants' listing with the actions taken in the film.

6. Cover any issues to clarify Herzberg's concepts.

7. Ask the group to list potential jobs they are responsible for. Select one function that has potential for enrichment and:
   1) Analyze motivation and hygiene factors in that job.
   2) Identify potential motivators to be added to the job.
   3) Identify any potential barriers or restraints that need to be considered in enriching the job.
   4) Develop a plan and schedule for the addition of motivators.
   5) Identify authority and responsibility requirements to implement the job enrichment plan.
   6) Determine criteria and methods to be used to evaluate the effects of the enrichment.
   7) Set plans in motion to carry out the application, monitoring and reporting.

APPENDIX 4.3 TEAM DEVELOPMENT

Tape Analysis Guide - 1

Problem-Solving Effectiveness and Time Utilization

As you listen to the tape, use the Managerial Problem-Solving Chart (Table 4.4) to make a flow chart of the sequence of points your group covered in its discussion. (Omit the reference to divergent and convergent thinking.)

When the tape is completed, show the chart you have made to the rest of the group. Also give your feelings about the following questions to the group (pass out a copy of chart to each group member so that they may follow the points during your comments):

1. How effectively was the time used during the meeting?

2. How could more effective use of time have been made?

3. How rational and logical was group problem-solving?

4. In what ways might group problem solving have been made more effective?

5. How effective were the communications in the group?

6. What was the role of emotional factors in the group meeting?

7. What else does the chart reveal about the way the group worked together? How might the group work more effectively in future meetings?

Tape Analysis Guide - 2

Task and Maintenance Activities

Review the Task and Maintenance activities on the Activity Observation Chart (Table 4.5). As you listen to the tape of your group's meeting, use the chart to record the activities engaged in by each of the members.

At the top of each vertical column on the chart, put the name or initials of each of the group members, starting with the boss. As you listen to the tape, make a hash mark in each person's column next to the Task and Maintenance Activities as he engages in them during the course of the meeting.

When the tape is completed, share your thoughts about the following questions with the group:

1. Who are the group members who are most concerned with Task activities? Maintenance Activities?

2. Which Task activities are used most often? Which are used least often?

3. What changes in Task activity usage would make the group meeting more effective?

4. Which Maintenance activities are used most often? Which are used least often?

5. What changes in Maintenance activity usage would make the group meeting more effective?

Table 4.4 Managerial problem-solving chart for plotting group problem-solving and time utilization

As you review the tape of the problem-solving conference, make a flow chart of the sequence of points your group covered in its discussion. In the left-hand column are possible areas of discussion, divided into three main groupings: Communicating, Problem-Solving, and Handling Emotional Factors. For each participant's contribution to the discussion, or for each brief exchange among members of the group, place a dot opposite the area in which it falls. Also, identify the substance of major problem-solving contributions as divergent (D) or convergent (C) thinking. Arrange these dots along the time continuum from left to right. Connect the cots and make brief notes above or below them to indicate subject-matter mentioned at key points in the discussion. You may need more than one chart/page for your tape analysis. At the end of the tape: (1) compare your individual charts, (2) analyze the pattern of your group's problem-solving discussion and (3) time utilization, and (4) evaluate the effectiveness of your team's efforts.

COMMUNICATING

1. Straightening out misunder- standings of meaning	
2. Nonrelevant comments	
3. Other (specify)	

PROBLEM-SOLVING

4. Organizing the group's efforts "How are we going about this task?"	
5. Gathering information (asking questions)	
6. Identifying or listing problems	
7. Specifying assumptions	
8. Determining causes for problems	
9. Searching for alternatives (listing ideas for possible solution)	
10. Analyzing or weighing alternatives	
11. Selecting alternatives (decision-making)	
12. Planning for implementation or follow-up	
13. Other (specify)	

HANDLING EMOTIONAL FACTORS

14. Interpersonal conflicts (arguments, disagreements, etc.)	
15. Reactions to pressures	
16. Joking, horseplay, etc.	
17. Other (specify)	

―――――――――――――――――――――――― (Time) ――――――――→

Group _____   Date _____

Table 4.5 Activity observation chart

As you observe the group in action, try to determine which activities are most evident among group members and what pattern, if any, these activities take. (Note: Any one group member may engage in several of these activities during the period in which the group is at work.)

A. Task Activities (*Getting the job done*)	Examples								
1. Initiating	Presents new ideas, suggests procedures or proposes alternate solutions.								
2. Information seeking	Seeks orientation or clarification for sake of self or group, offers constructive criticism.								
3. Information giving	States a belief or opinion on issues, gives own experience to illustrate a point.								
4. Clarifying	Restates an issue, reflects ideas, clears up confusions, indicates alternatives.								
5. Summarizing	Pulls together related ideas, restates suggestions after group has discussed them.								
6. Consensus testing	Checks with group to see how many are in agreement, tests for conclusions.								
B. Maintenance Activities (*Keeping the group working together*)									
1. Encouraging	Is friendly, responsive, warm and tries to be diplomatic, accepts contributions.								
2. Facilitating	Expresses feelings and thoughts openly, levels with group, supports the ideas and thoughts of others.								
3. Harmonizing	Reconciles disagreements, pours oil on troubled waters, gets people to explore their differences.								
4. Compromising	Admits error, tries to resolve conflicts, tries to maintain group cohesion.								
5. Gate-keeping	Keeps communication channels open, encourages participation of others.								
6. Setting standards	Expresses norms and standards for the group to achieve, uses constructive criteria to evaluate group functioning.								

6. How might attention to the carrying out of Task and Maintenance activities improve future group meetings?

Tape Analysis Guide - 3

Interpersonal and Group Relationships

Review the questions in the eight areas on the "Introductory Team Planning Session" sheet. Notice that they correspond to the eight categories on the "Team Perception Inventory."

As you listen to the tape, use the "Team Perception Inventory" sheet to jot down notes as instances in any of the eight areas as they occur during the taped meeting. (Use the open area beneath each rating scale for your notes.)

When the tape is completed, rate the group meeting on each of the scales for the eight areas. Show your ratings to the group, and share with them your reasons for rating the group as you did in each area. As often as possible, point out actual instances on the tape to illustrate each area.

The following questions may be helpful to you in giving your thoughts to the group:

1. To what extent did the group get beneath surface issues in the taped meeting?

2. What supportive or undercutting behaviors were apparent during the taped meeting?

3. Was all needed information made available?

4. How free were members to express their emotions and feelings during the taped meeting?

5. Were there any hangups or difficulties in the way the group worked together? Were they recognized and talked about?

6. Was maximum use made of individual and combined group resources during the meeting?

7. How were intellectual and emotional conflicts dealt with?

8. How committed did the individuals in the meeting seem to be to group goals?

Introductory Team Planning Session

1. SURFACE DISCUSSIONS   DEPTH DISCUSSIONS
    How will your team assure that you get beneath surface issues in your discussions?

2. INTRA-GROUP COMPETITION   INTRA-GROUP COLLABORATION
    How can your team promote a climate in which the members support rather than undercut each other?

3. GUARDING INFORMATION   SHARING INFORMATION
    How will your team see to it that all needed information is made available to the team by the members?

4. HOLDING BACK FEELINGS   EXPRESSING FEELINGS
    To what extent should team members be free to express feelings and emotions while working on a task?

5. UNAWARE OF PROCESS   AWARE OF PROCESS
    How will you assure that your team becomes aware of hangups in the way its members are working together and that it deals with such hangups as needed?

6. USING FEW TEAM RESOURCES   USING ALL TEAM RESOURCES
    How will your team assure that maximum use is made of the individual and combined resources of all members?

7. WIN/LOSE CONFLICT   WIN/WIN CONFLICT
    RESOLUTION   RESOLUTION
    To what extent will your team members confront emotional as well as intellectual conflicts? On what bases will conflicts be dealt with?

8. RESISTANCE OR APATHY TO TEAM GOALS   FULL COMMITMENT TO TEAM GOALS

How will you assure that members make their maximum contribution to the goals of the team?

Team Perception Inventory

Each member should indicate his perception of the team in the eight areas below by placing an X somewhere along the continuum for each item. If you place the X between any of the numbers, please also indicate your rating to the nearest whole number. (For example, if you place your X between 30 and 40 on a scale, you would also write 36 or whatever your rating.)

In making your rating, think of *your* perceptions of the team at this particular time in the course, based primarily on the most recent team activity. When you have finished your rating, make this sheet available to your team for group analysis.

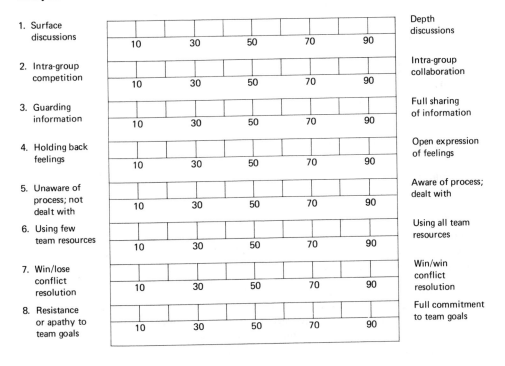

Tape Analysis Guide - 4

Styles of Leadership and Conversational Tone

Read the attached article "How to Choose a Leadership Pattern," by Tannenbaum and Schmidt. Concentrate especially on the Continuum of Leadership Behavior on page 96, and the section headed "Range of Behavior" on pp. 96-97.

As you listen to the tape, keep track of the changes in the Supervisor's leadership style and in the tone of the conversation as the meeting progresses. Use the charts on the Observer's Sheet to record these changes. You may wish to show movement either way on the continua by a continuous line, arrows, or consecutive letters or numbers.

When the tape is completed, show the diagrams you have made to the rest of the group and share your ideas about the following questions: As often as possible, give specific examples from the taped meeting to illustrate your comments:

1. What was the leadership style of the boss toward the start of the meeting?

2. Did his style change as the meeting progressed? What caused it to change?

3. What was the effect of the boss's style(s) on individual members of the group?

4. Were there times during the meeting when a different leadership style by the boss might have been more productive? When?

5. How would you describe the tone of the meeting?

6. Did the tone remain the same or did it change?

7. What relationship was there between the leadership style(s) of the boss and the conversational tone(s) during the meeting?

8. What changes in leadership style and conversational tone might make future meetings more effective?

Observer's Sheet

As you observe your group, focus your attention on two areas: (1) the Tone of the Conversation, and (2) the Styles of Leadership displayed by the supervisor.

1. *Tone of the Conversation*

On the following chart record the tone of the meeting on the continuum of rational and emotional factors. For example, the point at the extreme left of the continuum would indicate a very unemotional discussion of the facts.

The point on the extreme right of the continuum would indicate a nonrational emotion-packed argument, perhaps involving win/lose issues, personality conflicts, etc. The position in the middle would indicate a balance between rationalism and emotionality.

Indicate with an (A) the tone of conversation during the first few minutes and then draw a line to indicate changes in tone as the conversation continues. Indicate with a (B) the tone near or at the end of the conversation. Be prepared to describe the way the tone of the conversation varied throughout.

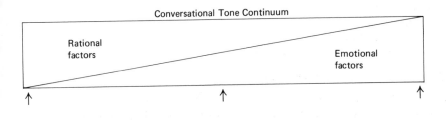

2. *Styles of Leadership*

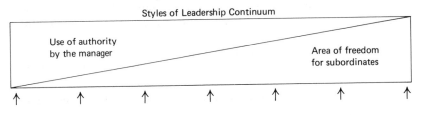

On the chart above, record the styles of leadership displayed by the supervisor. The seven points along the bottom of the chart correspond to the seven positions on Tannenbaum and Schmidt's leadership style continuum.

Indicate with an (A) the style of leadership displayed at the start. Then draw a line to indicate shifts in leadership style throughout.

Tape Analysis Guide - 5

Analysis of Quality of Listening

Review the instructions and chart on the Active Listening Exercise sheet.

Following your listening to the tape and keeping a score card of the boss's communications, report back on the number of "scores" in each of the thinking with, thinking for, thinking about, thinking against, and other, categories.

The following questions can be discussed with the group:

1. Did the category with the highest score represent the best approach to examining the issues being discussed?

2. How did the other categories come into play and what were the results in terms of resolving the issues?

3. Taking each of the categories in turn, what kinds of feelings on the part of both the boss and his employees resulted when the boss made a statement that fit into that category.

4. Taking the category that had the least scores, what was the reason for the low use of that category of communications. If that category had been used more, what would the consequences be

a) On the boss
b) On the employees
c) On the situation
   (resolution of the issue, time, etc.)

Active Listening Exercise: Observer's Role

Your main focus of attention should be on the boss during the exchange of communications. You should analyze the nature of the replies and comments made by the boss. You are to determine how well he is able to assist his employees in examining the "issues" they are discussing.

To help you assess the conversation, put a hash mark in the appropriate space below for each reply or comment the boss makes during the conversation. You may use this "score card" then as the basis for your feedback following the analysis.

	Thinking With	• Restating what participant said to let him know he was understood. • Pausing, nodding, waiting for further information • Asking for more information, but not directing conversation. • Guiding the participant in examining his own feelings & finding his own answers.
	Thinking For	• Interrupting participant-finishing the rest of his sentence. • Steering or directing the conversation • Giving advice • Restating what participant said, but changing its emphasis or implications.
	Thinking About	• Giving "pat" answers of an amateur psychologist type. • Analysing the participant's motivation. • Giving theoretical pronouncements of the "everyone feels that way" type. • Asking probing questions to determine the "real" problem.
	Thinking Against	• Arguing or disagreeing • Implying or stating that "you shouldn't feel that way." • Implying or stating a threat to the participant. • Being defensive-justifying himself.
	Other	

Tape Analysis Guide - 6

Communicating, Problem Solving, and Handling Emotional Factors

Review the factors listed under communicating, problem solving and handling emotional factors on the Team Feedback and Generalization Guide. After you have an understanding of the factors, listen to the tape and make notes on any of the factors that are pertinent to what is happening in the taped session.

Feedback your reactions and opinions to the other members using your notes as a resource. It would probably be helpful to give them copies of the "Guide" so they understand what factors you were examining. You may want to ask the group their reactions to some of the questions under each of the three basic areas.

For example, you may feel that there was evidence at one point on the tape that the group had some difficulty in determining the most important problem at hand. You might tell the group what you heard and ask them: "Does this indicate that we had some problem in determining the most important problem at hand?" This approach will allow the group to discuss the evidence and you can test their reactions against your own. The group will probably be more receptive towards accepting your analysis if you use the questioning technique.

Team Feedback and Generalization Guide

The following questions are concerned with the three basic areas of managerial problem-solving activity: Communicating, Problem-Solving, and Handling Emotional Factors. How you function in these areas as individuals and as a problem-solving team determines your effectiveness.

Take this opportunity to explore these questions as candidly and openly as you can among yourselves with particular reference to the task your team has recently completed. Try to analyze your individual and group strengths and weaknesses and to make definite plans to increase the effectiveness of your problem-solving team. (The questions are guides for discussion - spend the most time with the ones that are most applicable to your particular situation.)

COMMUNICATING

Reading: Were there any mistakes or problems caused by ineffective or inaccurate reading? How were reading requirements divided among team members?
Writing: Were any problems caused by lack of written communication or unclear writing?
Visualizing: Did your team make use of visualization and display techniques as effectively as it might have? What improvements in this area would be helpful?
Speaking: Was the oral communication among team members clear, concise and effective? How might it be improved?
Listening: Were team members listening to each other with a desire to understand? Does anyone feel he was being ignored or misunderstood?

PROBLEM SOLVING

Gathering Information: Did any team members have problems gathering or processing information relevant to the task? How might "Information-processing" difficulties be prevented?

Identifying Problems: How effective was your team in determining the most important problem or problems at hand? How could your team identify problems more quickly and effectively?

Considering Alternatives: To what extent did your team specify and consider several alternatives before deciding to take action? How might you improve individual and team creative searching for alternatives?

Making Decisions: What problems did your team have in analyzing and selecting the best alternatives? How might individual and team decision-making be improved?

Taking Action: What problems did you experience in implementing or following through on decisions made by the team or by individual team members? How might team performance be improved?

HANDLING EMOTIONAL FACTORS

Levelling: How open were team members in owning up to their emotions and discussing them with other members of the team? Were there instances when team-members sought to "bottle-up" or ignore their feelings? What were the results of such behavior on individual and team effectiveness?

Awareness: Were team members sufficiently aware of what was happening on all levels during team activity and discussions? What factors seem to be affecting or distorting awareness?

Climate: What kind of climate has been created in your team? To what extent do the team members feel relaxed, or pressured; accepted or rejected; useful or unneeded? Is each individual making the contribution to team effectiveness that he feels he can make? Do one or two team members seem to be dominating other team members?

Conflicts: Were there interpersonal conflicts between members of the group? How are conflicts handled in your group? Are they recognized, brought out in the open and discussed? Or ignored, repressed and denied? What role can conflicts play in your group's problem-solving effectiveness?

Tape Analysis Guide - 7

Group Process Observation

A good way to systematically get data to respond to the nine questions on the Instructions to Observers of Group Process form, would be to review and understand the questions and then write the names of the individuals in the group across the top of a piece of note paper. As the tape is played, you can take intermittent readings on the group and write "key words" that suggest the actions of each of the persons during the taped meeting. For example, an analysis could look like this:

	Fred	Jim	Bill	Sam
First 5 Minutes	Interrupted Bill	Amplified what Fred said	Started discussion	Quiet
Second 5 Minutes	Told Bill that purposes of meeting were misunderstood	Asked Sam for his opinion	Talked to Jim while Bill was speaking	Told Bill and Fred they ought to talk one to one after meeting

You can feedback your analysis to the group using your notes and any additional information the group members have to contribute. (It would be helpful to pass out copies of the questions to each group member during your comments.)

Instructions to Observers of Group Process

1. To what degree did everyone participate?
   How did the discussion get started?
   To what degree did people listen to each other?
   To what degree did they interrupt?

2. To what degree did the group focus on the task?
   Which members seemed most eager to move the group ahead?
   To what degree did "subrosa" or side conversations take place?

3. To what degree was an effort made to lay down any "ground rules" to govern the discussion?

4. To what degree did individuals tend to resist the assignment? Which members were most resistant?

5. To what degree did one or two individuals tend to dominate?
   Who were they?
   To what degree did questions or comments tend to be directed simply to one or two individuals?

6. To what degree did individuals pick up contributions of others and build on them?
   To what degree did people ask for clarification?

7. To what degree did the less talkative or more silent members appear to be interested and alert?
   To what degree did these individuals appear to be: bored, apathetic, antagonistic?

8. To what degree did conflicts arise?
   How did conflicts arise?
   How were conflicts resolved?
   To what degree did you detect a tendency for cliques and sub-groups to form?

9. What impact did the time deadline have on the group's working effectiveness?

Tape Analysis Guide - 8

Group Interaction Chart

This chart is designed to assist in an analysis of the interaction between individuals who are in the process of communicating with one another.

Prior to beginning the analysis, write the name of the leader in the first left hand column and the names of each member in each of the subsequent columns. Thus, each of the columns on the horizontal represents a member. The vertical dimension represents time.

To conduct the analysis make a mark in the column when that person contributes a communication. Proceed by connecting with a line each mark with the mark that follows. As the interaction continues between the participants, you will have a series of connecting lines that move downward on the chart.

As each person contributes, you can indicate the type of communication next to the mark by coding it with the following symbols:

? - if a question was raised
! - if an answer or interpretation was given
0 - if the communication was neutral
X - if directions were given

At the end of the interaction, you can total the number of contributions from each individual, assess what symbol was most characteristic of their contributions, and by scanning the chart, determine whether communications were mostly between leader and member, member to member, or equally participated in by members.

You can also see something about the quality of communications. For example: were the communications mostly questions asked by leader and answers given by members or vice versa?

Use as many of the interaction chart forms as you need to complete the analysis. In reviewing the results of your analysis, you may want to discuss the following questions with your group:

1. In the quantity of communications, was the leader or any one member(s) the primary communicator? What were the reasons for this?

2. Did any member(s) have fewer communications than others? Why was this?

3. Was the interchange mostly between leader and individual members or were there interchanges between members?

4. Did the leader mostly ask questions or did he mostly give answers or interpretations?

5. Did members (which members) ask questions directed towards the leader?

6. Is there any evidence that the interchange between the leader and any one member could have been handled on a one to one basis without involving other group members?

7. What guidelines does the Group Interaction Chart (Fig. 4.1) suggest for improving future meetings?

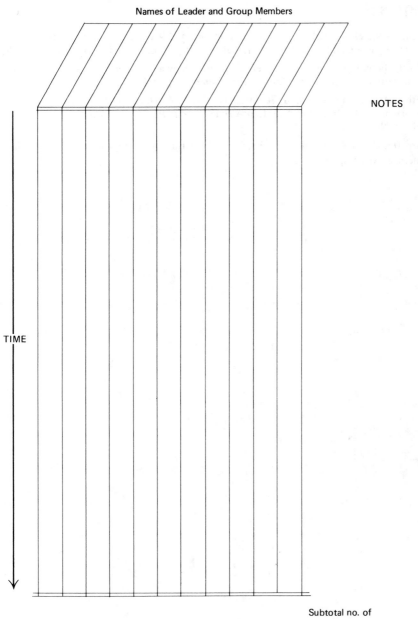

Fig. 4.1 Group interaction chart

FOOTNOTES

1. Rush, Harold M.F., "Behavioral Science Concepts and Management Application," Studies in Personnel Policy #216, National Industrial Conference Board, New York, 1969.

2. Schuttenberg, Ernest M., "The American Airlines Stewardess College, A Case Study in Organization Development," *The OD Practitioner,* September 1968.

3. Mather, Alan F., and Ernest M. Schuttenberg, "A Team Development Project - A Case History of an OD Project at American Airlines," *Training and Development Journal,* Vol. 25, No. 2, February 1971.

4. Marr, Douglas H., "What We Have Learned About Job Enrichment," Unpublished paper, American Airlines, August 1970.

5

ORGANIZATION DEVELOPMENT IN AN AEROSPACE SETTING

How does one make the transition from a standard training program with limited objectives to a broad-based systems change effort? The author describes how he turned a request for training into an OD program looking at such dimensions as decision making, conflict management, communication, risk taking, interface management, motivation/rewards, and quality of team relationships. The project conducted in an engineering organization consisted of three modules — orientation, management concepts, and laboratory learning covered in an off-site workshop. This course later became an integral part of the management development program. Despite adverse conditions in the industry, the program continues in a revised form now using in-house consultants exclusively.

Organization Development in an Aerospace Setting

MICHAEL HILL

PROGRAM DEVELOPMENT

Early in 1968, our management development unit was asked to develop a program for first line engineering supervisors. In our attempts to reach mutual agreement on what was to be included under the term "Management Development" we started down a path that was to bring us to extensive use of laboratory methods in training and the use of OD interventions in planned efforts to act directly on the work climate of given work teams.

Our initial contacts were with high level engineering administrators. It soon became clear that what they had in mind was a traditional training course: Some orientation sessions on company policies and procedures and some exposure to the principles of management.

We were something less than enthusiastic. We had just completed such a course for one of the other units in the division. Results were disappointing in that there was little visible impact on work relationships. We knew from theory, research, and recent experience that transfer of training from the classroom to the job is neither easy nor automatic. We were convinced that unless some specific effort could be made to work this transfer problem we would not get a reasonable return for our investment in time, money and effort.

Then there was the "climate" problem. Again, we were convinced that individual effectiveness is only partially a function of a person's insight, knowledge, and skill. A manager can develop skills that "the system" will not permit him to use. Organizational effectiveness, then, depends not only upon individual skills but on how these skills are linked together within a work group. We had research going back to 1955 which showed clearly that the most potent factor in the behavior of any supervisor is the attitudes and behavior of his boss.[1] It seemed pointless to teach new decision-making techniques if the supervisor was to return to an environment where his boss made all the decisions. If we were to teach

Michael Hill is an organization development consultant with Block-Petrella Associates, North Plainfield, New Jersey. He was previously a staff consultant in management development with Boeing Company, Vertol Division in Philadelphia, Pennsylvania. He received the Ph.B. and M.A. degrees from the University of Chicago where he has completed all requirements for a Ph.D. except his dissertation.

skills associated with more participative management styles, we would be doing lower levels of management a disservice unless all levels of management understood and were committed to the values inherent in this approach and were prepared to encourage and reward the behaviors involved.

We took our concerns to our own supervisors up to the director level. We were not against using traditional training methods to work toward traditional training goals. We were against presenting training programs that made no visible impact on organizational effectiveness. What we asked for was (1) approval and support for training course designs that would include explicit efforts to insure on-the-job application of course concepts and skills and (2) approval to use laboratory/OD methods as considered appropriate.

We were lucky. Our top management had been cautiously exploring the use of some of the newer OD technologies. Richard Beckhard had been in to talk with our general manager and his staff. Frederick Herzberg had run a seminar for our middle managers. Gordon Lippitt had taken some of our top level managers off to a four day workshop. There was something less than widespread enthusiasm for the use of OD methods but there was some interest and a willingness to experiment. Our decision to seek understanding and support of high level managers within our own unit was crucial. Without this support, we could not have approached other units in the division with the kind of determination it takes to get this kind of program off the ground.

In subsequent contacts with engineering managers, we repeated our rationale for a broader based management development program. It took some doing but we got cautious approval for an experimental pilot program. Our proposal included:

a) Accomplishment of a needs analysis to develop a data base for course design
b) Development of a lab-type course dealing with interpersonal skills
c) The assignment of line managers to act as a steering committee to work with the training staff on the details of diagnosis, design and implementation
d) The employment of an outside consultant to avoid the obvious pitfalls associated with the initial introduction of laboratory methods.

Our proposal was accepted but there was some delay in the appointment of line managers to act as our steering committee. We asked for the committee in May 1968. The members were appointed in Feb. 1969. During this period we went ahead with our needs analysis and had completed a prototype design for a five day interpersonal skills lab.

When the committee was finally assembled, there was something less than enthusiasm for the task at hand. Its members felt that they were being asked to rubber stamp a program that had already had a lot of high level visibility. This was not altogether true. The committee had a free hand to recommend policy in this area and, eventually, they did. But feelings are facts. It took months of hard work on our part to overcome the suspicion and distrust generated by their appointment after diagnosis and design had been completed by "outsiders."

Our rationale for asking for a steering committee was a reflection of values inherent in OD. We did not want to play the role of outside experts who had magic tricks to fix things that got bent. We did want to establish our role as technical consultants and facilitators.[2] Our goal was to engage line managers in joint diagnosis of management issues, to jointly design programs that would deal directly with these issues, and to work with us to evaluate results. We knew that commitment depends on ownership and that ownership results from involvement in the decision making process that leads up to any program.

In short, we goofed on this issue. We had plenty of "good" reasons. We did not have the authority to appoint such a committee; everyone was especially busy at the time; the administrator who initiated the request wanted to see some preliminary designs before involving line managers, etc., etc. But we knew better. In retrospect, I think we went along with the "good" reasons because we were afraid that if we made strong demands before we had a chance to demonstrate the technology we might not get anything at all. We had some bumpy meetings with the committee at first, but we worked it out (confrontation of real issues!) and our association has since been productive.

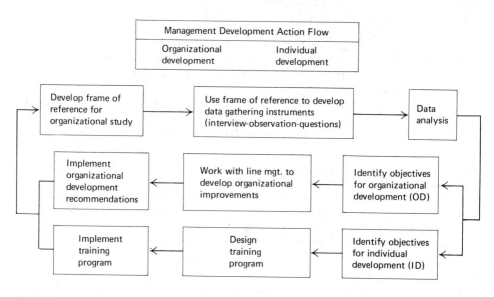

Fig. 5.1

Our overall strategy was presented to the committee as outlined in Fig. 5.1. The approach here was to develop an overall frame of reference to guide our efforts. Using line manager experience, we would try to identify organizational issues that would be most productive to examine. We would then use this information to design data gathering instruments. Data analysis could be arranged to point up issues that would respond to either individual training or OD interventions.

The committee balked; too much, too soon! Parallel ID/OD development seemed too ambitious. A strong preference was expressed for implementation in series, i.e., let's get the interpersonal skill training off the ground and then look for opportunities for OD team building. We did not press too hard on this issue as we felt it would work either way. It did. We completed our first instrumented lab in October 1969. We did our first OD team building lab with a family work group in April 1971.

We followed, with some deviations, the general outline presented in Fig. 5.1. We began with a set of organizational dimensions that were used successfully by Block-Petrella in a previous study dealing with a similar engineering environment:

Organization Dimensions

1. Decision making
2. Conflict management
3. Communication
4. Risk taking
5. Interface management
6. Motivation and rewards
7. Quality of team relationships

We used these dimensions as an outline for an interview program. We interviewed a vertical cross section of line engineers and engineering managers. The results provided us with some preliminary conclusions concerning major organizational issues. We then used these data to guide our design of a questionnaire to further explore these issues as a point of departure to program design.

We used a differential perception model for our questionnaire.[3] A sample question is presented in Fig. 5.2. We distributed the questionnaire to a sample of engineers from each engineering unit at three levels: line engineers, lst line supervisors and middle managers. The approach was to get some measure of the "value structure" of the organization in terms of the organization dimensions mentioned earlier. The left side of each question tried to get some measure of how managers thought things ought to be for best results. The right side of each question dealt with the "environment structure" i.e., how things were perceived to be in actual practice. This would allow us to arrange data analysis to show: (1) Level of consistency within and between levels of management on both value/environment structure, (2) value/environment structure congruence and (3) level of discrepancy between "real/ideal" scores on each dimension, within and between management levels.

Our rationale here was that a consistent value climate enables managers to develop a clear picture of desired behavior patterns and to act accordingly. Inconsistencies in the value climate tend to pull individuals in conflicting directions. It becomes difficult for a person to maintain a consistent behavior pattern in support of company goals when one manager condemns the same actions that are praised by another. Ideally, an effective organization should have a relatively clear picture of a "competent performer," a standard against which a man can measure himself and guide his efforts to improve. Markedly different evaluations of his performance tend to create uncertainty. Work energy is then expended in developing strategies rather than productive problem solving.

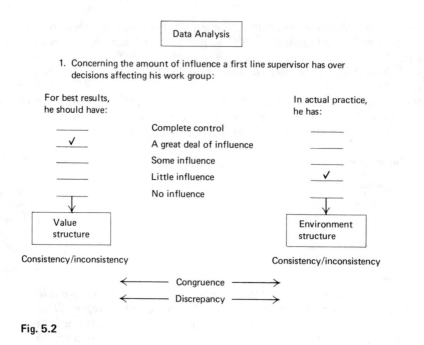

Fig. 5.2

We wanted to get some measure of the organizational climate to insure that training efforts would be consistent with management philosophy. The questions we worked with were: What is current management philosophy? What are the management style preferences of line managers? How do they think things ought to be for best results? As we asked questions on each of the organization dimensions listed, each answer gave us one element of a larger pattern we would call the "value structure." In a similar way, we could get some measure of how the actual work environment was perceived by the various levels involved.

Where we found a high level of consistency in value/environment structure and a low level of congruency between value and environment structures, we could then design training experiences that would help managers to get where they wanted to go. Where we found marked inconsistency and lack of congruence, we would present these issues to responsible managers for resolution using OD methods.

We had what we thought was a tight design but things did not work out exactly as we had planned. We were able to use the results of the study for program design but the committee felt that we should delay the introduction of OD until we got some experience with lab training methods. This series vs. parallel approach has worked well for us, i.e., the use of traditional cognitive material to serve as a base for the introduction of an instrumented lab, then later, the use of the instrumented lab to provide points of entry for OD team building. We are aware that other approaches have worked. OD team building has worked in other companies without any cognitive or lab-type preliminaries. But it worked our way too. We have come to believe that some level of cognitive understanding of interpersonal skills is helpful. OD team building efforts involve confrontation of real issues. Confrontation requires some level of interpersonal skill. Interpersonal behavior skills do not simply emerge on demand. They require some discussion, some conceptual understanding, acceptance as relevant and useful, and some practice in a low-threat environment.

After considerable work with our committee, we came up with a four element program. It had a little something for everyone: the administrators got their orientation course (traditional methods); the line managers got their management concepts course (cognitive plus experiential exercises to illustrate concepts); and we got a chance to run one pilot program to demonstrate laboratory methods. With these considerations in mind, our program sequence was as follows:

Phase 1 — Administrative Skills.

This is basically an orientation course designed to present knowledge about existing administrative systems and procedures. The course is presented on a need basis only to newly appointed supervisors.

Phase 2 — Management Concepts & Skills.

In Phase 2, the purpose and methods are analytical. The materials are analytical in that they present a set of ideas, facts, concepts, research findings and theories about management skills and interpersonal processes. The ideas presented represent a selection from the literature of behavior science to include those elements considered most relevant to the needs of current industrial management.

The prime purpose is to increase the manager's knowledge about and understanding of management relations by presenting a series of ideas concerning factors that tend to restrict or enhance effective interpersonal relationships.

The methods used are those best suited to achieve the objectives of this phase, i.e., to increase knowledge and understanding of management concepts. Concepts are presented in lectures and lecture/discussions with case materials, in-basket exercises and role playing being used to illustrate and clarify concepts presented.

Phase 3 — Interpersonal Relations.

In Phase 3, the approach is experiential. No new concepts are presented. Using communication as an example, the manager is engaged in a case, an exercise or a business game that will require him to deal with a communication problem. Where in Phase 2 the focus was on understanding various elements of the communication process (analytical), in Phase 3, the manager is asked to act in a situation that includes all the factors presented in the analytical materials — and a great many more intangibles many of which have successfully eluded positive identification.

The problem in the experiential setting is not to apply the standard recipe but to examine the total ongoing situation in terms of analytical concepts presented earlier in an effort to determine the kind of behavior that will prove most effective in the particular situation at hand.

The purpose here is to avoid the pitfall discussed earlier which assumes that analytical "knowledge about" communication will, by some mysterious chemistry, automatically produce skill in communication. It will not. We will learn to increase our skill in communication only by communicating in an environment that provides for instant feedback concerning the effect of our efforts. The environment must also provide an opportunity to make mistakes and to try new behaviors in an atmosphere of reduced threat.

In Phase 2, the manager learns from the experience of others. In Phase 3, the effort is aimed at a different kind of learning. Here the effort is to create a workshop environment where the manager can learn from his own experience by acting in a real situation, observing the consequences of his actions, consciously reflecting on observed consequences and trying new behaviors in the light of insights so obtained.

Phase 4 — Organization Development.

In Phase 4, we try to deal with the problem of insuring application of acquired skills in the on-the-job environment. We can state as axiomatic that there will be little or no transfer of learning from the classroom to the job unless the organization climate is supportive of the attitudes and skills taught in the course. The most potent factor in the behavior of a supervisor is the attitudes and behavior of his boss — and his boss up the line. There is simply no point in presenting a supervisor with new decision making techniques if his boss makes all the decisions. It is highly inadvisable to develop skills associated with participative management if the supervisor is to return to an autocratic, do-what-you-are-told environment. If a supervisor wants to hold his job, he must respond to the situation as it exists, not how it ought to be. If we develop the skills of participative management, the organization must be committed to the values inherent in this approach and be prepared to support and reward the behaviors involved.

The primary objective of any management development program is to increase organizational effectiveness. Phase 2 and Phase 3 of our program concern *Individual Development.* In Phase 4, the focus is on *Organization Development,* that is, the development of organizational units of people in the actual on-the-job situation. The rationale behind this two element approach is that for the individual manager to apply the skills presented in Phase 2 and Phase 3, the organizational climate must encourage, support, and reward the use of skills acquired.

Individual development works toward the goal of developing managers who will be able to contribute more to the achievement of organizational goals. Organizational Development attempts to create on-the-job conditions in which the manager can make these contributions.

The strategy of individual development is to present concepts and develop skills leading to increased individual effectiveness. The strategy in organization development is to develop a process that will help the organization diagnose its problems, plan ways to solve them and implement these plans effectively and economically.

We ran our course five times. Committee members attended the first two sessions and personally evaluated all sessions in discussions with participants. We dropped Phase 1 (Administrative skills) due to cutbacks in our work force. Phases 2 and 3 went through a number of revisions to end up as a two-element course: Four days of management concepts and skills (cognitive), and a four-day instrumented lab (experiential). No OD team building was attempted at this stage. We had run the course for a hundred engineering managers. The committee's review of end-of-course evaluations and private discussions with participants resulted in a strong recommendation to continue the course to include all levels of engineering management.

While we were working with engineering, a series of events had occurred on the manufacturing side of the house that led to a request for a "management development" program. They already had a working committee of line managers who had been examining other corporate programs. As part of their review, arrangements were made for three line managers from manufacturing to attend the engineering course. Their response was positive. We went to work to develop a program using our experience with engineering as a point of departure.

The course is organized into four major elements: (1) Introduction (Monday morning), (2) A cognitive element dealing with management concepts and skills (Monday afternoon through Tuesday night), (3) A two day instrumented lab, and (4) An exchange with top management which, in effect, became a low profile OD intervention.

We tried to apply the lessons learned working with engineering: (1) We worked closely with the line manager committee on all elements of course design; (2) We carefully briefed top managers on the opportunities, and the potential problems, inherent in this kind of approach; (3) We strongly recommended and got approval for a one-time pilot program to be attended by the Vice-president – Operations and his staff, all members of the steering committee, and a vertical slice of line managers from selected manufacturing units. This made up a group of about thirty managers including representatives from the vice-president level to first line supervisors.

Results of the pilot program were positive. We have since run the five-day program for 285 managers. After the pilot program, the course was offered to all division units. Each group now includes participants from Engineering, Manufacturing, and all support units.

Since we began this effort in April 1968 we have completed sixteen sessions of the course for a total of 385 managers from all division work units. We had built up some understanding and acceptance of experiential methods using the instrumented lab and we had a formal commitment to try OD team building as a planned follow-on to the more formal course. In June 1971, I put together a brief summary of the overall program.

The purpose of this paper was to present a brief summary of ideas presented earlier as they related to team building. We repeated time and time again the basic postulates of organization development: that team building was not "training" as normally defined; that team building dealt with basic values and attitudes;

that success was more a function of personal involvement and commitment to the values inherent in OD as against learning management "techniques."

It may be helpful at this point to summarize our rationale concerning the overall program, which we described in the following manner:

General.

Since January 1971, we have completed eleven sessions of our management development training course. We plan to continue this effort until all line managers have completed the program.

While we believe that this individual training is important, we have taken some care to emphasize that long experience with industrial training tells us that transfer of training from the classroom to the job is neither easy nor automatic. Unless we make a specific effort to solve this transfer problem, it is not likely that maximum return for our efforts will be achieved. What we call Team Building, then, is a planned effort to insure on-the-job application of concepts and skills that will help to build more effective work relationships.

Our five-day course deals with individual training. Here we begin with the notion that the effective manager is a learning, growing person who has a built-in desire to improve his understanding of management processes. Here we ask, "How can the line manager best learn about concepts and skills that will help *him* do a better job?" Our answer was to remove him from the work setting and have him join with other managers to consider and discuss current management concepts and to get some practice with basic management skills.

With team building, our basic objectives remain the same but the focus changes. Here we try to deal directly with the transfer problem. The rationale here is that individual effectiveness is only partially a function of a person's insight, knowledge, and skill. A manager can develop skills that "the system" will not permit him to use. Organizational effectiveness, then, depends not only on individual skills but how these skills are linked together. With team building we ask: How can we get a collection of individuals, with unique capabilities, to learn to work together as a team, to learn how to make maximum use of available talent, to learn how to communicate with each other, to learn how to make team decisions that lead to personal commitment, to learn how to examine its work relationships and revise them as necessary?

If we accept the task of improving our on-the-job work relationships, we must also accept the fact that improvement implies change. For individuals to make changes toward more effective relations, they must work to create an organizational climate that supports and rewards desired changes. Team building is an effort to work directly on the "climate problem." In our management development course, the individual goes to school. In team building, the effort is aimed at "training the system" to support the kind of change that is considered desirable.

The basic strategy in team building is to work with actual work teams, at all levels including nonsupervisory workers, toward the goal of developing a process that will help a working unit to diagnose its problems, plan ways to solve them and implement these plans quickly and effectively.

MANAGEMENT CONCEPTS AND SKILLS

The five-day course we are working with is organized into two major parts.* The first part (Monday and Tuesday) is devoted to the presentation of three basic concepts: Process, Perception, and Feedback.

The prime purpose is to increase the manager's knowledge about and understanding of management relations by presenting a series of ideas concerning factors that tend to restrict or enhance effective interpersonal relationships.

In the remaining three days (Wednesday, Thursday, Friday) the methods are experiential in that participants are engaged in exercises that are designed to provide an opportunity to get some experience in the application of the concepts presented earlier.

Team Building.

In the team building phase, we try to deal with the problem of insuring application of acquired skills in the on-the-job environment. We can state as axiomatic that there will be little or no transfer of learning from the classroom to the job unless the organization climate is supportive of the attitudes and skills taught in the course. The most potent factor in the behavior of a supervisor is the attitudes and behavior of his boss — and his boss up the line. There is simply no point in presenting a supervisor with new decision making techniques if his boss makes all the decisions. If we teach the skills of participative management, the boss must be committed to the values inherent in this approach and be prepared to support and reward the behaviors involved.

Team Building Designs

Team building efforts try to deal directly with in-fact relationships within a given work group. The term "work-group" can be defined in various ways but most generally it is used to mean (1) an organization chart work group, i.e., a supervisor and his subordinates† or (2) a supervisor, his subordinates and other support people who report to a different manager but who have important interface relations with the work group.‡

Team building activities are usually based on an *Action-Research Model* consisting of three basic steps:

1. Collection of relevant work data,
2. Feedback of data to the team,
3. Action planning based on the feedback.

Team building efforts can be used to work a wide variety of problems, e.g., improving relationships of team members, setting goals, developing collaborative decision-making processes, resolving interface issues, etc. The specific focus is determined by the nature of work issues that emerge from the data collection

---

*Appendix 5.1

†Appendix 5.2

‡Appendix 5.3

stage. The first step, then, is diagnostic. If we want to straighten something out, it seems reasonable to find out where it is bent — and this requires that openness about problem issues is encouraged by the power figures involved. We are confident that the talent, knowledge and energy to solve most work issues already exists within most work groups. The problem is normally not more knowledge but our ability to get the real issues surfaced.

We have completed several OD Team Building programs using standard OD type interventions with six managers. In each case, the request was generated by a line manager who had completed the course and who wanted to explore the use of OD methods to work directly on the working climate of his work unit. All these efforts dealt with family work teams. In some cases, we worked with a manager and his staff. In other cases, we worked with a single manager and all of his subordinates (nonsupervisory employees) including secretaries.

As before, results were evaluated by our steering committee who made regular reports to top management. In addition, managers who had tried the team building approach reported their evaluations directly to top management. Results, to date, have been positive. A memo has been written to all managers announcing the availability of assistance to work team building programs on a volunteer basis.

CONCLUDING REMARKS

The effort described in this paper took over three years. The staff involved one in-house trainer and the assistance of an outside consultant for the first year. In the second year, budgets tightened considerably. We discontinued use of outside consultants; we discontinued use of off-site conference facilities; we shortened the course from eight days to five days without major reduction in impact. The current program, a five-day course plus team building labs as they emerge, is being run by two in-house trainers plus a lot of understanding and support from line managers.

APPENDIX 5.1

Monday	Tuesday	Wednesday	Thursday	Friday
1. Opening comments	1. Theory X/Y quiz	1. NASA exercise Score results Discussion Team effectiveness Quiz Process quiz	1. Johari Window exercise	1. Prepare for exchange (Likert profile)
2. Course overview	2. Theory X/Y lec.		2. Process results	
3. Introduction	3. Score quiz			
4. Mgt. theory & practice	4. Theory X/Y movie			
5. Likert profile	5. Maslow Hierarchy of Needs			
	6. Herzberg quiz, lecture, movie			
Lunch	Lunch	Lunch	Lunch	Lunch
1. Content/process	1. Management grid	1. FIRO-team compatibility exercise.	1. LIFO-management style questionnaire.	1. Exchange with top management
2. Task/maintenance	2. Talk on grid	2. Score questionnaire.	2. Score questionnaire and discuss.	
3. Micro-lab	3. Score quiz	3. Process results		
4. Asch experiment	4. New truck case			
5. Paraphrase	5. Feedback lecture			Course critique
Dinner	Dinner	Dinner	Dinner	Conclusion
1. Perception lecture	1. Grid feedback exercise	1. Group development exercise	1. Group role inventory	
2. Perception		2. Process results	2. Process results	

Table 5.1 Management development course for Boeing-Vertol supervisors

APPENDIX 5.2

Team Building with Family Work Groups

The length and specific focus will vary but good results can be achieved in one day.

8:00 - 8:15	*Opening Comments* by top management.
8:15 - 8:45	*Introduction.* Conference leader present workshop objectives, schedule, discuss ground rules, identify specific end product.
8:45 - 12:00	*Data Collection.* Working in small groups, participants are asked to discuss: What significant problems are faced by team members in getting their jobs done? What is bugging who? What behaviors, procedures, ways of work, etc. should be different to make us more effective?

Small groups are asked to summarize the results of this discussion on Flip Charts and pick a spokesman to present the results to the other groups.

12:00 - 1:00	Lunch
1:00 - 2:00	*Information Sharing.* Small group spokesmen present results to other groups in general session. No problem solving in this period. Only clarifying questions allowed. Object is to understand what is being presented.
2:00 - 6:00	*Priority Setting and Action Planning* Get consensus on the 3 or 4 most important issues. Develop action plans that will lead to resolution of issues identified. Plans must be 1) written down, 2) distributed to all team members and 3) stated in operational terms: What is the goal? Who, specifically has agreed to do what, when and with whom? How and when will we evaluate progress?

Pick a specific date for a follow-up meeting. The purpose of this meeting to be:

1. Review progress in the agreements made.
2. Renegotiate those that have not worked as well as expected.
3. Revise action plan.
4. Set another evaluation meeting.

APPENDIX 5.3

Team Building, Interface Work Groups

8:00 - 8:15	*Opening Comments* by top management
8:15 - 8:45	*Introduction.* Conference leader present workshop objectives, schedule, ground rules, identify specific end product.
8:45 - 11:00	*Data Collection* Each group, working separately, describe 1) its own image of itself and its own view of problem issues and 2) its image of the other group and its view of how the other group sees the problem issues. Summarize results and pick a spokesman.
11:00 - 12:00	Each spokesman reports results to the other group. Only clarifying questions allowed. Object is to understand views of other group.
12:00 - 1:00	Lunch
1:00 - 2:00	Groups continue to meet separately. Each group asked to consider what kind of behavior on their part may have lead the other group to form the image it has. Pick a spokesman to report results.
2:00 - 3:00	*Information Sharing.* Groups meet in general session. Spokesmen report to total group.
3:00 - 6:00	*Priority Setting and Action Planning* Get consensus on 3 or 4 of the most important issues between the groups. Develop action plans. Plans must be 1) written down, 2) distributed to all group members, 3) stated in operational terms: What is the goal? Who, specifically, has agreed to do what, when, with whom? When, how will we evaluate progress?

Pick a specific date for a follow-up meeting the purpose of which will be:

1. Review progress on the agreements made.
2. Renegotiate those that have not worked as well as expected.
3. Revise the action plan.
4. Set a date for the next progress meeting.

FOOTNOTES

1. Fleishman, E. A., E. F. Harris, and H. E. Burtt, *Leadership and Supervision in Industry,* Columbus, Bureau of Educational Research, Ohio State University, 1955. This study has become a classic in the field. For related studies, a brochure giving brief extracts of available monographs can be obtained from: Center for Business and Economic Research, College of Administrative Science, Ohio State University, Columbus, Ohio, 43210. *See also:* Halpen, Andrew W., "The Leader Behavior and Leadership Ideology of Educational Administrators and Aircraft Commanders," *Harvard Educational Review,* Vol. 25, No. 1, Winter 1955.

2. Hill, Michael, "The Manager as Change Agent," *Personnel Journal,* Vol. 50, No. 1, January 1971.

3. The differential perception approach has been used extensively as a framework for research design and as a model for OD interventions. For use as an *OD model,* the Addison-Wesley Series on Organization Development contains a wide variety of models that have been used by experts in the field. *See:* Schein, Edgar H., *Process Consultation: Its Role in Organization Development,* 1969, p. 71; Bennis, Warren G., *Organization Development: Its Nature, Origins, and Prospects,* 1969, p. 4; and Beckhard, Richard, *Organization Development: Strategies and Models,* 1969, p. 33. *See also:* Blake, R. R., H. A. Shepard, and J. S. Mouton, *Managing Intergroup Conflict in Industry,* Houston, Gulf Publishing Co., 1964, pp. 155-195. For use as a basis for *research design* see: Lowshe, C. H., "Of Management and Measurement," *The American Psychologist,* Vol. 14, June 1959, pp. 290-294.

6

ORGANIZATION DEVELOPMENT
IN A BANK SETTING

Taking a broad approach, the author describes OD projects he is knowledgeable of in different banks. His cases are drawn from banks with OD positioned differently in the organization with somewhat varying responsibilities. He discusses such topics as task maintenance, client expansion and selection, definition of OD tasks and product line, and measurement of OD effectiveness. He concludes by speculating on the future of OD with particular reference to third party consultation, consulting styles, and its relationship to the human potential movement. He cites two possible approaches to the OD role: (1) make the OD man a part of temporary task groups as a group facilitator; (2) focus on consulting or counseling, probably with higher level management. In either event, he sees OD as being able to increase one's awareness of what is happening in the organization and to develop better insight into how to function more effectively as a member of it.

Organization Development in a Bank Setting

THEODORE SCOTT

INTRODUCTORY COMMENTS

This chapter represents a "state of the art" report of my experiences, observations, and impressions regarding several of the larger New York City banks. I have worked in a couple of them; others I have visited.

This nonspecific approach was taken in order to afford a free opportunity to discuss what I think are the major OD issues, without raising defenses in my own and other banks by applying labels.

My audience is assumed to be either professional or would-be change agents such as OD, management development, and training personnel.

The basic outline of the chapter is as follows:

Part 1 – How did we get here?

A brief historical sketch of typical OD development in banks.

Part 2 – Where are we now, anyway?

A. Some typical current activities or interventions.

B. Some areas of concern for OD staffs.

1. The problem of task maintenance.
2. How to survive and grow.
3. Defining OD product lines and emphases.
4. Self-maintenance – values and ideals.
5. Measurement

Part 3 – Where are we going?

A. Two possible paths.

B. Other influences.

C. An Evaluation and Summary.

Theodore Scott is an organization development consultant with Bankers Trust Company, New York City. He was previously with the Bank of New York in a similar capacity. His experience includes counseling, community development, and management development. He holds an M.A. in Human Relations from New York University where he is pursuing additional graduate study in human development.

Before launching into Part 1, let me define some terms which will be used extensively.

1. Organization Development or OD, refers to a consultative activity directed primarily at systemic change. The change sought is in organizational assumptions, relationships, and work patterns. OD approaches these primarily through data-gathering, problem-solving procedures which result in intervention tailored to the needs of particular groups or systems. A large number of diverse activities thus constitute OD to the extent that they fit these characteristics.

2. The term "line" refers to persons involved in the regular or primary work of the organization. These can be individuals involved in banking or trust work; they are for the most part operations or "back office" personnel.

3. The term "manager" for the most part signifies someone of official status (around 10% - 15% of the average New York City commercial bank's total staff is official).

4. "Staff" refers to persons whose function is a secondary one of supporting the line by providing specialized assistance which makes the line more able to pursue its primary tasks.

PART 1 — THE DEVELOPMENT OF OD IN BANKS

OD has its start usually by the fact that someone in the training or personnel area hears and becomes interested in the field. Occurrences like this began twelve or fourteen years ago, at the start of the OD movement itself. This person begins to read about OD, which seems to offer powerful alternative ways of influencing an organization as opposed to traditional training and education methods; he also meets persons engaged in the work. He begins to do such work, and starts on a years-long process of proving the worth of the idea to the organization. Depending on the size of the bank and his location in it, the *de facto* OD man tries various strategies: labs, lunches, personal visits, pilot programs, consultants, or "name" contacts. All of this is dedicated to exposing significant individuals, echelons or groupings of management to the concepts and values of OD. This process is almost always tortuous at times. Apparent allies often behave unexpectedly. Successes do not produce hoped-for responses. Political wisdom either grows rapidly in the OD faction or there is a shuffle.

If the process goes well, the OD function comes to be defined and understood as such in the organization. It is found under various titles: Training, Management Development, Human Resources, Manpower, or Organization Planning. The overall umbrella is still almost always Personnel.

Established OD groups exhibit these sorts of concerns: how can the OD staff avoid becoming overly familiar with and to the organization; how can they continuously update their skills; what areas of the organization should be concentrated on; how can impact be maximized with minimum adverse effects; how can continuity and quality be maintained; ultimately, how can one establish and keep a good name in a system where having a good name is important, while maintaining integrity? Much of the chapter will be devoted to discussing aspects of this internal process of OD.

An Alternate Schema of Development

1. OD evolves out of a training function as people in that area begin to concentrate more on managerial skills or people management skills than previously. Motivation theory, communication, problem solving, conflict management are taught in a learning laboratory context. Managers and supervisors are told that the training area is willing to provide on-job assistance in applying these learnings.

2. The training area people begin to tailor their regular, broad-brush seminars upon request to the needs of specific groups. (In addition, contractual understandings providing consulting assistance are negotiated with managers who wish to follow up on their course work.) For example, a workshop on job enrichment is developed, or a course on communication, or further work on transactional analysis, using real-time examples and material.

3. Contractural understandings to provide consulting assistance begin to be negotiated with managers who wish to apply their insights further.

PART 2 WHERE ARE WE TODAY IN OD?

Every person in the field has his particular skill bag, containing such items as appraisal, job enrichment, problem solving and decision making, transactional analysis, and planning. Some combination of these makes up the content of interventions in response to organizational needs. Listed following are some samples of typical OD interventions:

Example 1:

OD personnel in Bank X became involved in assisting a senior operating manager who wished to establish and improve accountability and control procedures. For his needs, a thorough-going MBO program carried down to the supervisory level was deemed most appropriate (see Forms 6.1 and 6.2*). This program served to solidify existing programs being carried out by the OD staff within that area; it also triggered some middle-level managers into requesting further assistance from the OD group in planning, job redesign, information flow, and survey feedback activities.

Example 2:

In Bank Y some very typical work in team building with an investment group yielded over time the insight that (a) the team was interested in new marketing ideas and (b) they were missing systematic data from customers about their needs. A data collection and processing procedure was developed which enabled the group to explore some new and potentially very fruitful marketing and service strategies (Form 6.3).

---

*Forms cited appear in Appendix 6.1 at the end of this chapter.

Example 3:

In Bank Z a middle-level manager requested internal OD cooperation with an external consultant in pursuing a job enrichment project in a large operating file area (Form 6.4). The agreement worked out between all three parties was that the external consultant would train the internal OD man on how to run a job enrichment program. This would be carried out by including the internal man as a co-consultant to the project. Over a one-year period the files area was extensively reordered. This cooperative relationship between external and internal consultants has been carried out in Bank Z both in other job enrichment efforts and in team building (Form 6.5), problem solving interventions (Form 6.6).

Example 4:

Bank A has no centralized OD staff. However, several individuals with OD training and inclinations have been involved in a sizeable management training and development activity in its large banking operations area. Some of this work leads to consulting with middle-level managers (Form 6.7).

A continuing problem is that needs of banks today in the whole area of proper human utilization and basic concerns such as communications and employee morale are so great that one can begin anywhere and make an impact that has some value for the line. The issue is how to do what is most appropriate, and in what order to do things.

Current OD Concerns

1. Task maintenance. When an OD group has been going for a few years, maintenance concerns gain weight. A principal cause for this comes out of the nature of the work. OD staffs are continuously initiating new efforts. Since energy output and involvement is almost always highest when something is just beginning, older programs tend to sag. As the number of mature or concluded change efforts increases, investment in maintaining them does also. However, the rewards generated within an OD staff are most often for initiation and short-term success, not long-term maintenance. To aggravate this situation, line managers have not at present a very well developed idea of how to incorporate change. Therefore, unless the change initiator keeps checking up on older, formally concluded programs, their effects are likely to fade.

An OD staff is saved from retribution on this score by several factors. The effects of OD efforts become blurred quickly in the welter of pressures, changes, unforeseen developments, and shifts which line managers face. In most cases, program measurement and accountability have not been clear cut, and the failure of one intervention may have been blunted by the success of others.

One staff is attempting to meet the maintenance problem in this way: staff members write up objectives for each intervention in which they are engaged, giving desired end results, steps to get there, completion dates, and achievement measures. These are checked upon and changed periodically. Also, the staff has developed some fairly clear ideas as to the capacities of its various members. No one is allowed to handle more than three or four major projects. New ones are not added until the older ones have been concluded under conditions which reasonably satisfy the objectives.

2. Client expansion and selection. Bank OD practitioners seem always in a spiral somewhere between naked concern for survival and real hope that their efforts are having some impact on the organization. Obviously, this comes out of being a relatively new, still not very well understood endeavor, which originates from outside the main power arenas of the corporation. This gut-level peripheral feeling, plus the idealism resident in most OD people, leads to a peculiar combination of political sensitivity, creativity, influencing games, and self-improving activities. Thus the OD staffs that I have been involved with have a growing product line of skills and seminars which can be tailored to a wide variety of management needs.

OD personnel are very careful when possible in selecting their clients within the organization. The emphasis is on getting clients with respectability, power, and connections. A frequent maneuver involves using lower-level people as a bridge to upper management. Example: One large New York City bank became well-known in OD circles years ago through a very carefully constructed and documented team-building intervention in an area of trust operations. The success of that effort influenced senior and middle-level managers in the bank to permit a much broadened OD program in subsequent years. Example: In another bank, an extensive retraining program was conducted for securities operations personnel not long after Wall Street's 1968-1969 back office crisis. The program included considerable exposure to OD concepts, values, and practices. Success of the program for many has been equivocal; nevertheless, the OD staff gained numerous contacts throughout the bank during the course of conducting this effort. These are paying off currently in the form of a series of specific-impact programs requested by managers.

Most OD efforts, as is now clear, are by no means pure, being heavily interlarded with management development, training, etc. To some extent this is history's fault, but it also makes sense as an aid to survival. A program which has both packaged products and consulting skills can meet a wider range of requests. This is important in maintaining credibility.

Not withstanding the effects of such strategies, OD staffs will probably continue to have expansion and selection concerns. Illustration: review the second example just listed above. Although managers throughout the securities and trust areas of that particular bank still make requests for OD assistance, there continues to be noticeable cynicism about such ideas as team building, confrontation, negotiation, and participative management. This attitude surfaced in the initial large-scale program. A similar situation exists in other banks with a longer OD history. Part of this seems to stem from the too-extensive promises and claims made by OD personnel, part from poorly designed or conceived interventions, and part of it is just normal resistance to cultural change.

It is possible to become very cynical about line resistance to change. One temptation is to dehumanize line people by making them into images of Machiavelli, or letting them be no more than Anthony Jay's hunting animals. The problem is extremely complex.

To discuss only one aspect of it, staff people in organizations have multiplied in number, knowledge, and exposure over the past decade. Diverse concerns such as OD, controllers, industrial engineering, methods research, planning, and training are impacting upon the line. In not a few instances, concerns and powers previously resident in the line have been usurped by staff personnel. During this time, also, work has been standardized, controls have been tightened, and the sense of pressure has increased. All this has come close to putting many line personnel into a posture of feeling deprived, judged, and intruded upon. They have become experts in various forms of reaction and resistance. Any large "packaged" OD program, for example, particularly arouses negative response. Following practically any broadsided or widely applied packaged program, one hears comments such as these: "I basically knew it before." "Didn't add anything new." "Doesn't quite fit my situation," and the usual clincher, "What is top management's commitment to this program, really?"

Whatever the difficulties, though, expansion must continually occur, both in particular activities, and in the acquisition of new skills. Line managers in organizations where there is now some OD history have become more sophisticated and can do a considerable amount on their own. Only by staying ahead and acquiring new skills can the OD person still be relevant. A few of these possibilities are discussed in the section on futurecasting at the end of the chapter.

3. Definition of OD tasks and product line. The concern about expansion and survival of which we have spoken has led bank OD people into a strong concern for constantly re-examining the quality of their service to the line, and to recurring attempts to define their tasks in the organization. Together with the political stratagems which have been employed, these have been helpful in maintaining and expanding OD. For example: One OD staff has spent considerable time of late defining its product line. The process has been one of clarifying the discipline or technique attached to a particular skill such as team building. Care has been taken to define a given OD skill, explain its purpose, and lay out the process followed in doing it. The staff is engaged in this product review primarily because of feedback from managers which indicated they were vague about the specific capacities of the group—this notwithstanding a good success record which touched on a large number of managerial people in the organization. Such a definitional task can give an OD group confidence in its conceptual clarity; that confidence can aid the expansion of its activities.

4. Self-maintenance. A fair number of the New York OD people I know have strong ideals. Almost invariably, they are liberal in outlook, and socially aware. Most seem genuinely committed to the pragmatic melding of human values with corporate concerns expressed by OD movement fathers such as McGregor, Argyris, and in recent years, Herzberg. They really believe it can work. Meanwhile, the average bank exhibits these sorts of cultural norms: short-term perspective; no particular objectives; detail oriented; rigid hierarchy; a "cover your rear" mentality; scrambled communication patterns; fractionalized work, leading to the attitude of "let the other guy worry about it."

The stage is thus set for a dissonance which many have experienced. It is a potentially awkward area where personal world and organizational reality meet. The appropriateness with which an OD staff handles this dissonance experienced by its members has, in my opinion, a direct relationship to its energy and effectiveness among line personnel, who are often struggling with similar issues.

Several quite popular ways are in use to handle the personal values-corporate structure interface. (a) Pair your own staff with other OD personnel, other bank staffs, or members of a larger professional network. (b) Hire an outside "consultant to consultants" for regular discussion of how and where the *organization* impacts upon you. Or work on how *you* connect with the organization, with the aid of a personal therapist. (c) Develop your wife (husband) and/or lover as a private consultant.

A common ethical program revolves around proper management of the earfuls of information which come to every consultant. Line managers have a persisting urge to use the consultant as an information pipeline to, from, or about other managers. The challenge is being able to give appropriate bits of information to one person while at the same time maintaining the essential confidentiality of another relationship.

5. Measurement. As everyone knows, efforts to measure OD programs are unceasing and largely unproductive, except in a few cases where large amounts of time, skill, and money have been invested. For purposes of the everyday OD man in banking, two major types of program measurement are used: (a) system performance of "hard" information such as volume statistics, productivity indices, error rates, (b) perceptual information or "soft" data such as general attitude surveys or interpersonal and intergroup surveys. An ideal program is one which impacts positively on both categories. For this reason, job enrichment efforts have been very popular in banks for the last two or three years. The definiteness and even mechanistic nature of these programs makes it possible to systematically analyze their impact as evaluated by the normal control data produced by a system. Attitude surveys (pre and post) are also available from consultants specializing in this activity.

The concern for measurement for an OD program can also be met by taking time at the start to carefully define what one is doing, how long it will take, and what the desired or probable results will be. At this time, the degree of hard or soft measurement required can be thoroughly discussed and agreed upon. For the basic measure is still management's response to an OD activity. Attention to contractual details and parameters can lead to measures which are satisfying and meaningful to both line and staff.

Example: A middle level manager in Bank B invited an OD consultant in to discuss some concerns he was having as the new boss in his area. Their conversation surfaced a need in the manager to sketch out his objectives for the next six months. The following measures or progress indices were specified: (a) He would be able to identify the issues and would have developed definite plans for dealing with them as a result of the consultation; (b) the consultant would have carried out a team building operation between the manager and his staff in which major tasks and task-related interpersonal issues had been surfaced, discussed, and to some significant degree resolved.

Note: The importance of these measurement indexes, which were arrived at jointly by the manager, his consultant, and the manager's superior, was not in their specific content, but their acceptability and worth to the parties involved.

Interestingly, the people most likely to be concerned about measurement are OD personnel or other staff people such as controllers, or planners. Line managers generally evaluate a program as much by how they feel about the value of the intervention as by indicants like error rates or productivity. This may be changing somewhat; senior managers in recent years have been more interested in tangible results (meaning at least some "hard" data), given the squeeze on people and budgets.

One of the largest banks in the city, which intriguingly enough has no OD staff, but which instead relied on a large corporate training unit, has used highly sophisticated measures for years now in evaluating its courses. Certain terminal behaviors are asked for and, if the training area agrees, are delivered, complete with pre- and post-measurements. This approach has had the noteworthy effect of allowing the training center to confront managers on such problems as the fading of skills or the loss of learning due to adverse line culture. Thus the programs have many impacts similar to those of OD efforts in other banks.

PART 3—SOME THOUGHTS ON THE FUTURE OF OD

The third party, consultative stance of OD is at once a distinguishing characteristic and also a severe liability. It gives the OD person the valuable status of being an independent mind at the same time that it makes him peripheral and questionable. My hunch is that in the future we will handle this inherent instability by movement in two directions. One path will lead the change agent into utilitarian integration into the organization by making him part of functional teams, which are charged with specific tasks by the line. The other path will make the OD specialist yet more of a consultant or counselor. This will be possible as sophistication of line people increases to the extent where such a position is clearly understood. In this fashion, the OD person would function very much as an idea man, organizationally related to top management.

In one instance, functional integration into an ongoing project group has already occurred. An acquaintance who once held a "traditional" OD consulting job now has a position on the organization planning staff of one of our larger banks. In this job, he is part of a team which examines proposed reorganizations. The point of that staff group's involvement and its authority are clearly specified. There is no question when the planning group is to be involved and on what level it will deal with the issues. He feels that he is involved in matters of real consequence for that bank, in a way that employs many of his skills as a consultant and a change agent. But he is primarily a functioning member of a team given a planning assignment by senior management. That assignment has necessitated his learning more than OD change skills alone.

There are numerous areas where the comparative change competence of OD personnel can be used: interdisciplinary staff teams, project teams charged with bringing new computer systems on line, other groups studying man-machine interfaces, groups studying new business ventures. The barrier which seems to stand in the way of involvement of such depths and scale has two aspects: the ignorance of many OD people of the complexities of machine technologies, finance, etc.;

and management's relative ignorance of human systems and its reluctance to add that factor so overtly into complex business arrangements.

A problem for the future of banking OD is the onward sweep of the human potential movement, in recent years into such exotic and as yet unapplied realms of bioenergetics, primal therapy, and gestalt. Tavistock approaches are not being used. Meanwhile, we are still trying to get managers to accept and use the most basic OD skills and procedures. Folding in the new learning and new approaches without disrupting continuity will be a large challenge for the future.

An Evaluation and Summary

At a minimum, managers seem better able to play the corporate game as a result of exposure to OD. They play better in the sense that they have more behaviors to choose from, and that they see and process human-related data more effectively. At best, they are able to arrange for the people in their areas a much more rewarding daily environment, the sense that communications are better, motivation is improved, and the overall operation more stable in the face of stress.

At worst, managers are left cynical and unchanged except in the direction of a greater capacity for deception.

One of the most rapid areas of growth for OD people seems to be towards a more sophisticated approach to the actual needs of managers. Careful attention to survival has made OD programs more appropriate in the sense of being less value-loaded and more attuned to complex realities. The peril, naturally, lies in the potential loss of distinctive perspective. My impression is that the distinctiveness remains, aided by better listening and a willingness to handle more variables. But the extent of the peril is not clear.

In any case, bank OD people do not seem any longer to be looking for one-shot ways through the organization's complexities to the pinnacle of success. There is more of a long-haul mentality. Big programs have been tried and found wanting in a number of locations. Mostly, the emphasis is upon smaller scale, carefully designed involvements which have specific results. The expectation is to coordinate these smaller efforts to produce continuing pressure for and adaptability to change within the organization. From the small pieces a larger mosaic of accomplishment will hopefully emerge.

Organization		Organization Development Division	Objectives – 1972		Page
Key objective no. 1. Provide OD consulting and program resources.		Remarks:			
Critical objective no. 1. 1 Provide intensive departmental consultation					
Code	Specific and program objectives	Staff/time	Achievement indices		Complete
1.2	Corporate Trust Operations Increase management skills of officers and supervisors.	1 1/2 days through June then 1 day/ week.			
	– Implement new management systems, MBO, Job Enrichment, team development.	J. Jones C. Wills J. Johnson	Officers managing 75% and supervisors 50% – Both groups able to accomplish 75% of objectives.		12/31/72
	– Complete installation of MBO system through supervisory level.	S. Jones	All objectives documents will have objectives, programs and schedule of 2/3 quantifiable.		1/31/72
	– Plan for job enrichment complete and implemented with all supervisors.	S. Jones C. Wills	Plan completion time, job satisfaction increases by 10% - supervisors continue process as part of managing.		Plan complete by 4/30. Program complete by 12/31/72.
	– Team development completed with teams 1-2-3	S. Jones	Each team able to critique and improve its own process in handling		12/31/72
	– Training and development of managers.	S. Jones C. Wills	Plan complete on time: courses and seminars held as scheduled, with bosses following up & supporting on job behavior changes.		Plan complete by Apr. All training courses underway by 10/30/72.
	– Plan for management development complete and implemented.				

Form 6.1 OD project planning and evaluation guide

Form 6.2 OD product line

Name:	Management by Objectives
Purpose:	To predetermine results to be accomplished. This is done by first establishing a *position charter* containing key and critical objectives, then an *action plan* containing specific objectives, performance standards, programs, schedules, and budgets, and then by following up with appropriate *review and correction.*
Primary Focus:	The position charter, action plan, review and correction process.
Measurement Factors:	*Position charter* contains the key objective and critical objectives with performance standards. The action plan should grow out of the position charter, be linearly traceable top to bottom. The specific objectives should be stated as end results, be measureable (quantitatively or qualitatively) by use of performance standards, be realistic, challenging, and innovative. The programs, schedules, and budgets for each specific objective should be coordinated with the appropriate areas.
Procedural Steps:	The key objective or primary result for enterprise as a whole and each component is derived from a *commitment analysis* which includes an economic or purpose commitment, product or servile commitment, market commitment, geographic commitment, functional and perhaps social, investment, or personnel commitment. From the key objective, a *critical performance analysis* is done to determine the primary work, technical and managerial, which must be accomplished to meet the key objective. Then critical objectives are established which state the most important continuing results which must be accomplished in each critical performance area to achieve the key objective. These critical objectives should have appropriate performance standards and are long-term, ongoing objectives. The key and critical objectives for each position comprise the *position charter.* Next, *needs analysis* is performed to determine what stands in the way of achieving the critical objectives. Then specific objectives, short-term, measureable results, are established to overcome the identified weaknesses or opportunities stated in the needs analysis. The specific objectives have performance standards. Finally, each specific objective has a program of action steps, a schedule or time frame, and a budget. Together, these elements comprise the action plan.

Form 6.3 OD product line

Name:	Survey Feedback (Instrumented)
Purpose:	Systematic gathering of attitude, opinion, or evaluation information which, once collected, is introduced into an organization to provide:

1. measures of managerial effectiveness,
2. identification of problems and probable solutions,
3. a forum for involving employees in the analysis and solution of problems.

Primary Focus: Agreed on characteristics of the organization at a particular level. For example, management systems, styles, rewards, policies, team work, supervision, environmental conditions, job content.

Measurement: Instrument must be statistically reliable (accurate) and valid.
Ownership of the process by the target group.
Ownership of the process by the task force.
Communication of the data to those who were asked to provide it.
Actual resolution of problems as identified.

Procedural Steps:
1. Agreement by top group on total process.
2. Develop an instrument with task force (task force includes representatives from each level in the target population).
3. Administer instrument.
4. Professional analysis of data for clarification.
5. Feedback data analysis to department head and task force.
6. Task force selected is given task:
   a) Study data and find out what problems exist.
   b) Communicate results to all employees.
   c) Determine what is going on that's positive and what needs to be changed.
   d) Recommend solutions to problems.
7. Task force meets with line managers to discuss recommendations.
8. Line managers decide actions to be taken.
9. Line managers meet with all people to explain:
   a) Results of survey.
   b) Recommendations of the task force.
   c) Action plan:
      - those actions to be taken immediately and by whom.
      - those actions to be taken in the future and by what date.
      - those actions which will be difficult and why.

Local and Corporate Survey:

The advantage of a corporate survey is that it provides normative data for comparing profiles with other groups. It is also typically a more well-developed instrument.

The advantage of a local survey is that it does not diminish the need for corporate surveys. Local surveys should focus on specific characteristics of the organization not covered by corporate surveys. Local surveys development should follow the procedural steps established and should be used in addition to, and not in lieu of, corporate surveys.

Form 6.4 OD product line

Name:	Job Enrichment
Purpose:	To increase the utilization and work motivation of people by re-structuring clerical jobs and supervisory roles.
Primary Focus:	Enrichment principles (acknowledgment, recognition, responsibility, work itself, advancement) as distinct from "maintenance" factors (salary, environment, benefits, relationships).
	Clerical jobs considered in terms of vertical loading feedback, career path, client relationships, module and natural work unit.
	Supervisory roles and assumptions regarding people and work.
Measurements:	Increased productivity and/or reduced errors; job satisfaction as measured by attitude surveys; lower turnover and reduced absentee-ism; reduction in the number of management levels and change in supervisory roles.
Procedural Steps:	1. Contract negotiations with, and commitment from, area management structure.
	2. Initial job analysis and development of control statistics.
	3. Supervisory work shops on motivation covering such things as: enrichment principles, job restructuring techniques, application of principles and techniques to specific roles. (Green lighting and red lighting).
	4. Implementation of selected job changes by appropriate groups of supervisors.
	5. Evaluation.

Form 6.5 OD product line

Name:	Team Development
Purpose:	To help a presently functioning or newly established work group function more effectively on tasks which must be done in a group.
Primary Focus:	Any one or all of the following group processes:

- Mission definition and goals
- Decision making
- Leadership
- Interpersonal relationships
- Meeting procedures — agenda setting, time usage, interim assignments, keeping on the track, etc.

Measurement Factor: The team's ability to understand, critique, and improve the above processes.

The consultant can use such techniques as group feedback, his own observation, Group Meeting Questionnaire, Likert Questionnaire, and the Billie Alban Instrument.

Procedural Steps: Focus directly on key group processes primarily using past data.

1. Meet with manager to define apparent problem.

2. Communicate purpose/procedure to participants.

3. Gather data from all participants through a written instrument and/or interviews.

4. Feedback to manager.

Workshop: 5. Workshop with manager and participants to discuss data — identifying the real problem(s), discussing possible action alternatives, choosing the best solution, and formulating programmatic steps.

6. Implement action steps.

7. Review results and take necessary corrective actions.

Ongoing: Focus on key processes as the team works on live, specified tasks:

1. Determine with the manager and the team the *setting* for observation and team development.

2. Establish with the team the *ground rules* under which the team will review its group process.

3. Systematically *assist the group in self-diagnosis and corrective action* regarding its group process.

4. Follow-up as necessary.

Form 6.6 OD product line

Name: Team Problem-Solving Meetings

Purpose: To arrive at a common diagnosis of problems; to analyze the barriers and opportunities and *plan* action steps or programs to be implemented; to solve the identified problems.

Primary Focus:
- Common diagnosis
- Analysis of barriers and opportunities
- Action plan including problems and outline of accountability for each
- Follow-up

Measurement Factors:
1. Diagnosis of problems agreed upon by each member of management team.
2. All relevant barriers and opportunities are uncovered.
3. All alternative programs are explored.
4. Follow-up sessions are held to test progress.

Procedural Steps: The procedural steps follow the same order as the purpose and primary focus.

1. Arrive at a common diagnosis and statement of the problems.
2. Analyze each problem in terms of constraints which, if removed, would solve it and/or opportunities which, if explored, would solve the problem.
3. Develop an action plan consisting of the appropriate programs and schedules and statements of accountability.
4. Follow up individually and in future problem-solving sessions to test progress.

Form 6.7 OD product line

Name: Third Party Consultation

Purpose: To improve the working relationship between two people by: 1)
                               facilitating mutual understanding of some of the problems which ex-
                               ist in a relationship and 2) exploring new ways to handle the issues.

Primary Focus: Troublesome or unclear aspects in a work relationship; for instance,
                               understanding of mission, cooperation and work issues, role clarity,
                               power and influence, game playing, positive and negative feeling.

Measurement Factors: Consensus between parties involved and the consultant that there
                               has been:

                               1. increase in understanding of mission,

                               2. increase in collaboration, decrease in destructive competition,

                               3. increase in role clarity,

                               4. increase in openness and confronting behavior, decrease in game
                                  playing,

                               5. increase in positive and perhaps decrease in negative feelings,

                               6. agreement on appropriate distribution of power and influence,

                               7. capacity to critique the relationship on an ongoing basis,

                               8. increase in joint work output.

Procedural Steps: 1. Agreement and desire of both parties to work on their relation-
                                  ship using a third party.

                               2. Consultant interviews each party separately and feeds back the
                                  data to the pair.

                               3. Discussion of the data including analysis of its meaning, open up
                                  feelings and perceptions of each other, and mutual diagnosis of
                                  the problem.

                               4. Informal follow-up as appropriate with each individual.

                               5. Follow-up session with the peer to test feeling about the relation-
                                  ship now, and new issues which might have emerged.

7

ORGANIZATION DEVELOPMENT
IN AN INSURANCE SETTING

How does an OD practitioner establish his new role in an organization? The author describes how he initiated a management education program utilizing case studies dealing largely with behavioral science applications to problems of management. Part of the plan was to identify problems confronting the participants. This led to some interesting results when fed back to top management. This accounting illustrates what usually happens whenever a group identifies problems it lacks authority to solve and instead confronts management with them. Some changes did occur as a result of this effort. Perhaps the greatest learning occurred in the OD consultant himself, who found out how difficult it is to establish an OD function and uncover anxiety-producing problems that he then finds himself in the middle of.

Organization Development in an Insurance Setting

JAMES C. FALTOT

GETTING STARTED

If you accept the premise that Organization Development (OD) is not a totally new phenomenon, but rather a consolidation of many training and behavioral science techniques into a discipline, then it follows that many different activities fall under the umbrella of OD. These activities can range from the more traditional forms of training to the more recent techniques of team-building and transactional analysis. In fact, the more traditional interventions often provide a platform for more innovative approaches to organizational problem solving. It is the intent of this chapter to explore how this very process occurred in a New York City life insurance company.

I joined the Guardian Life Insurance Company of America in March of 1970. As I understood it, my job was to determine the training needs of the organization and by either engaging outside resources or developing my own programs, upgrade the performance of the home office staff. Special emphasis was to be placed on the managerial and supervisory personnel. This was the first time in Guardian's one-hundred-ten-year history that someone was given full-time responsibility for training and development.

In the beginning I spent long hours talking with my boss, the vice-president of Personnel, about the Guardian, its history, organization, personalities, etc. We realized that in order for me to form my own impressions and become active in the organization, I would obviously have to meet and become known by the appropriate management people.

The question of getting exposure in a new organization faces most OD practitioners at one time or another in their careers. Our first step in getting exposure for me was to set up a series of interviews with those employees who were college graduates with less than two years' company service (Guardian had been experi-

James C. Faltot is a doctoral student in social psychology at the University of Delaware. He was most recently Personnel and Organization Development Specialist for Philco-Ford Corporation, Philadelphia, Pennsylvania. Prior to that he was in charge of corporate training and development for Guardian Life Insurance Company in New York City and held a similar position with Insurance Company of North America in Philadelphia. He holds a B.A. in Speech and Dramatic Arts from Temple University, Philadelphia, where he has also done graduate work in psychology.

encing a large amount of turnover in this particular group). The second step was to schedule training sessions on the general topic of communications with middle management personnel. Another one of our early efforts was an orientation program for new employees. Although personnel people presented the sessions, we used middle management figures to evaluate the program and help us shape its content. Department managers also gave functional overviews of their operations as a part of the tour which followed the orientation. These vehicles enabled me to meet some of the key people with whom I would work later.

One project, more than any other, was to plant the seeds for the introduction of OD into the Guardian. The Guardian was suffering from a malady common to many enterprises, a management structure comprised of people promoted to managerial ranks based on their technical competence. This situation was caused by a tradition of promoting the best worker to the job of supervisor. I think it is fair to say that the best salesman is not necessarily going to be the best sales manager. The jobs require different skills, therefore the performance of the jobs is, or should be, measured by different standards. However, in the absence of such standards, it would be reasonable to assume that the best worker would make the best manager. Suffice to say that at the time I arrived on the scene, the Guardian was in the process of deciding what it was to be a manager in the enterprise. We felt that this issue was critical, that unless it was understood and supported, the manager's job was not that of merely being a super-technician, all our management development efforts would go down the drain.

Prior to my joining the company, my boss had made contact with a former colleague about putting together a management education program for the Guardian. The choice of an outside consultant is a critical step in any OD effort. The selection made by my boss was perfect: in addition to being a professor of management, this particular consultant had been Vice-president of Training and Education for Life Office Management Association (the life insurance industry's A.M.A.) and had also had working experience in a life insurance company. The consultant's background enabled him to relate to the specific problems facing the Guardian's managers. Just as importantly, his credibility in the eyes of our management was enhanced by his insurance knowledge.

Although my boss and the consultant, working in tandem, got the support of the president for a management education effort, the actual start of the program was to be delayed until March of 1971, three months after the president would have assumed the position of chief executive officer of the company.

Although we had hoped to begin the program in October of 1970, it was felt that to delay it five months would help the president in articulating a new philosophy of management for the Guardian. In retrospect, the delay seems even more fortuitous, because in February of 1971 the president announced a new company organization, based on a profit-center concept. This new structure was to be an added bonus for us — for it was based on the delegation of responsibility by product line, a concept which was embraced by our approach to management.

During this time, I was trying to compile a Manpower Planning and Development Report for presentation to top management. We hoped to accomplish several things by communicating our efforts in these areas: first, we wanted to get top management thinking in terms of its human resources, not just for today, but for tomorrow as well; and second, by projecting our anticipated manpower losses for the upcoming five years, get them to realize how urgent it was for them to start thinking in those terms.

I had the usual difficulty in collecting data for the report — no one ever maintains records with your project in mind. When the report was ready, we decided to have a "dry run" for some middle management personnel, selected for their reputation of being frank. I included in this group one of the young college graduates I had interviewed earlier. After the presentation, they were asked not only how they reacted personally, but also how they thought top management would react. We received invaluable feedback on the report from this group. After the presentation to top management, we talked to each member of this group, told them how we had altered our report as a result of their suggestions, and gave them our impressions of how it was received.

The most important result of the report was to put the upcoming management education effort into perspective in terms of a total management development effort for both present and future managers. Data collected from this kind of manpower forecasting provides management with concrete evidence for taking action in regard to human resource development and utilization.

The Management Education effort was divided into two parts. The first half of the program was designed as an orientation or appreciation session for top management (at the Guardian this meant every officer from first vice-president up through the president). The sixteen participants were taken away from the office for three days of seminars on the management process. The reason for these sessions was twofold: first, we wanted to give the participants a "preview" of the sessions their managers would be attending later, thus building a common vocabulary for further discussion; and secondly, we hoped that the participants would analyze their own managerial practices. Also, the attendance of top management would, to some degree, indicate support for the concepts and approaches later presented to middle management. This was especially true concerning the president's attendance at the program. In fact, the president opened both the three-day seminar for top management and the eight-day program for middle management by stating his views concerning company directions and his approach to management. At the three day seminar, once his address was over, he became a participant in the program.

So the Guardian Management Seminar was held in March of 1971. Larger insurance companies (Guardian's home office staff numbered approximately nine hundred employees) have been conducting management education efforts since the early 1950's. Although the Guardian had been successful in terms of assets (over five billion dollars insurance-in-force in 1970) and growth, it was this very growth into multiple product lines and diversified investments (not to mention additional staffing) which indicated a need for leadership based on strong management skills as well as heavy technical expertise. This need was understood as early as 1964, as evidenced by memoranda to the file concerning discussions of the problem with several members of top management. Finally, seven years later, a decisive action step was being taken.

The management education effort for both top and middle management, as communicated to the participants, had four objectives:

1. To develop better understanding of the job of managing and the administrative process.

2. To provide knowledge of the concepts, approaches and methods that can be utilized by executives and managers when performing their managerial functions. (This statement recognized the fact that the participants would still have technical responsibilities in their jobs.)

3. To foster an awareness of the changing environmental factors that have an impact on the manager's job. (This objective obviously promotes a basic OD concept.)

4. To provide a framework for further study and continued self-development.

The program design itself leaned heavily on the case-study method. The seminar for top management was divided into six half-day sessions. Each session focused on a particular aspect of the job of managing. The sessions were comprised of three activities. During the first part of the session the consultant presented material relevant to the topic and set the stage for the case. During the second part of the session the participants broke down into discussion groups to discuss the case which had been read beforehand. Following the group discussions, each group secretary would report his group's findings to the group at large. The consultant would then lead a discussion of their findings and summarize the major points.

Table 7.1* lists the major topics, along with the case and readings, used for the six sessions, each of which was a half-day program.

The selection of cases, of course, is critical to the success of such a program. Their relevance to the actual problems of the organization is what makes the program more realistic and less theoretical. For this reason, it is advisable to select cases that do not dwell upon technical information of an industry foreign to the participants. This does not mean, however, the cases must be restricted to one industry. For example, The Case of the Missing Time is a good case for opening a management program because it deals with the universal problem of a manager trying to find time to manage.

The interaction among the top management people during the discussion sessions was spirited. This lively interchange made for exciting and meaningful sessions. According to several participants, the management program was successful if only to provide a framework in which these executives could learn about how their peers approached problems. The president later confided to us that he was extremely pleased by the seminar and planned to have an annual off-site program for his top management team.

The week after the top management seminar we began conducting the middle management program. This program was comprised of eight one-day sessions held over an eight-week period at the Guardian.

---

*Tables cited appear in Appendix 7.1 at the end of this chapter.

The basic design of the program was the same, topical material, followed by group discussions of cases, followed by feedback reports. In addition to the supplemental readings, the participants were asked to read selected chapters from *Management in the Modern Organization* by Theo. Haimann and William G. Scott (Boston: Houghton & Mifflin Co., 1970). Due to the additional time provided us, we were able to handle two cases in each session and delve into issues in more detail during the middle management program.

As in the seminar for top management, the Guardian's middle management group was enthusiastic especially during the discussions of the cases. There was, however, some initial defensiveness in this group as evidenced by an unsureness as to why this program was being conducted in the first place. This defensiveness disappeared as the participants became more comfortable with the consultant. In fact, as the program went on, the more frank and open the discussions became, particularly when it involved relating a case problem to the situation at the Guardian.

One way to demonstrate the differences between the two groups would be to look at the responses of the two groups to questionnaires they completed during the sessions on motivation (see Tables 7.2 and 7.3). Both groups agreed that money was the factor which motivated them the most (Herzberg take note!). Middle management listed "chance for promotion" second whereas top management didn't list this factor at all. Obviously, chances for promotion lessen the higher up one goes. Both groups felt freedom on the job to be important. Although factors 22 and 24 are similar, 24 expresses the viewpoint of someone who works for someone else.

Although both groups wanted the opportunity to do interesting work, only the top group mentioned the chance to turn out quality work as a motivating factor. Top management showed concern for being respected and knowing what is going on in the organization. This would seem reasonable in that top management people would like to be respected for themselves rather than for their positions. Also, there is a fear that by being in such a position one loses touch with what's happening down in the organization. Middle management approached the respect issue by showing concern for feeling that their jobs are important.

This kind of data could be put to use in many ways. For example, it would have been interesting to have each group answer how they thought the other group had responded. Comparisons of the responses could then lead to inter group understanding. Unfortunately, we never capitalized on this data.

However, during one of the other sessions with middle management, data was collected and later used for a company-wide OD effort. During one session devoted to a discussion of symptoms of an ailing organization, middle management let loose with a verbal barrage in a highly vitriolic manner.

Basically, the participants felt that there was a gap between the "ought to" of management as presented in the seminar and the "what is" of management as practiced at the Guardian. We quickly realized that although the management program was aimed at improving the managerial performance of the *individual* participants, there were certain *organizational* obstacles which were preventing optimum managerial performance as well.

During this session, we listed these organizational obstacles as perceived by the middle management group. All obstacles centered around two basic areas:

1. A lack of interaction between top and middle management resulting in a lack of trust, a feeling that top management had no confidence in middle management's ability to manage, poor vertical communications, lack of delegation, etc. For evidence, the group pointed to the use of a staff agency, Profit Improvement (known as PIP team) for cutting costs, rather than making local management responsible for cost reduction activities.

2. Middle management did not know the long-range marketing and financial plans of the company. They felt they were not functioning under clearly defined operational objectives which would contribute to the attainment of the long-range goals.

After listing the obstacles, middle management, in effect, "dared" us to take this information back to top management. This, in and of itself, was significant to me. It showed me that middle management felt that *they* could not confront top management and wanted us to do it for them.

We accepted the role as middle management's communication vehicle because 1) we realized that unless we did, these feelings would not get communicated; and 2) it was our feeling that this data would provide us the opportunity to get involved in a total organization development effort.

During the remaining weeks of the management program we worked on formulating strategies for presenting this feedback to top management. It was requested that the consultant and I write an analysis of the problem along with some alternative courses of action. It seemed to us that the root cause for most of the obstacles described earlier was a lack of definition in the Profit Center Officer's job.

Most organizations have a structure like the one shown in Fig. 7.1. And though that's how they look on paper, in practice we usually expect them to operate as depicted in Fig. 7.2.

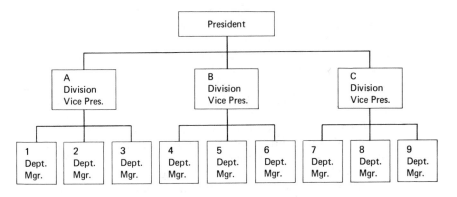

Fig. 7.1 Traditional management structure

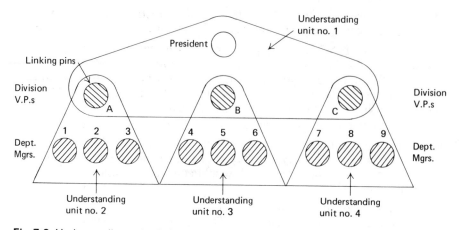

Fig. 7.2 Understanding unit—linking pin structure (From *New Patterns of Management,* by Rensis Likert. Copyright 1961 by McGraw-Hill. Used with permission of McGraw-Hill Book Company.)

The traditional structure in Fig. 7.1 presents a static picture of the organization. The attempt in Fig. 7.2 is to show the structure in operation. The idea here is that the relationships between the "boxes" cause people to operate in functional groups within the organization. Each of these groups is called an "understanding unit" (the terms understanding unit and linking pin come from Rensis Likert). The "linking pins" – in the Guardian's case the Profit Center officers – have two organizational roles to fulfil. First they are members of an understanding unit comprised of their peers and boss. Secondly, they are leaders of the understanding units comprised of the department managers within their respective divisions or profit centers. They, in effect, act as the communications link between the two groups. It was our feeling that the profit center officers were not operating as effective linking pins, hence the poor vertical communications, unclear objectives, etc.

In preparing for our meeting with the president and one of his executive vice-presidents, we outlined three sequential steps which would have to occur in order for any development effort to take place. First we would have to get agreement from them that there was a problem. (If *they* see no problem then there's no need for a solution.) Secondly, we would have to obtain a commitment from them that they wanted to do something about it. (Does the problem hurt enough to take action on it?) And finally, we would have to get agreement on a course of action (regardless of whose plan it was).

There was an interesting decision made during this period of analysis. As a result of the reorganization in February of 1971, the personnel function now reported to a senior vice-president in charge of Administrative Services. Obviously, he had not been involved in the planning for the management education programs. The question now arose as to whether we should invite his participation in the presentation of our report. We opted not to include him because he was filling one of the profit center officer positions we were zeroing in on. (I'm still not sure whether this decision was right or not.)

The long awaited meeting took place in June in the president's office. We first restated the objectives of the management education effort. We then provided these men with the feedback we had obtained from the groups and the specific obstacles to effective management outlined by middle management. The initial response to these obstacles was one of defensiveness particularly concerning the use of the Profit Improvement team. After stressing the point that the issue was not whether the feelings of middle management were justifiable or not (the point being that the issues were real for *them*), we managed to get agreement that there was indeed a problem, enough of a problem that these executives were willing to take action to correct it. (It took a long time to get to this point, longer than we had anticipated.) The question then obviously became what kind of action? At this point, these two executives began to verbalize possible approaches to the problems. Many divergent solutions were expressed and the meeting ended without agreement on a unified approach. The president asked for a written report outlining our proposals for overcoming each of the obstacles which had been identified. We left the meeting feeling pretty good about what had happened.

Essentially, our written proposal recommended an approach which combined team-building and Management by Objectives (M.B.O.) We wanted to initiate an M.B.O. program as a vehicle for improving the vertical relationships in the organization. Our plan was to set up a series of meetings of the different understanding units for the purpose of establishing objectives. The consultant would act as a resource concerning the process being used by the group to establish their objectives. We felt that this approach would accomplish two goals:

1. It would aid in the definition and communication of both long-range financial marketing objectives and operational objectives for the company, thus providing standards for measuring performance; and

2. it would facilitate interaction between top and middle management thus improving lines of communication through the use of the understanding unit and linking pin concepts.

Unfortunately, our report did not explain *how* these sessions would be set up — the interrelationships between understanding units were not defined. We realized that the president required structure in order to proceed (as evidenced by his request for *a* solution to *each* obstacle), however, we provided him with details on supplemental activities such as performance appraisal and mechanized communication vehicles rather than details on our basic approach of improving vertical relationships through the objective-setting process.

Needless to say, we did not get the president's approval to proceed. At this point my boss's boss, the senior vice-president of Administrative Services, was brought into the process. We learned *from him* that the president was not pleased by either our meeting or written proposal. We had obviously misread his response at the meeting. He was, however, still convinced that some kind of action had to be taken in order to correct the situation at the Guardian.

The first step in restructuring our proposal was the inclusion of the senior vice-president in our efforts. His involvement in the project added the dimension of "clout". We realized that if we could convince him that our proposal was viable, *he* would convince the president. We spent several days, the four of us, working together restructuring the proposal, to include identifying the understanding units at the Guardian. Using the company's organization charts, we prepared overlays depicting the understanding units and linking pins.

Next we wrote sample corporate objectives and showed how profit-center, divisional, and departmental objectives would be established in order to support a corporate objective.

Next we outlined a series of objective-setting meetings showing how the process is not just objectives moving down through the organization, but how they can move back up through the structure as well. We also demonstrated how an understanding unit can evaluate the objectives of one of its member's groups (remembering that each member is also the leader of another Understanding Unit). This process allows for the integration of objectives between the profit-center and divisions. In addition, we discussed the long-range implications of our proposal, particularly the maintenance and company-wide communication of objectives and the obvious concern of performance appraisal by objectives.

Armed with this new material, my boss and the senior vice-president met with the president and received the go-ahead for the project. After this meeting, we tackled two more problems. First we put together material to aid the president in running the first objective-setting session, a meeting of his profit-center officers for the purpose of determining company directions and goals. The point here is that the sessions were to be run by the head of each understanding unit, not by the consultant or us. Secondly, we prepared for a meeting with all the top management participants from the first management education effort. We wanted to present them with the feedback from the middle management program and the design of the management improvement program which was to begin shortly. This session was held in October of 1971 followed shortly thereafter by the objective-setting session.

It was at about this time that I left the Guardian. I have maintained contact with the Guardian and can report generally on what has happened as a result of the sessions. Objective-setting sessions have been conducted at the corporate, profit center, and divisional levels. Vertical lines of communication have been opened and there has been a real attempt to delegate downward.

Objectives have been set albeit they have not been communicated laterally throughout the company. For example, although the Group Profit Center has established objectives, they are not known by those in the Life Profit Center. The reason for this appears to be that the linking process between the understanding units has worked effectively downward. However, when objectives have been brought back up through the structure, it has been through the *individual* reporting relationships rather than through the next higher understanding *group*.

Four concrete actions have resulted from the Guardian's efforts:

1. The need for a Marketing Vice-president was identified. An appointment to this position has been made.

2. Joint meetings of both top and middle management are now held in order to communicate company directions and results in terms of accomplishment against objectives. (In fact, attempts are being made to link accomplishment against objectives to salary administration.)

3. The role of the profit improvement team has changed. Profit centers are now responsible for setting cost-reduction objectives as well as profit and volume objectives. Line managers have been appointed to the profit improvement team, now a resource for reaching cost-reduction objectives.

4. Additional development activities such as supervisory training, job enrichment, and further management education efforts are now taking place.

If there is one message to be learned from the experience at the Guardian, it is that OD efforts can develop out of other kinds of activities. They need not begin as pure OD projects. We did not design the management education project at the Guardian with the idea of laying groundwork for innovative OD efforts, however, when the opportunity for an OD intervention presented itself, we capitalized on that opportunity. The change efforts inherent in an OD project are often viewed by management as less threatening if they are generated by more traditional kinds of activities. One interesting sidenote: the term OD was never used outside the change team itself.

Due to many variables such as lack of time or resources, not all opportunities for OD interventions can be pursued. For example, at the Guardian we missed a real opportunity to make a contribution during a conversion of policyholder records to a computerized system. This project would have demanded people with divergent skills. In fact, I think this type of project will be the future arena for corporate OD efforts and I foresee the use of corporate interdisciplinary change teams comprised of not only people with OD skills, but systems experts, financial analysts, and industrial engineers as well.

Over two years have passed since I joined the Guardian, and considering that the company did not even have a training and development function at that point, it is a tribute to the receptive and flexible management of that company that it is so actively engaged in OD activities today.

APPENDIX 7.1

Table 7.1 Topics, cases, and readings used in management education program

SESSION ONE

Topics
The Management Viewpoint
The Management Job
The Management Process

Case
"The Case of the Missing Time"
Intercollegiate Clearing House
Harvard Business School
Soldier's Field Road, Boston, Mass.

Readings
"Skills of an Effective Administrator"
Robert L. Katz
Harvard Business Review
January-February 1955

"The Management Process in 3-D"
R. Alec Mackenzie
Harvard Business Review
November-December 1969

SESSION TWO

Topics
The Changing Patterns of Management
Systematic Approaches to Managerial Think-
ing
Problem Solving and Decision Making

Case
"The Puritan Life Insurance Company"
(Case provided by consultant)

Readings
"How to Analyze That Problem"
Perrin Stryker
Harvard Business Review
July-August 1965

"The Decision Process in Administration"
Robert D. Calkins
Business Horizons
Fall 1959, Vol. 2, No. 3

SESSION THREE

Topics
Approaches to Planning
Factors Affecting Planning
Strategy and Structure
Organizing the Enterprise

Case
"The Delaware Corporation"
Executive Programs
Graduate School of Business
Columbia University, 1955

Readings
"Personal Values and Corporate Strategies"
William D. Guth and Renato Tagiuri
Harvard Business Review
September-October 1965

"Putting Action into Planning"
Robert H. Schaffer
Harvard Business Review
November-December 1967

SESSION FOUR

Topics
Organizing the Unit
Organizing the Job
The Process of Delegation

Case
"Zebra National Bank"
Intercollegiate Clearing House
Harvard Business School
Soldier's Field Road, Boston, Mass.

Readings
"The Task-Force Approach to Business
  Problems"
Neal M. Draper
Management Review
May 1963
"Too Many Management Levels"
Elliott Jacques
California Management Review, 1965

SESSION FIVE

Topics
The Human Factor in Management
Theories of Motivation
Motivation and Management

Case
"Tom Harper"
(Case provided by consultant)

Readings
"How Money Motivates Men"
Charles D. McDermid
Business Horizons
Winter 1960, Vol. 3, No. 4

"On Being a Middle-Aged Manager"
Harry Levinson
Harvard Business Review
July-August 1969

SESSION SIX

Topics
Patterns of Communication
The Changing Nature of Control

Cases
"McNamara's Case"
"B1 – B2"
(Cases provided by consultant)

Readings
"Control Means Action"
Arnold F. Emch
Harvard Business Review
July-August 1954

"Management's New Role"
Peter F. Drucker
Harvard Business Review
November-December 1969

Table 7.2 Motivation instrument used in management education program (Used by permission of Leslie E. This and Gordon L. Lippitt, Project Associates, Inc., Washington, D. C.)

"FACTORS WHICH MOTIVATE ME"

Please indicate the six items from the list below which you believe are most important in motivating you to do your best work.

	Top Management Ranking	Middle Management Ranking	Factors
1.			Steady employment
2.	5		Respect for me as a person
3.			Adequate rest periods or coffee breaks
4.	1	1	Good pay
5.			Good physical working conditions
6.	3 (tie)		Chance to turn out quality work
7.			Getting along well with others on the job
8.			Having a local house organ, employee paper, bulletin
9.		2	Chance for promotion
10.	3 (tie)	5 (tie)	Opportunity to do interesting work
11.			Pensions and other security benefits
12.			Having employee services such as office recreational and social activities
13.			Not having to work too hard
14.	6		Knowing what is going on in the organization
15.		4	Feeling my job is important
16.			Having an employee council
17.			Having a written description of the duties in my job
18.			Being told by my boss when I do a good job
19.			Getting a performance rating, so I know how I stand
20.			Attending staff meetings
21.			Agreement with organization's objectives
22.	2		Large amount of freedom on the job
23.		5 (tie)	Opportunity for self-development and improvement
24.		3	Chance to work not under direct or close supervision
25.			Having an efficient supervisor
26.			Fair vacation arrangements
27.			Knowing I will be disciplined if I do a bad job
28.			Working under close supervision

Table 7.3 Sample display of group differences on motivational factors

Factors	Workers	What Supervisors Thought	Differences Between Rankings
Good working conditions	<u>9</u>	<u>4</u>	<u>5</u>[1]
Feeling "in" on things	2	10	8
Tactful disciplining	10	7	3
Full appreciation for work done	1	8	7
Mgmt loyalty to workers	8	6	2
Good wages	5	1	4
Promotion & growth with company	7	3	4
Sympathetic understanding of personal problems	3	9	6
Job security	4	2	2
Interesting work	6	5	1
			42[2]

In explaining the data, the following can be noted:

(1) The smaller the difference, the greater the agreement among the groups on the individual factor rankings.

(2) The smaller the sum of the differences, the greater the agreement among the groups on the total factor rankings.

8

ORGANIZATION DEVELOPMENT IN A UTILITY SETTING

The following case describes the evolution of an OD program from one that offered cafeteria-type courses covering a wide variety of subjects to an organic approach of diagnosis and intervention into the client system. The author describes two projects (one in engineering, the other in personnel). Both projects involved gathering data on the organization and feeding it back to the clients who then identified the problems they wanted to work on. The consultants used a number of instruments that provided the groups with additional data about themselves. The consultants served as facilitators to the groups to identify problems, solve the problems identified, and plan action to resolve them. Participants in both projects expressed feelings of better communication, increased understanding and greater awareness of their roles in the organizations. Both groups point to concrete examples of how their effectiveness as a team has increased significantly. As a result of these successes the OD group has obtained new clients who were influenced by the word of mouth testimonials by participants. The problem now is one of maintaining the momentum thus generated while finding ways to make an increasing impact on the organization.

Organization Development in a Utility Setting

KATHLEEN L. WAKEFIELD

ESTABLISHING A ROLE

Mountain Bell is an organization of approximately 34,000 employees including 7,000 management people. Its geographical territory includes seven mountain region states (Arizona, Colorado, Idaho, Montana, New Mexico, Utah, Wyoming) and El Paso County in Texas. The nature of the business is telecommunications.

The organizational development group at Mountain Bell has been successful in effecting organizational change. There is evidence to prove that they have been able to help accomplish organizational improvements in several departments in Mountain Bell. Some of the kinds of changes that the OD group has contributed to are:

1. Positive attitude changes towards the work and the environment — an initial attitude survey in one department showed that there were only ten percent positive responses towards the work and the environment. After being involved with OD for about two years, the attitude survey revealed a 90 percent positive response towards the work and the environment.[1]*

2. Lower turnover — People who had been looking for other jobs have decided to stay because "good things are happening around here" as a result of OD activities.

3. Improved quality of production — Clients and line managers have stated that the quality of work has improved in departments involved in OD.

4. Organizational norms have changed — Personnel are no longer defending the status quo in groups that have been involved in OD. Individuals felt that the changed environment and norms would now support such actions as requesting job reassignments if they felt their jobs were unnecessary or in some rare

---

*Appendix 8.1

Kathleen L. Wakefield is currently on the staff of M.O.R.E. for Women in New York City. Previously she held positions in training and organization development with Western Electric and the New York City Department of Sanitation. She holds an M.B.A. in organization behavior from Drexel University, Philadelphia, Pennsylvania. The author expresses appreciation to W.L. (Bud) Paullin and Lowell G. Fowble of the Organization Development Staff, Mountain Bell, Denver, Colorado for their help in the preparation of the manuscript.

instances requesting a demotion into a job that would be more appropriate for their skills.

5. Individuals are taking more responsibility and are more proactive towards their jobs — In some departments that have been involved in OD some middle management positions have been eliminated because lower management is taking more responsibility and making more decisions.

6. Individuals are more influential upwards — In departments that have been involved in OD people have learned that they now have more influence and they can use it to accomplish organizational change.

The OD group has been able to accomplish these normative and operational changes by using an organic approach to change efforts following the classical model of diagnosis and intervention. Since 1969 over 400 management personnel (22 groups from 14 departments) have been involved in various OD activities. Each group has gone through a data gathering and feedback (problem analysis) phase and the appropriate OD intervention has been jointly selected by the organizational development specialist (ODS) and the group. The organic approach to solving the problems that have been found to exist in the organizations has led to the use of a wide range of OD interventions. These interventions include: Job Enrichment, Management by Objectives, the complete structural reorganization of one department, new job assignments, personal growth activities, interdepartmental problem-solving efforts, team building and educational efforts.

The OD group is currently responsible for both OD and management training. The group sees itself as being involved in: (1) Acting as facilitators for normative and organizational change, (2) Being agents of free and informed choice to help people choose the way they want to operate from among various alternatives, and (3) Applying behavioral science concepts to problems that are found to exist in the organization. They have found that their goals and the dual functions of management training (with the goal of personal growth) and OD (with the goal of creating organizational change) are compatible and complementary. Some of their more successful OD activities have involved managers who have gone through management training programs and have supported OD activities.

As a result of their experiences with the various groups involved with OD activities the OD group has identified several factors which are seen as critical to the success of OD activities. The most important of these are stated in general terms; (1) The group that wants to be involved in an OD effort must have a clear statement of presenting problems and a willingness to work on those problems. Groups that have gone into OD because it was the vogue or just to find out if there were problems in the group have tended to have unsuccessful experiences. (2) There should be one or more "disciples" of OD values in the organization (preferably the head of the organization) to help keep the organization enthusiastic about the project and to provide the necessary ongoing support. (3) The contract between the ODS and the client organization must be clearly spelled out. (4) Credibility must be built quickly by providing immediate "success experiences" for the client organization. In the contract with the organization, provisions should be made for two or three short term steps which will permit the organization to experience the feeling of quickly achieving positive results. (5) The involvement of one ODS throughout all phases (diagnosis intervention, follow-on and consulting) in a specific OD project seems to contribute to the success of a change effort.

The following case studies will illustrate the ways in which the OD group functions.

CASE STUDY – ENGINEERING DEPARTMENT

This project involved the engineering department of one state consisting of 44 management personnel. The organization has been involved in OD for about two years with measurable and visible results. The attitudes of people in the organization have changed (initially there were only ten percent positive responses to the work and the organization, now there is a 90 percent positive response to the work and the organization), morale is higher and the quality of the work is improved. People in this organization exhibit the kinds of commitment towards OD that are seen, felt and remarked on by individuals that have contact with this organization. The efforts have been so successful that many of the engineering managers are encouraging the new department head to continue the involvement.

In October 1969, the department head met with the OD group to discuss the concerns he had with his organization. He had attended an OD presentation earlier and thought the OD group might be able to assist him. He outlined several problems in his department, as he saw them. They were: (1) He felt that the jobs in his organization were not challenging enough and were not fully utilizing the talents of his people. (2) He felt there was some difficulty in the appraisal program since it was difficult to find adequate ways of assessing merit salary treatment and discover high potential. (3) He felt that there was a need for general management theory in modern management methods since most engineering people didn't have much management background. The initial contract with the OD group was for a diagnostic and education effort. Phase 1 would involve five one-day diagnostic and education sessions held about one month apart. The education effort would involve the concepts of the Managerial Grid, Hertzberg's motivation-hygiene theory along with some inputs based on the work of Rensis Likert, Chris Argyris, George Odiorne, and Douglas McGregor. The diagnostic effort would be undertaken to assess the climate, attitude, and morale in this department which would indicate whether or not the department head's assumptions about the problems in his department were accurate. Phase 2 would involve feeding the diagnostic data back to the participants, having them analyze the data and come up with priorities as to the aim and thrust of future efforts. Phase 3 would implement these priorities through a concrete action plan.

The initial session included input on Blake's material on the Managerial Grid and John Gardner's article *Organizational Dry Rot*.[2] An instrument was used to determine the conferees feelings about their company in relation to Gardner's nine rules for organizational renewal. [3]*

---

*Appendix 8.2

An adaptation of Argyris' questionnaire on self-actualization helped individuals to focus on their perceptions of what the job had (actual) as well as what they wished the job had (ideal).[4]* This data was fed back to the group at the next session. (Data collected at one session was always fed back and worked with at the next group meeting).

At the second session the group used Blake's instrumented package to determine their own management styles. They also used an instrument to determine the department's management style and stance towards such things as getting results and cost consciousness.[5]†

During the third session motivational theory was introduced to lead into the concept of job enrichment. These concepts were to be used by the supervisors to help them analyze the jobs of people who reported to them. These job assessments were to be used as case studies at the fourth session.

At the fourth session feedback on a boss-subordinate questionnaire proved to be extremely helpful by pointing out the difficulties bosses and subordinates were having in talking about job related issues.[6]‡

The fifth session was basically a wrap-up of the entire process. The collected data was fed back to the group to be analyzed. The data revealed the following problems in the organization: (1) Many of the jobs needed changes to become responsible positions since they were seen as relatively meaningless by the people who held them. (2) People were experiencing a high degree of frustration because their needs were not being met by these jobs. (3) The goals and objectives of the department, within various units in that department and for individuals were not clearly defined. (4) There was not a good open relationship between the boss and the subordinate regarding job-related matters. People did not know how they were doing or where they stood in terms of performance. (5) Present appraisal methods were not meeting the needs of either the subordinate or the boss. Appraisals appeared to be based primarily on personality characteristics rather than performance factors. (6) Some people felt they were not able to utilize their talents to any degree at all on the jobs they now held. (7) People did not believe that anything would happen with this data and did not believe anyone was serious about making changes.

At this time the educational and diagnostic phases were completed and the contract between the client organization and the ODS needed to be renegotiated. The data collection had supported the department head's basic assumptions that the jobs weren't challenging and that the appraisal system left something to be desired. The contract needed to be renegotiated for OD interventions in terms of what to do about the problems. The department head and his six immediate subordinates met with the ODS and decided to take a look at restructuring jobs to make them more responsible, accountable, and motivating. A task force of lower level management was appointed to analyze the entire department structurally and to make recommendations as to how it might be reorganized into a more effective organization with a primary goal of making jobs more meaningful.

---

*Appendix 8.3
† Appendix 8.4
‡ Appendix 8.5

The ODS met with the task force and higher management when the task force report was completed at the end of three months. Jointly this group critiqued the report and discussed the recommendations. It was decided to undertake a drastic reorganization of the department in an attempt to restructure it along more functional lines. Jobs would combine four or five functions, they would be more responsible and they would provide feedback to the individual in terms of how he was doing. An individual was selected to devote his full time efforts to see that the new plans were carried out.

The second major change at this time was the introduction of an MBO approach to jobs and appraisals. This would force the clarification of group and individual goals as well as clarify and make explicit the department's objectives and goals. The appraisal program would now be based upon results instead of being based on personality traits as it had previously been. MBO made particular sense at this time because management personnel were in the process of setting goals and objectives for their newly designed jobs.

Another education session was held by the ODS to specifically zero in on the Management by Objectives concept with primary thrust on a new appraisal program. The basic objectives of this one-day session were: (1) To develop criteria necessary for an objective, workable management evaluation system. (2) To provide a framework to aid the managers in implementing this phase. (3) To develop a follow-up system which would include additional coaching and training.

The introductory lecturette described some of the drawbacks of the current appraisal system. The group task was to form a list of the characteristics of their worst and best subordinates. The concept of the four areas usually used for evaluation (personality, background, behavior or skills, and goals or results) was used by the group to analyze these characteristics. A lecturette then stressed that output or results is what should be measured. The purpose of management by objectives and the method were discussed. Conferees paired up to work with a "new boss exercise" by preparing a list of major responsibilities which had to be measurable, appropriate outputs (not activities). They were to apply three measurements or indicators to each output and establish the priorities for the outputs. Further input was provided on how to measure the three types of goals (regular, problem solving, and innovative). Conferees worked in pairs to practice using these concepts.

The final lecturette discussed the importance of the dialogue between the boss and the subordinate, the need for a memo specifying the goals, and the need to keep updating the goals. A tape of a typical goal setting and follow-up session was played and discussed. The final segment of the session was a discussion of how management by objectives can be tied into the present reward system.

The engineering department has been involved in this OD effort for more than two years. The ODS's current role is one of being available for consultation at the request of the department. The department head was recently transferred to another organization and took immediate steps to involve his new organization in an OD effort.

There have been several positive outcomes of the OD effort in this department. Data collected by several methods including personal interviews, a questionnaire devised by the engineering department itself, a post-test using the same attitude questionnaire that was given before the project began, and anecdotal data revealed the following results: (1) There has been a positive response to the effort from the participants. Comments include such ones as: "A better relationship exists between my boss and myself;" "I know where I stand with my boss now;" "I have a better idea of what is expected of me as a manager;" "I feel as if what I'm doing is important;" "I have a much better awareness of the relationship between my job performance and my salary treatment;" "I think generally everyone's attitude is improved, objectives are clear and people feel more equal;" "Communications are much better between the boss and myself and the supervisors at the first level of management." (2) An attitude survey depicting the feelings of the people towards the organization and the work has gone from an initial ten percent positive responses to 41 percent positive responses (about one month after the job enrichment concept had been introduced) to a total of 90 percent positive responses (about four months ago). (3) The management force has been reduced due to the restructuring of jobs. (4) People who were seriously considering leaving the company have decided to stay because of the effort. One highly regarded young college graduate had other firm job offers and would have left except that he felt good things were beginning to happen. (5) The quality of the work leaving this department has improved. The department provides engineering data and specifications to an outside supplier. The company receiving the work indicates that it is of higher quality than before and the error rate is less causing fewer delays and less confusion in getting jobs done. (6) The people in the department exhibit a genuine commitment that is felt and commented on by individuals and groups that come into contact with the organization. This commitment is further evidenced by their desire to continue the process under the new department head.

The department head who was initially involved in OD for about two years commented, "We now have more managers involved in making better decisions. I'm now free to do my job — overall planning and setting broad long-range objectives. You have to let the manager manage and that means letting them make decisions. You can't have one man making them all at the top." One of his subordinates recently commented, "I think we have finally learned to communicate with each other — I now run my job, and make my own decisions. I'm part of what goes on around here and I like it."

CASE STUDY — PERSONNEL DEPARTMENT

This project involved the personnel department in one state. As a result of OD activities the entire climate of the organization has changed. Data showing the positive results of the OD project were collected by various methods such as a pre- and post project attitude questionnaire, informal interviews and anecdotal information. The organization was small enough so that results, such as significant changes in work flow operations and individual behavior, could be directly observed. People are much more involved with their jobs, there is greater job satisfaction, communications are much more open, attitudes have improved and people are experiencing personal growth. Individuals outside of the organization as well as organizational members have commented on the exciting things that have happened as a result of the involvement in OD. There is a visible commitment to the concepts and values of OD.

The department head, who was relatively new in his job, attended a personnel managers' conference where the OD group had delivered a presentation on the objectives and practice of OD. During the next six months he became intrigued by the idea of the possibility of applying OD principles to some of the problems he saw in his organization. He contacted the OD group to discuss his organization's problems and to determine if their involvement would be appropriate.

The department head's leadership style was oriented toward Theory Y principles. He was experiencing frustration with the passiveness and dependency he perceived at lower levels in his organization. The areas he presented to the OD group as problems in his organization were: (1) Too many decisions are passed up to me — they should be made at lower levels in the organization. (2) The lower levels of management are more passive and dependent than is desirable. They need to learn how to become more pro-active. (3) The climate in parts of the organization is apathetic; in other parts it is hostile and defensive. The organization needs more openness, confronting and cohesion. Communications need to be improved.

The department head appeared to be very open regarding the kinds of approaches in which he would be interested and was very committed to team development. It was decided at this meeting with the OD group that the department head would discuss this conversation with the two men reporting directly to him to determine if they wanted to be involved in the OD process. One of the men chose not to become involved so that his part of the organization was not a direct part of the OD process.

When the OD group decided to become involved with the personnel department their decision and their subsequent planning were based on the basic assumption that the lower levels of management were not inherently dependent, passive and resistant but had adjusted to bureaucratic life by behaving that way.

The basic strategy for the project was a team building process which would involve lower levels as well as higher levels of management in determining the changes that needed to be made in the operation of the department. The key to the project was the formation of an action plan by the team members with virtually no restrictions, limitations or reservations placed on them. The initial plan included holding one day sessions with the entire group on a monthly basis. The monthly meetings would include the following activities: (1) Diagnostic activities to point out problem areas, (2) Discussion of diagnostic results, (3) Action plans to resolve problem areas and (4) Input on theory which was appropriate to the group's concerns and needs.

The initial strategy was not highly structured since the problems of the organization were not yet well diagnosed. As problems were uncovered instruments, designs, tasks and theory would be used to deal with them.

The ODS planned to make extensive use of the information from the diagnostic tools, information gathered from formal and informal interviews and conversations, as well as his perceptions of what was happening in the group process to help him form his ongoing diagnosis and plans.

The action plans formed at the monthly meetings would provide tasks which subgroups and individuals would work on during the month and report during the next session. This approach would tend to make problem solving activities the responsibility of the people most directly concerned with the problems. It also permitted a wide variety of approaches and presented the possibility of dealing with many problem areas. The regular day to day involvement of the group members in carrying out the action plans would also tend to help make OD a way of life rather than something that happened once a months.

The ODS's contract with the client did not include a definite date for the completion of the project. It was felt that this depended on how the project and the group evolved.

The ODS felt it was critical that something significant happen at the first meeting so participants could see in a behavioral sense that they had power and influence and could cause things to happen if they exerted effort toward that end.

At the first session the department head spoke of his commitment to the process of team development and his concerns with the organization. The group was asked to individually answer the following diagnostic questions which would be used to help devise an action plan. The questions were: (1) What does the department do well? (2) What needs improving? (3) What are the barriers to effecting this improvement? The individual answers were discussed in a fishbowl arrangement. Half of the group sat in an inner circle discussing the questions (participants) while the remainder of the group listened (observers). The roles were then reversed with the participants becoming observers and the observers becoming participants.

The problems identified at this stage tended to be very task related. Some people in the group were willing to be open at this time and did help to move things along by confronting some of the issues which were not directly task related. Two task problems were jointly picked as priority items. The first item was not a large problem but it had been annoying people for some time. By the second session it had been solved by the task force.

The second problem involved some things that needed to be done by the department head and by the second session this problem was well on the way to being solved. The day was concluded with a critique of "task-process" issues such as the role of the boss in the session and the decision-making process.

By the second session the ODS was aware that one of the big problems in the group was an untested assumption — the lower levels of management were saying that they wanted to make more decisions " . . . but you (higher management) won't let us," while higher management was saying, " . . . we want you to make more decisions but you won't try." Another problem seemed to be a lack of open communications — people were not letting problems out in the open so the organization was unable to know where people needed help in solving their problems. It seemed as if people needed to get a sense of themselves and a sense of belonging before they were able to deal with some of the task problems which existed in the organization.

At the second session the information from an actual-ideal questionnaire was fed back to the group. The questionnaire focused on such factors as cooperative teamwork, leadership styles, and communications. At first the group did not appear to be ready to deal with the causes of the problems and the discussion almost came to an end. When the group started to deal with the data a significant turning point had occurred.

At the third session the group was given some theoretical input on Gibb's Modal Concerns.[7] Gibbs discusses four basic concerns in a group: acceptance, data flow, goal formation, and control. A greater degree of group effectiveness is obtained when these concerns are identified, worked with, and resolved. When a group is first formed the primary concern of the members is acceptance – this concern is basically one of fear reduction and trust formation. Data flow, the next concern, has to do with the quality of communication and the expression of feelings and attitudes. This concern finds expression in the decision-making process in the group. Goal formation, the next concern, deals with the work of the group, the reason for getting together. This concern has to do with doing work, creating things, growing, learning, and getting things done together. Control, the final concern, has to do with the organization of the group. If the first three concerns have been worked through and largely resolved, the control concern seems to take care of itself. The group was given instruments[8]* to rate how they felt about themselves and the group on the concerns of acceptance/membership, feedback/data flow, productivity/goal formation, and control/organization. The design revealed that individuals not only lacked feelings of potency but also feelings of belonging.

At the third session, a design was used to deal with several untested assumptions that were affecting the group. The objective of the design was to form a "work-behavior contract" among the supervisors of the organization. First line supervisors were in one group while all other supervisors were in a separate group. Each group was to be explicit concerning what kinds of behavior they wanted from the other group, specifically what they wanted the other group to start doing, stop doing, or do differently. The groups worked separately on their lists then met together to negotiate these lists. Both groups presented their lists and then began to work together to resolve the lists. It appeared that both groups wanted the same things but the problem was how to get there. Together the groups formed action plans and work behavior contracts. During this session the ODS's role was primarily to help the group members be clear and specific in their discussion.

The following sessions continued to deal with helping people learn that they could exert influence. The subgroup tasks were also helping to deal with some of the task problems as well as the interpersonal problems. Some of the supervisors had exhibited leadership styles that were creating barriers to effectiveness and these were dealt with in various ways.

As a result of indicators such as activities at the monthly meetings, as well as the feedback about the subgroup activities and the daily affairs of the group members, the ODS felt that the group had become more proactive, communica-

---

*Appendix 8.6

tions were more open and the group was capable of being self-sustaining. At the sixth session he posed the question to the group, "What else do you want from me?" Discussion revealed that the group did feel as if they were ready to continue on their own. They felt free to contact the ODS or upper management if they felt a need for their assistance. Since that time the ODS has attended one half-day total group meeting and a session of one subgroup as well as being available for consultation.

The outcomes of the project which have been viewed as measures of success of the OD approach are:

1. Lower levels of management are much more proactive. When a problem arises people have a tendency to try to deal with it themselves rather than take it to their boss. Decisions are being made at a lower level of management. People have a sense of potency because they have been able to make things happen. As a specific example, a few months after the formal sessions ended several first level supervisors decided some problems were occurring that deserved the attention of their peer group. They rented conference facilities, purchased airline tickets, set the agenda, and invited higher level organization members outside their department as the personnel group needed this interface. The supervisors did not feel the need to ask for approval to hold this meeting.

2. Two middle management job positions were eliminated because problems were handled and decisions were made sufficiently well at lower levels to eliminate two positions in the middle.

3. Greater job satisfaction and better interdepartmental coordination have occurred as a result of the restructuring of work assignments. As an example, employment supervisors were made responsible for specific departments in the state rather than dealing with requests from the entire state on the basis of when calls come in.

4. Previously untapped resources are now being used. In one case a supervisor, through her own initiative, developed and began training interested line managers in a cultural awareness (minority employee) program.

5. One black woman who had felt unable to communicate with some of the group felt many of the acceptance concerns and communications problems she was experiencing were resolved.

6. Communications are much more open. People tend to discuss the impact they are having on each other and discussions are much more direct, confronting and candid than before. Work teams are now meeting to review job problems and causes.

7. Attitudes are improved and people are experiencing personal growth. Here is a quote from a letter the ODS received eight months after the effort began.

   "The year preceding OD, I had been a poor excuse on our team. I had developed a terrible inferiority complex, a closed mind, and lost all my self-confidence. My main concern was whether or not I would be accepted by the group. I found out when I am open and candid I can establish a feeling of trust with others. I am a happer person on the job as well as off the job after the sessions. I have this wonderful feeling of having found myself. I believe I will be a much better employee and member of the team."

The OD group has gained entree into departments in Mountain Bell through a variety of approaches. Presentations at staff and line management conferences have been an effective way to interest management in the objectives and strategies of OD. These presentations, which include experiential designs and demonstrations where possible, have led to several projects. Public relations has been cooperative in placing articles about OD activities in the company magazine and the management newsletter. Upper management has encouraged entree in several instances by supporting OD efforts. The most successful method for obtaining new clients seems to be word of mouth testimony from a satisfied client telling what they accomplished using OD. A video tape of two departments telling about their OD experiences was effective in helping top management become interested in involving themselves in OD. When requests for educational efforts are directed towards the OD group they try to provide diagnostic experiences as part of the educational efforts. These diagnostic experiences have helped to cause some organizations to become involved in OD activities.

The OD group has been effective in influencing the organizational norms in ways other than straight OD projects. Mountain Bell is currently involved in a Manpower Action Plan which has several facets including an inventory of current manpower, resources and talents, a forecast regarding new job skills required, replacement figures, a new (and more explicit) performance and potential appraisal system, improved career pathing and planning for all employees, and a study of employment and recruiting procedures in getting the "right" kinds of people once the needs are determined. The OD group has had considerable influence on various segments of the Manpower Action Plan. The group had sole responsibility for the development and implementation of the performance and potential appraisal system. The performance appraisal portion was designed as an MBO approach.

The OD organization has responsibility for the orientation week for management-trainee college-hires as well as an orientation for their bosses. They also have a follow-on session with trainees once each quarter throughout the trainee's first year with the company. This provides the group with an excellent opportunity to influence the young managers in the company.

There are several areas in which the OD group feels things need to be done and they are beginning to increase their efforts in these directions. These include: (1) There is a great need for a better integrated effort throughout the company to increase the impact on all segments of the company. (2) OD at the top is moving too slowly. In order to have a more systematic effort the top officers need to become more deeply involved. (The Cabinet has had contact with an outside consultant regarding involvement of the top team. This involvement is a result of OD successes lower in the organization.) (3) More needs to be done with interdepartmental confrontations as well as between corporate staff groups and the state line organizations. (4) There is a need to help task forces learn to work more effectively more quickly. (5) More must be learned about institutionalizing OD norms. (6) There is a need to learn better ways of keeping an OD effort alive and well when key personnel (e.g., a department head) are transferred or promoted.

Additionally the OD group sees a need to expand its role and functions. It has been action oriented in its approach, and wants to maintain that stance, but concurrently became more involved in planning and research of some major corporate projects, such as inputs pertaining to studies of corporate organizational structure, and the appropriateness of various departmental roles. An example of the latter involves the Personnel Department where there is a growing need to examine and perhaps redefine its mission.

APPENDIX 8.1*

Job Questionnaire

Instructions:

Please answer each question so as to show how you feel. You can do this by placing an "X" at the point on each scale which best describes your opinion, as in the example below.

	Very few	A few	Quite a few	A great many	All
None			X		
0	1	2	3	4	5

The only correct answer is your frank opinion.
There is no need to sign this questionnaire or to identify yourself.

Start Here:

1. Think about the specific duties of your job. How often have you felt unable to use your full capabilities in the performance of your job?

Almost always	Very often	Fairly often	Not very often	Very seldom	Almost never
0	1	2	3	4	5

2. How many functions do you perform on your job which you consider relatively unimportant or unnecessary?

Almost all of them	Most of them	Quite a few	A few	Very few	None of them
0	1	2	3	4	5

3. As you see it, how many opportunities do you feel you have in your job for making worthwhile contributions?

Almost none	Very few	A few	Quite a few	A great many	Unlimited
0	1	2	3	4	5

*The material presented in Appendixes 8.1 through 8.6 is reprinted by permission of the Mountain Bell Training and Organization Development Organization.

4. How often do you feel that your job is one that could be dropped?

Almost all the time	Most of the time	Quite often	Very seldom	Almost never	Never
0	1	2	3	4	5

5. How much say do you feel you have in deciding how your job is to be carried out?

None	Almost none	Very little	Fairly large amount	Very large amount	Unlimited amount
0	1	2	3	4	5

6. How frequently have you felt in your job that you could accomplish more if you could have complete freedom of action to accomplish your objectives?

Almost all the time	Most of the time	Quite often	Not too often	Very seldom	Almost never
0	1	2	3	4	5

7. How frequently on your job have you received some type of recognition for your accomplishments?

Almost never	Very seldom	Not too often	Quite often	Very often	A great many times
0	1	2	3	4	5

8. How often does your job, as presently structured, give you opportunities for personal recognition?

Almost never	Very seldom	Not too often	Quite often	Very often	A great many times
0	1	2	3	4	5

9. How do you feel about your present assignment as a job where you can continually learn?

Nothing more to learn on it	Practically nothing to learn	Can learn something but not much	Still can learn a little	Can still learn a lot on it	Can still learn a great deal
0	1	2	3	4	5

10. How do you feel about your general association with your company as an opportunity for learning a lot?

Provides no chance for learning	Provides almost no chance	Can learn something but not much	Can learn a little	Can learn a lot	Can learn a great deal
0	1	2	3	4	5

11. Outside of any regular measurements of your job (indexes or performance standards), how often have you inwardly felt you have achieved something really worthwhile?

Very seldom	Once in a while	Fairly often	Often	Very often	All the time
0	1	2	3	4	5

12. To what extent is it possible to know whether you are doing well or poorly on your job?

No way of knowing	Almost no way of knowing	To some extent	To a large extent	Great extent	Entirely possible
0	1	2	3	4	5

13. To what extent is it possible for you to introduce new (untried) ideas on your job?

To no extent	Almost no extent	Very little extent	Fairly large extent	Very large extent	A great extent
0	1	2	3	4	5

14. How often have you found the kind of work you are now doing to be interesting?

Almost never	Very seldom	Not too often	Quite often	Very often	Almost always
0	1	2	3	4	5

15. Based on your past experience in your present job, how often have you thought that you would like to quit or change jobs?

Very often	Often	Fairly often	Once in a while	Very seldom	Almost never
0	1	2	3	4	5

16. To what extent do you consider your present assignment helpful for a person who wants to be advanced in this business?

Almost no extent	Very little extent	Not very helpful	Fairly helpful	Very helpful	Extremely helpful
0	1	2	3	4	5

17. If you wish to make any comments about your job, your chance for achievement, recognition and personal growth, please use the space below or the back of this sheet.

APPENDIX 8.2

How do you feel about your company in relation to Gardner's nine rules for organizational renewal as outlined in "How To Prevent Organizational Dryrot"?

Below are scales on which to place your rating of your department for each of the nine rules or criteria. Please refer to the article for complete definition of the particular rule.

Rule 1: Recruitment and Development Programs

1	4	7
Poor	Fair	Excellent

Comments: _____

Rule 2: Environment for Individual

1	4	7
Very inhospitable		Very hospitable

Comments: _____

Rule 3: Provisions for Self-criticism

1	4	7
"We don't want to hear"	"Mostly we hear what we want to hear"	"We seek out and encourage self-criticism"

Comments: _____

Rule 4: Fluidity of Internal Structure

1	4	7
Rigid inflexible, unchanging		Viable, fluid, changes with times

Comments: _____

Rule 5: System of Internal Communications

```
1                          4                          7
L_____L_____L
Poor                      Fair                    Excellent
```

Comments: _____

_____

Rule 6: Prisoners of Procedures

```
1                          4                          7
L_____L_____L
```

Procedures all   Procedures are
important   guides to help
(How we do it more   but not ends
important than   in themselves
whether we do it)

Comments: _____

_____

Rule 7: Vested Interests

```
1                          4                          7
L_____L_____L
```

A lot of   Some vested   Very little
vested interests   interests   vested interests,
                                            high cooperation

Comments: _____

_____

Rule 8: Interest in What is Going to Become

```
1                          4                          7
L_____L_____L
```

Tend to live   Systematic
in past   planning
and present   for the future

Comments: _____

_____

Rule 9: Individual Motivation, Conviction, Morale

```
1                          4                          7
L_____L_____L
```

LOW – people   *HIGH* – people care,
don't care   are concerned &
generally apathetic   involved with
                                    their work

Comments: _____

_____

APPENDIX 8.3

Part 1

On the following two pages is a list of conditions representing various aspects of a job. If you were looking for an ideal job, within a field for which you are qualified, which of these items would you consider to be important?

On the attached answer sheet in *Column A:*

Place a "1" by those items which you feel are extremely important.

Place a "2" by those items which you feel are fairly important.

Place a "3" by those items which you feel are only slightly important.

Place a "4" by those items which you feel are of no importance at all.

Part 2

Now that you have indicated the importance of these conditions in an ideal job situation, would you please indicate to what extent you feel these conditions are characteristic of *your present job.*

On the attached answer sheet in *Column B:*

Place a "1" by those conditions which always are characteristic of your job.

Place a "2" by those conditions which frequently but not always are characteristic of your job.

Place a "3" by those conditions which rarely are characteristic of your job.

Place a "4" by those conditions which never are characteristic of your job.

Column A

Importance in ideal job —
1 = extremely important
2 = fairly important
3 = slightly important
4 = not important at all

Column B

Characteristic of actual job —
1 = always characteristic
2 = usually characteristic
3 = rarely characteristic
4 = never characteristic

	Col. A	Col. B
1. Being able to set my own job objectives	____	____
2. The amount of money I can make	____	____
3. Having new and varied tasks from day to day	____	____
4. Having a job that is secure	____	____
5. Having a responsible and challenging job	____	____
6. The physical surroundings where I work	____	____
7. Being able to perform the work in my own way	____	____
8. Knowing where I stand with my boss	____	____
9. Having an opportunity to do quality work	____	____
10. Feeling satisfied that I've achieved something at the end of a day	____	____
11. Working with harmonious, well-related people	____	____
12. Receiving recognition for a job well done	____	____
13. Having a supervisor who is technically competent	____	____
14. Having an opportunity to learn and grow professionally	____	____
15. Being kept informed by my boss	____	____
16. Having an opportunity to experiment and innovate	____	____
17. Having attractive fringe benefits, i.e., vacations, medical care, retirement plans, etc.	____	____
18. Having a feeling of knowing what I do matters to the overall success of the department	____	____

APPENDIX 8.4

The following questionnaire is designed to help diagnose the leadership style of a particular work group. We would ask that you answer the questions as objectively as possible to indicate the way you see your organization actually operating at the current time. Check the appropriate answers on the scale for each question.

1. How much confidence is shown in subordinates?

   None   Condescending   Substantial   Complete

2. How free do they feel to talk to superiors about job?

   Not at all   Not very   Rather free   Fully free

3. Are subordinates' ideas sought and used, if worthy?

   Seldom   Sometimes   Usually   Always

4. Is predominant use made of: (1) Fear, (2) Threats, (3) Punishment, (4) Rewards, (5) Involvement?

   1, 2, 3   4, Some 3   5, 4 Based on
   Ocasionally 4   4, Some 3   & 5   group set goals

5. Where is responsibility felt for achieving organization's goals?

   Mostly   Top and   Fairly   At all
   at top   middle   general   levels

6. How much communication is aimed at achieving organization's objectives?

   Very little   Little   Quite a bit   A great deal

7. What is the direction of information flow?

                     Mostly   Down, up
   Downward   downward   Down & up   & sideways

8. How is downward communication accepted?

   With   Possibly with   With   With an
   suspicion   suspicion   caution   open mind

9. How accurate is upward communication?

                     Censored for   Limited
   Often wrong   the boss   accuracy   Accuracy

10. How well do superiors know problems faced by subordinates?

                     Some
    Know little   knowledge   Quite well   Very well

11. At what level are decisions formally made?

Mostly at top	Policy at top, some delegation	Broad policy at top, more delegation	Throughout but well integrated

12. What is the origin of technical and professional knowledge used in decision making?

Top management	Upper & middle	To a certain extent, throughout	To a great extent, throughout

13. Are subordinates involved in decisions related to their work?

Not at all	Occasionally consulted	Generally consulted	Fully involved

14. What does decision-making process contribute to motivation?

Nothing, often weakens it	Relatively little	Some contribution	Substantial contribution

15. How are organizational goals established?

Orders issued	Orders, some comment invited	After discussion, by orders	By group action (except in crisis)

16. How much covert resistance to goals is present?

Strong resistance	Moderate resistance	Some resistance at times	Little or none

17. How concentrated are review and control functions?

Highly at top	Relatively highly at top	Moderate delegation at lower levels	Quite widely shared

18. Is there an informal organization resisting the formal one?

Yes	Usually	Sometimes	No —same goals as formal

19. What are cost, productivity, and other control data used for?

Policing, punishment	Reward & punishment	Reward, some self-guidance	Self-guidance, problem solving

APPENDIX 8.5

Place an "X" in the one area in each question that best describes your feelings toward your boss.

1. How much confidence does your boss have in you?

None	Some but not too much	Quite a lot	Complete

2. How free do you feel to talk to your boss about your job in its entirety, i.e., responsibilities, objectives, problems, frustrations, etc.

Not at all	Some but not very	Rather free	Fully free

3. Are your ideas sought and used, if worthy?

Seldom	Sometimes	Usually	Always

4. How responsible do you feel for achieving departmental goals?

Hardly at all	Some	Quite a lot	Very

5. What is the direction of communications?

Downward	Mostly downward	Down & up	Down, up & sideways

6. From information you receive from your boss, how accurate would you say downward communication is?

Often wrong	Limited accuracy	Usually accurate	Extremely accurate

7. How accurate is upward communication?

Often wrong	Censored for boss	Usually accurate	Very accurate always

8. How willing does your boss seem to be in helping you to solve problems you face on your job?

Not very	Limited interest	Usually interested & helpful	Very interested & helpful

9. To what degree does your boss understand your problems?

Hardly at all	Only somewhat	Quite a lot	Completely

10. How involved are you in making decisions related to your job?

| Not at all | Occasionally consulted | Usually consulted | Fully involved |

11. How are your job objectives established?

| Orders by boss | Orders, some comment invited | After discussion, by orders | By mutual (yours & your boss') agreement and understanding |

12. How are control data (quality of work, quantity of work, etc.) used?

| For policing then as punishment | Reward & punishment | Reward, some self-guidance | Self-guidance problem solving |

13. How often have you felt unable to use your full capabilities in performing your job?

| Very often | Fairly often | Very seldom | Almost never |

14. As you see it, how many opportunities do you feel you have in your job for making worthwhile contributions?

| Very few | Only sometimes | Quite a few | Almost unlimited |

15. How frequently have you felt in your job that you could accomplish more if you had more freedom of action?

| Most of the time | Quite often | Very seldom | Almost never |

APPENDIX 8.6

A.   Rate the degree to which the acceptance concern seems to be resolved within the team.

B.   Rate the degree to which YOU feel accepted as a fully contributing member of the team.

1. Concern for Acceptance/Membership

A.   1   9

     Low   5   High

B.   1   9

     Low   5   High

Sign Posts (Indicators)

Low

- Mistrust, fear — people are cautious
- High anxiety, nervousness
- Some are rather withdrawn, hidden in the woods
- Others are overly aggressive to be sure they are heard
- People say only those things known to be safe and acceptable to the group
- Conflict is suppressed, smoothed over, denied, avoided
- Overabundance of harmony — rather superficial

High

- Opinions expressed openly
- Willingness to confront conflict
- People feel free and do contribute "far out" ideas (different from majority of group)
- Genuine concern for ideas and feelings of each other
- Atmosphere is informal, group work is satisfying
- People genuinely respect each other
- Acceptance of people for what they are

A. Rate the degree to which the feedback concern seems to be resolved within the team.

B. Rate the degree to which YOU feel able to give and receive feedback with team members.

2. Feedback/Data Flow Concern

A. 1   9

Low   5   High

B. 1   9

Low   5   High

Sign Posts (Indicators)

Low

- Feedback not given openly
- When feedback is given it is often given in a strategic way (Your contribution has been marvelous — perhaps we could give John a chance).
- Facades exist
- Many innuendos and hidden meanings seem to be present
- Feedback is of the barbed humor variety which comes through in a punitive manner
- Group norm seems to be if you can't say something nice, don't say anything at all.
- Other norms (implicit not explicit) — "Let's leave feelings out of this and stick to the facts."
- People keep their feelings hidden under the guise of "not wanting to hurt someone."
- Ideas plop due to lack of support, examination, and/or understanding.

High

- Feedback given in a candid, straightforward fashion
- Feedback is meant to be helpful to the person's development and the group's functioning
- Feedback is seen as necessary and helpful and members solicit feedback

A.   Rate the degree to which the productivity concern is resolved within the team.

B.   Rate the degree to which YOU feel you are able to be productive and creative within the group.

3. Productivity/Goal Formation

A.   1   9
      |_____|_____|
      Low   5   High

B.   1   9
      |_____|_____|
      Low   5   High

Sign Posts (Indicators)

Low

- Involvement low — some people apathetic
- Evidence of win-lose competitiveness among some
- Considerable bickering over irrelevant points
- Questions of capacity of team to deal with issue
- Members concerned over degree of influence they can exert
- Defense of "my ideas."
- Members wanting "credit" for ideas
- Goals ill-defined

High

- Personal needs and team objectives are integrated
- Diversity of ideas encouraged — creativity comes from amending, support, encouragement, and confrontation
- Thrust is to solve problem with best solution rather than win one's own point of view (collaborative not competitive)
- Consideration of many alternatives, even though different from "mine"
- Goals clearly defined, understood, and people are committed to them

A. Rate the degree to which the control/organization concern is resolved within the group.

B. Rate the degree to which YOU feel an *equal* responsibility for the control and organization of the group.

4. Control/Organization

A. 1   9
    └────────────────────────────┴────────────────────────────┘
    Low   5   High

B. 1   9
    └────────────────────────────┴────────────────────────────┘
    Low   5   High

Sign Posts (Indicators)

Low

- Some people are passive — wait for the other guy to assume the responsibility
- Some people constantly fight the "authority" figure or other team members in an arbitrary way
- Some are rather "clinical" about it, i.e., "you people go ahead — I'll do it my way anyway and I'm not going to get involved with you"
- Some want to be shown and told exactly how to do things
- Others fight any semblance of structure or procedure

High

- People are interdependent
- Resources are identified and used well
- People assume various leader roles when the need arises rather than expecting someone else to take the responsibility
- Members regulate their own contributions and exercise self-control
- People participate freely
- Members are pro-active — take initiative

FOOTNOTES

1. Job questionnaire developed by Mountain Bell Management Training and Organization Development Organization (Appendix 8.1).

2. Gardner, John, "How to Prevent Organizational Dry Rot," Harper's Magazine, October 1965.

3. Organizational Renewal questionnaire developed by Mountain Bell Management Training and Organization Development Organization (Appendix 8.2).

4. Actual-ideal job questionnaire developed by Mountain Bell Management Training and Organization Development Organization (Appendix 8.3).

5. Leadership style questionnaire developed by Mountain Bell Management Training and Organization Development Organization (Appendix 8.4).

6. Boss-subordinate questionnaire developed by Mountain Bell Management Training and Organization Development Organization (Appendix 8.5).

7. Gibbs, Jack, "Climate for Trust Formation," in L. Bradford, J. Gibbs, and K. Benne, *T Group Theory and Laboratory Methods*, New York, London, and Sydney: John Wiley and Sons, 1964.

8. Modal concerns questionnaire developed by Mountain Bell Management Training and Organization Development Organization (Appendix 8.6).

9

ORGANIZATION DEVELOPMENT IN A FEDERAL GOVERNMENT SETTING

The following case is a story of how an organization moved from buying packaged OD programs from the outside (i.e. , the Managerial Grid) to developing its own in-house program using its own staff to conduct it. This program began with train-the-trainer programs for the internal resource staff. What followed was a series of team-building sessions for intact work groups covering such topics as organization culture, personal evaluation, problem solving and plans for follow-up. This program gave a different perception of what the evolving OD function was to be. The author describes some of the problems he encountered while attempting to change his role in the organization. Others can benefit from this accounting of his successes and failures that are typical when establishing a new OD role in an organization.

Organization Development in a Federal Government Setting

JOHN FARRELL

Beginning in the year 1967, one region of one of our smallest federal agencies began a program which I believe represents the most in-depth attempt to actually apply — as opposed to discuss — the collective behavioral science based organizational research, analysis, and change-technology, known generically as organization development, of any public agency in the United States. This chapter will attempt to recount some of the more significant events of those five years: How the program began and evolved and how some of the many problems that its creation caused were dealt with. This program, the objective of which was in large measure to make the operating organization a more rational, understandable system, particularly to the various employees of the organization itself, often created additional confusions and anxieties. An attempt will be made here to relate these as well as the more lofty and laudable objectives of the effort. Hopefully, trainers and managers from public agencies, particularly those who are considering an organization development program for their agencies, will be able to gain some relevant insights into what life might be like in an OD program.

REGION 2 OF THE BUREAU OF RECLAMATION*

The Bureau of Reclamation is a small, technically oriented conservation agency. Its mandate from the Congress of the United States directs it to facilitate the development of the arid western lands through water resource development. "Water resource development" translates, in reality, to the planning, construction, and operation of systems of dams and canals. The primary objective of these water systems is to provide irrigation water for the farmlands of the adjacent areas, although hydroelectric power and municipal and industrial water have become increasingly important benefits of the various projects. The bureau is somewhat unique among federal agencies in that it is only involved in the seventeen

---

John Farrell is Director of Staff Development at Kaiser Permanente Medical Center, San Francisco, California. He was previously an Organization Development Specialist with the U.S. Bureau of Reclamation in Sacramento, California. He holds a B.A. in history from Long Beach State College (California) and has done graduate work in psychology and public administration at Sacramento State College.

*The name has since been changed to Mid-Pacific Region.

westernmost states of the continental United States. Within these seventeen states, the bureau is divided into seven regions. The focus here will be on Region 2 of the bureau which is headquartered in Sacramento, California. Because it is, in part, a construction agency, the bureau's various regions have a fluctuating workforce and a semidecentralized organization. Region 2, during the four-year period of 1967 — 1971, had a workforce which fluctuated between approximately 1500 to 2300 full-time employees. Of these, approximately 600 employees are located in the bureau's regional headquarters in Sacramento.

IMPACT OF JOB CORPS PROGRAM

In 1967 the bureau became a part of the Job Corps program. This experience was to have a great impact on the bureau since, for the first time in its history, the agency was to be involved in a dramatically different program from those to which it was accustomed. Building and operating dams and canals is primarily an engineering enterprise. True, the bureau employs significant numbers of geologists, economists, agricultural specialists, and accountants, but these professions are also extremely technical in nature. Now for the first time, the bureau was concerned with a different product, assisting educationally disadvantaged young men to significantly increase their educational and vocational skills. The focus here is not to be on the Job Corps program itself, but rather to illustrate that the introduction of this agency to organization development was preceded by its involvement in a comprehensive change effort which was not directed toward the agency itself, but which inevitably left its mark on those associated with it. It is my pronounced bias that, had the bureau not been prepared for a change effort by attempting to facilitate change in others, no OD program would have emerged. Engineers as a group are, comparatively speaking, conservative folk. If we consider as well that the great majority of the bureau's managers come from rural America and average somewhat above fifty years in age, it might be assumed that the climate for a comprehensive organizational change effort was not particularly bright.

The Job Corps program required the influx of a large number of behavioral science-oriented people into the organization, principally teachers and counselors. In Region 2 we had two Job Corps centers and, in the main, they operated separate and apart from the remainder of the organization. With the exception of the teacher-counselor group, however, the staffs of these centers were by and large made up of pre-Job Corps employees of the bureau. Many of these employees later returned to the more traditional jobs within the organization. Of these men, with respect to the region's subsequent OD program, one was to be particularly helpful. He was regional Job Corps coordinator at that time, but he was subsequently to become a division chief and more importantly, to be in charge of the personnel and training offices within the region. Much of what was later to transpire with respect to the region's OD effort took place with his support and advocacy. Once again illustrating, that in addition to a fortunate sense of timing and an understandable, sequential organization change strategy, another essential ingredient of any viable organization change effort is the support of influential people in high places.

INTRODUCTION TO ORGANIZATION DEVELOPMENT

In 1967 I was serving as Assistant to the Regional Training Officer. The Job Corps people had become interested in Robert Blake's and Jane Mouton's Managerial Grid Program (Scientific Methods, Inc. of Austin, Texas) as part of their management training. I attended a Phase 1 seminar, along with a young line engineer, in order to take a look at that program in general and in particular to see what it might have that would be useful to the non-Job Corps portions of our organization. We came away very much impressed. Shortly after this time I became Regional Training Officer.

The managerial grid seminar which I attended had been jointly conducted and sponsored by the U.S. Bureau of Land Management, the U.S. Forest Service, and Region 1 of the Bureau of Reclamation. All of these agencies were responsible at the time for staffing and administering Job Corps conservation centers. During the next few years we cosponsored several seminars with each of these agencies. For the first two years, 1968 and 1969, our OD effort consisted pretty much of grid Phase I's.

In 1969 our own "home grown" OD program began to take shape. The first step was to expand the trainer base. Another of my biases is that the average line manager can be trained in a reasonable period of time to be an in-house OD consultant. It was my belief that the region could become self-sufficient with respect to OD "experts", thus equipping itself to completely manage its own organization change effort.

IN-HOUSE TRAINER TRAINING PROGRAM

During the course of our first year and a half of grid training, I had been keeping my eyes open for program participants who looked like good potential candidates for more indepth training in group leadership and team building skills. In early 1969, I approached regional management with a proposed six-month training program for seven line employees from within the organization. Briefly, the proposal was as follows: Each participant would have two one-week training lab experiences and one two-week lab experience over a six-month period. The first one-week lab was to be an in-house program with the seven participants together to sample the process and see if it was their cup of tea. They also would get to know each other pretty well and be in a better position to see if they would be comfortable working closely together over an extended period of time. In essence, the first lab was an "I'm in" or "I'm out" affair (although an established ground rule was that anyone who felt strongly about dropping out could do so at any time with no questions asked). The second and third labs were to be taken from those scheduled by N.T.L. The second lab (one week) was to be a basic human relations lab. My reasoning here was that a group trainer must have a feeling sense of the participant's perspective in a group context, particularly when the tension level is frequently very high. The third lab, the one lasting two weeks, was scheduled late in the six-month training program. My objective here was to gain access to as much OD technology as possible while at the same time giving us the opportunity to come in contact with a wide variety of OD practitioners and OD implementation strategies. In other words I hoped we could steal as much useful material as possible. The two-week labs we selected were, therefore, from among N.T.L.'s Laboratories for OD practitioners. We sent one or two persons to each of four different training sessions and, as we had hoped, came away with a great deal of useful information.

The design of the in-house facilitator training program was as follows: the three laboratory experiences just described, a series of six one-day training sessions with an outside consultant as trainer, and, toward the latter part of the six-month training period, a one-week team building session in which the trainee served as co-facilitator. The six one-day sessions focused on communication skills and were spread out over the six-month period of training. These sessions provided us the opportunity to develop our skills as effective communicators and, at the same time, allowed us to keep in touch with each other regarding the progress and problems we were having with a rather rapid inundation of process-oriented material. For most of us this experience was very much like a journey into another world. It meant a great deal to us to be making the journey together.

The seven part-time, in-house trainers then became part of the Training Advisory Group working with the region's top management in planning and designing the region's ongoing organization development program. This relationship is still continuing and is, I believe, one of the major strengths of the current program.

In 1970 the Regional Training Office doubled in size. From one full-time trainer we expanded to two. We also started our second in-house train-the-trainer program. Eight line employees began a year-long training program.

In evaluating our first in-house trainer training program, which was in large part a result of pressure to meet a growing demand for more and more OD training, we realized that a six-month course was just not long enough to provide the background we felt necessary to meet the developmental needs of an in-house resource person. This was not to say that our first program was unsuccessful. On the contrary it was most successful, both in the eyes of the participants themselves and in the eyes of management. It was successful, however, largely because of the dedication of the participants. They worked weekends, nights, and occasional hours during the week while at the same time carrying on full-time jobs. We all felt, however, management included, that to ask a program participant to exhibit this amount of dedication in order to be a part of the program was simply unrealistic. With the immediate pressure off us with respect to a staff of trainers we could afford to be more deliberate. The new program was to be of one year's duration. The first six months was to focus on the participant himself — his needs, leadership and communication styles, and how he felt and reacted in a group context. The second half of his training would focus on group-leadership skills, problem-solving techniques, and OD strategy in general. Eight participants began this training and completed the first half. The program is still continuing and it is expected that there will be a new class of six to ten participants starting each year.

TEAM BUILDING

The focus of the region's OD effort after the first two years, which emphasized orientation to the concept of organization development, has always been team building. During the first years we worked toward getting the individuals in an existing work unit through one-week seminars which emphasized group problem solving. In order to do this we held as many as three seminars (of up to eighty participants each) per year. We also took advantage of problem-solving seminars sponsored by other government agencies. This approach enabled us to get as many as one hundred and twenty employees per year through the introductory seminar. As soon as an entire work unit completed the first seminar (this could take anywhere from six months to a year and a half since all the members of the work unit would not go to the same seminar) we scheduled a one-week team building session.

The team building week is divided into four parts: Organization culture — an examination of the general working conditions of the unit, review of work priorities, and individual assignments; personal review — a review of the interpersonal relationships within the unit based upon the expectations and responsibilities of the various team members; problem solving — a listing of the major problems facing the unit and a preliminary prioritizing of these problems followed by the selection of one problem to work through during that week; and lastly, plans for follow-up sessions to continue the team building effort.

The design of the team building session followed a relatively unstructured format, other than roughly conforming to the sequence just described. At the outset, as we did with Phase I or orientation seminars, we followed the grid materials rather closely. We shortly, however, converted these weeks to a much less structured approach. Our methodology essentially became one of data accumulation-feedback-analysis. Participants were asked to describe their views of the work situation in terms of (1) reality as they see it, (2) their own expectations and, (3) an "ideal" organizational situation. These questions soon flushed out the participants' assumptions, resentments and frustrations and, for the first time for most, the realization that they had little individual (let alone collective) idea of how they felt they *should* be operating. The relevance of this last bit of confusion became very apparent to all. "How can we do anything about our present frustrations if we have such a poor idea about where we want to go?" "What do others expect of us?" "How do we *know* what others expect of us?"*

These questions, as well as many others tend to surface rapidly. The communication and problem-solving process skills required of the facilitator in such an unstructured approach are of a relatively high order. The results — identification of significant "problem issues" (many of which had been previously viewed as "too sensitive" for discussion) and subsequent action on these problems — have indicated that the approach is a sound one.

---

*Those readers familiar with the managerial grid program will recognize that the four-step sequence is very similar to the grid approach. We soon abandoned the use of grid materials, however.

TEAM LEADER TRAINING

Another significant feature of the bureau's regional OD effort, but one which began rather late in the game, has been a three-part program for managers and supervisors which we called "Team Leader Development." This particular aspect of the program evolved as a result of the rather belated realization that many team leaders (e.g., managers/supervisors) who endorsed the *concept* of OD, and who had reacted enthusiastically to the orientation seminar, were dragging their feet about scheduling a team building session. We arrived at the tentative conclusion that these managers were holding back a more personal investment in our program because they were really quite confused about their individual roles in a "team" context. It is rather easy to demonstrate to a manager that high quality decisions can consistently come from a team which is pooling its resources to solve problems. It also is quite easy to demonstrate that the team's commitment to solutions is much higher if they themselves arrive at those conclusions rather than simply serving as data collectors or legmen for managers presumed to be more capable than themselves. What is more difficult to do, but what we now believe to be critical, is to be more explicit about what a team leader *should* do. Just what is his role after he has disavowed an autocratic leadership style?

Our first indication that we were on the right track came when we announced our first course for twenty team leaders. We had two and a half times as many candidates as we could accommodate. Our second indication that role confusion was a primary factor in manager reluctance was demonstrated by the fact that several managers who completed the course, but who had not previously been involved in team building, immediately scheduled team building sessions.

One of the primary benefits derived from the team leader training program was the establishment and strengthening of relationships between individual managers and members of the training staff. During these programs managers and supervisors were afforded the opportunity to observe the training staff in action. They were thus able to determine by personal observation whether or not they would be comfortable working with one or more of those trainers.

In rather quick review, this agency's regional organization development program consists, at this time, of OD orientation, team building, team leader development, an in-house OD resource training program, and a training advisory group for overall program coordination. Since my leaving the bureau in June, 1971, several inter-group (i.e., inter-divisional, inter-branch) problem solving sessions have also been held. Details on the design of these sessions are available from the agency.

ROLE OF THE ORGANIZATION DEVELOPMENT SPECIALIST

We evolved from a training approach to an OD approach. This, I believe, is rather typical of most organizations with a training department. The average supervisor or manager in such an organization sees training as the responsibility of the training department. The supervisor is preoccupied with day-to-day duties. He gets involved in training when a course announcement comes across his desk and he must decide whether to send a member of his staff to the course, or when he himself is to be sent to a program. The training department typically designs programs for the organization at large, though occasionally specific programs are designed for specific departments. Trainers want their programs to be broad enough in scope that they will be attractive to the largest number of potential participants. The subject matter of the courses is rarely, therefore, directly related to the work that the program participants actually perform. This is particularly true of management and supervisory courses, although to a large extent it is also true of technical courses. Trainees are exposed to methodology which they are to learn and then take back to their work units where the new methods will be implemented. The assumption is that the back-home work unit will adopt what the trainee has learned and the work of the unit will be more effective and efficient. The problem is that it doesn't work.

The mode of instruction just described is quite useful for individual learning. It does not work well for influencing behavior change in work units. In order to significantly influence the learning experience of work units it is necessary to work with *work units*. This effort requires that the work unit be systematically developed, that the evolution of the training toward stated goals be clear, and most importantly, that the work unit — as a group — has a legitimate opportunity to influence the entire process.

This focus on training and development, first of all, is a departure from tradition. That means simply that the organization must be helped to learn and become accustomed to this approach to training. It is a new experience for almost everyone in the organization and, as such, can threaten individual employees tremendously. For many people, particularly some of the older employees, this will be the first time they can *ever* recall being asked to take a hand in their own development. Individual reactions vary tremendously. Some respond with enthusiasm, some with caution and skepticism, others attack the effort out of fear and alarm. Throughout this introductory phase it is extremely important that the trainers react with patience and compassion. It is quite likely that at times they will be under pressure both by reluctant employees and managers who are distressed about an apparent erosion of their traditional degree of control. It is at such times that the OD trainer's background in communication skills and interpersonal relations must be utilized for his own emotional tranquility — and at times for his own survival.

PROBLEMS WHICH AROSE AS A RESULT OF THE OD EFFORT

One of the initial problems with the OD program which we had to face as an organization involved the relationship between our region and our bureau office in Washington, D. C. When we were coming close to focusing our training effort on an organization development approach we wanted to describe our intentions and get a clear indication from Washington that (1) they understood what we were planning to do and, hopefully (2) that they approved. The word we got back — via telephone — (and after a long silence) was that Washington did not wish to take a position. If we wished to proceed it was to be on our own hook; we were not to look to Washington for guidance.

Exactly what was going on in Washington was not clear. What *was* clear was that if we were going to proceed we would have to make the decision locally and live with the consequences. Throughout the history of our program it has remained a local effort.*

We didn't know, of course, but we surmised that part of our inability to get a more clear position statement from our Washington office came from one of the historic problems that has plagued OD efforts. This is the association that many people have in their minds about sensitivity training and organization development. This particular relationship, or lack of relationship, created one of the earliest crises in our program. The former Regional Job Corps Coordinator, who has already been mentioned, was attending the first of the three laboratory training sessions as a part of his involvement in the program. At the time, he was my immediate supervisor. I was one of the two trainers conducting the course.

About midway through the week the lab participants became divided about (1) whether this experience was sensitivity training, and (2) whether sensitivity training was evil or beneficial. My supervisor was not clear on either of these questions, but most of all he was distressed that we were in the throes of such a debate and that he didn't know the answers. We became involved in a very heated exchange which left our relationship strained for about two months. Afterward we were closer than we had ever been previously. Our argument forced us as an organization to face this issue. We did. We compiled a collection of writings on group-centered learning. Some were by authors who clearly advocated the experience, some by writers who were cautionary, and others that were truly alarmist papers. We held a meeting of the Training Advisory Group to discuss the issue. From this meeting came a clear understanding of the issue and our position on it. Essentially our position was to be as follows: We would at no time deal with the personalities of bureau employees. We would, however, focus on the observed behavior of individuals within the actual training session itself, and process this behavior in the terms of the individual's own stated learning objectives. This focus has worked out well in practice.

Another crisis situation involved the managerial direction of the OD program. It was my contention from the outset that for the program to truly influence organizational behavior it would have to actually *be* the region's program. This was the old issue of who is responsible for training — the training department or the individual supervisor or manager? I viewed it as critically important that management become an actual part of planning and administering the OD effort, rather than simply passing judgment on the recommendations of the training department. From my vantage point, the primary source of resistance to this concept came from one of our top managers. He was in a direct line authority relationship with me and therefore rather difficult to ignore. His position was that while it was highly desirable that management become involved in directing our program, it was not consistent with their own history that they actually would do so. He proposed, therefore,

---

*There are significant indications, however, that this situation will not prevail for much longer. Recently a group from Region 2 conducted an orientation meeting on the Region's OD Program in Washington, D.C. for the bureau's Central Management Group.

that the two of us provide program direction and that he would serve as liaison to other top managers and keep them advised. We had serveral heated exchanges over this issue and it never really became resolved between the two of us.

In actual fact, the top management group provided generous amounts of its time and became deeply involved in directing the program. The immediate crisis was resolved largely as a result of the very proactive stance of top management. My relationship with the manager in question, however continued on a very strained basis up until the time I left the organization.

It is in situations like the one just related that I had some of my greatest personal learning. Many of the reasons for the relationship breakdown were directly due to my conduct during the dispute. I believed then, as I do now, that my position on the issue was correct. That in itself was, and is, quite beside the point. It is extremely important that change agents model nondefensive behavior, and patience, when working with managers. Most managers are accustomed to relying on power when issues that are in dispute between them and their subordinates come down to the wire. The change agent must keep making his views known, but at the same time, pay particular attention to avoiding a win-lose confrontation. This, of course, is even more important when the manager in question is your boss. I handled the first part well enough, but I failed rather miserably with the latter.

When I first wrote the last paragraph it represented my concluding remarks on that situation. I believe, however, that I have some responsibility to elaborate further. The manager in question was as responsible as any single man in our agency for the advent and subsequent success of our OD program. He took a personal interest in me from very early in my employment with the bureau. I worked for the Bureau of Reclamation for several years before I became specifically associated with the training department. The relationship which I developed over time with this manager was one of the organizational veteran following the progress of the well-intentioned but organizationally naive neophyte. This relationship was not unique to me. He kept track of, and spoke often to, many young people in the organization. To a very real extent, much of what we were able to attempt was a direct result of this man's receptivity and very active support. After our program began to really gain momentum I became increasingly concerned with the process by which major program decisions were being made. I felt that it was vital to the program that upper management be intimately involved with identification of the issues needing resolution, the decision making process itself and the administration of the program. The training department, I felt, should function as a coordinative body and a provider of specific organization and individual development expertise. It should, however, be *management's* program, not the training department's.

My view of what happened between the manager in question and myself is obviously influenced by a variety of factors. Basically, I saw it as an issue of program control and direction. Who should do it? I thought a management *group*, representing the significant departments in the organization, would be appropriate. He did not disagree, but believed that managers in our organization were not accustomed to working as a group on such matters and therefore could not be relied upon to do so. He proposed that he and I work together to administer the program and he would be responsible for keeping the other managers informed.

This overture was in many ways a demonstration of his confidence in me. At the time, however, if I was mindful of that at all, it was overshadowed by my zeal to force the issue. I disagreed, and disagreed very forcefully. He responded with hurt and anger.

We had a variety of strained interactions from that time forward. I believe, however, that the deterioration of our relationship began at that point. I have thought often since leaving the organization of my role in that interchange as well as a good deal of my subsequent behavior. In doing so the line-staff relationship has become a good deal more clear to me. Line managers are charged with running the organization. It is *their* responsibility, not the staff man's. What distresses me most about the event is that it did not have to happen. It was not the fact that I disagreed with him that caused the problem. We had disagreed fairly often in the past. It was the *way* I disagreed.

The organization development specialist is a staff man. True, he is a special sort of staff man, but a staff man none the less. A good portion of his input to the organization is more behavioral than conceptual. If he cannot model the organizational practices which he is advocating his effectiveness will be severely limited. Of course the OD specialist is just as subject to the pressures of organizational life as the next man. His professed area of expertise, however, is the ability to help others, individually and collectively, to deal with these pressures.

I learned a great deal about myself from that interaction. I believe that it helped me to get a much better feel for the organizational role of the OD specialist.

The last problem area that I will address myself to is one which was inherent in the design of our program. I am referring to the role of the in-house part-time trainer who also has a regular nontraining job in the organization. The advantages of such an approach have already been referred to briefly. They are: (1) the organization becomes essentially self-reliant with respect to OD training expertise,* (2) the change effort is not merely a training department program, and (3) it demonstrates that line personnel can learn and utilize behavioral science based interpersonal skills training. There are several potential problems with this strategy, however. First is the pressure on the individual to carry out the responsibilities of two jobs. It was a matter of tremendous pride to the first group of seven trainers not to use their involvement in the program as an excuse for not meeting their nontraining responsibilities. In order to do this, however, it required a great deal of additional work on their own time. I recommend to any organization that is interested in experimenting with this aspect of our program that they make demonstrated reliability and follow-through one of the selection criteria for their candidates. We were extremely fortunate in this respect.

Another problem related to this approach involved the relationship between the part-time trainer and his line supervisor. These relationships varied tremendously among the individual in-house trainers, but in every instance was to become a problem at one time or another. We spent a good deal of trainer time

---

*This is not intended to mean that we did not use outside consultants. I will refer to our use of consultants shortly.

discussing the issue. We were never able to lay it to rest. The only conclusion we reached was that we would have to deal with this on a continuing basis and work through each new occurrence. The supervisor would be asked to lay out his specific production and behavior expectations to his employee. The employee would do the same. They then reached a contract on their mutual expectations. These contracts were continually being renegotiated. We would ask the supervisor for a certain amount of the employee's time. This would vary from a top figure of twelve weeks per year to a minimum of two weeks. Once agreement was reached we gave the supervisor as much lead-time as possible regarding the specific schedule of training activities. At first glance this approach might seem to put an undue amount of pressure on the trainer/employee. While there certainly is pressure, it was not as much as might be imagined for two reasons: (1) the supervisors who had employees as part-time trainers were, in most cases, proud to be making a contribution to the program, and (2) top management endorsed the program and knew which supervisors provided trainers (supervisors knew that it was in their interest to cooperate).

The last problem area relating to the in-house part-time trainers concerns the relationship between the individual trainer and his nontrainer peers within the organization. The program itself provided no guarantees for promotions or any other specific advantages to anyone who became a trainer. It inevitably led, however, to much more organizational visibility for the employee who took on the added responsibility. Therefore, a certain amount of resentment became focused on the trainers. I believe that this diminished gradually as time went on, however, as people became more familiar with the new organizational roles of these individuals.

REFLECTIONS ON ORGANIZATION DEVELOPMENT IN A PUBLIC AGENCY

My intent in the remaining portions of this chapter is to share some of my own opinions regarding organization development in general and my own experience with OD in a federal agency in particular.

Governmental agencies are, in concept at least, primarily reactive systems. That is simply to say that our governmental system provides that elected politicians make policy in response to public need. This policy is then communicated to agencies for implementation of specific programs. In actual fact it is rarely this tidy. The great majority of programs implemented by the Bureau of Reclamation were drawn up in considerable detail by the agency itself and then submitted to Congress for approval. Congressional hearings *are* scheduled prior to authorization and adjustments *are* made. The programs, however, are primarily the products of the agencies themselves. (The Job Corps program mentioned earlier was a notable exception.) This situation, that is a system which was set up to operate in one way but in reality operates in quite another, has some very interesting organizational ramifications. Federal agencies are dependent on congressional approval for their survival. If they cannot get approval for their programs they cannot continue to exist. An interesting factor in the Congress-agency relationship, however, is that there is seldom any individual or group that is more expert concerning the programs of the agencies than the agencies themselves. They accumulate the data that their proposals are based upon and they often influence, if not determine, the criteria upon which their proposals are to be judged.

The significance of this for an organization development program is that (1) the concept of governmental direction (i.e., by elected officials) is somewhat in question, (2) the agencies are in fact far more self-directing than often even they perceive themselves to be, and (3) most people within the agency, except some of those at the very top, relate to the agency as a reactive entity — which in fact is very often not the case.

From an organization development point of view, these observations, if we can accept them as essentially accurate, have considerable relevance. Most managers with whom I interacted viewed their jobs as carrying out the directions of a higher level — a reactive stance. Yet in actual fact, the agency, even on a regional level, was largely responsible for not only producing *but actually generating* its own product. The product, in the case of the Bureau of Reclamation, is recommendations for future dams and canals.

One of the primary sources of frustration to me as a change agent was my attempt to gain an understanding of the way the region operated. I attempted to see it as a rational system. By "rational system" I simply mean that I attempted to see our region as a system of interacting units which had defined functions and responsibilities and which produced products and provided services which resulted in the reclamation of the arid lands of our region. Over time, however, the original system (readers will note that I am still addicted to the concept that there was *at least* an original system) had become extended, contracted, interrupted, and convoluted by changing technology, changing skills, and changing objectives. The nature of many individual and collective relationships had not been systematically examined for many years. We found that in a good many instances, so much energy was required to make the wheels turn that there was very little left over to check out where we were going.

I have come to realize that this situation is not unique to this small agency. Quite to the contrary, most organization-change agents as well as most managers with whom I have spoken, both in and out of government, have come to see their organizations as essentially irrational systems. This realization has saved me a great deal of subsequent frustration, and in large measure this situation provides the *raison d'etre* of OD (and its practitioners).

This learning was not unique. Our OD program was to be largely a series of attempts to understand and influence our particular system and then to make the necessary adjustments when we found we had not taken every contingency into account. We learned a great deal. Perhaps most of all we learned to trust our bumbling efforts, to assume that we would make few decisions that were free from subsequent adjustment, and, perhaps most of all, that we could live with what happened. Lastly, we came to realize that little organization change takes place by studying the successful efforts of others or listening to experts' advice about what we ought to do.

Before closing I must say a word or two about our experience with outside consultants. We used outside consultants in two basic ways. In the first instance the consultant came into our program just prior to our first OD resource training program for internal people. We used him primarily to help design that program and later to conduct a series of skills training sessions for those trainees. He later led a team building session for our top regional management. He helped us a great deal. He was never, however, the prime mover in the design or conduct of any of the basic aspects of our program.

We also used several trainers skilled in team building facilitation skills to conduct several of our earlier team building sessions. All of these people did excellent work for us, particularly at times when our own resources were very thin.

In my opinion, learning that we could effectively identify, analyze, and solve systemwide organizational problems was, and has continued to be, the primary benefit of the bureau's OD program. The most unique aspect of our program, if indeed there is anything truly unique about it, was and is the program for developing internal resource people. This approach resulted in the active involvement of many very competent individuals from within the organization. This group has continued to grow in size and involvement. It now numbers approximately twenty-five people and includes top-level managers, middle managers, first-level supervisors and both engineering and nonengineering personel.*

Ours was a most uncertain course but I recommend it. We identified what we wanted, why we wanted it, how we were going to do it. Then we did it. We often had to scurry around trying to figure out where things went wrong, which we did, and learned we could make the adjustments required.

What has all of the effort done? I ask the question not because I have an impressive list of accomplishments to recount but rather because my conscience (and the editor) won't permit me not to. I have very little hard data to offer in support of our program. The results thus far seem to be almost entirely attitudinal. I believe that many operating relationships have been improved; certainly many individuals have said so.

I would like to believe that Region 2 of the Bureau of Reclamation does what it does at least as well as it did it a few years ago. I also believe that it does it more pleasantly.

---

*This last item has considerable relevance because the bureau has traditionally staffed its significant management positions with engineers.

ORGANIZATION DEVELOPMENT
IN A STATE MENTAL HEALTH SETTING

The role of a consultant is not new to mental health systems. Consultation is an ongoing service provided by most mental health systems. However, an OD consultant encounters some unique problems when he consults with mental health workers themselves. Practically everyone views himself as being an expert on human behavior and cites his credentials to prove it. The author describes his approach to such issues as (1) identifying the client, (2) diagnosing the situation, (3) intervention styles, (4) values (i.e., of the consultant, of the system), (5) psychological contract (between consultant and client), (6) the relationship between training and OD, and (7) evaluation of the consultant's effectiveness. Written in a very personal style, the author describes some of the issues he grapples with as a consultant to a helping organization. Although the context in mental health systems may differ from other organizations, the problems of an OD consultant are not unique.

Organization Development in a State Mental Health Setting

ARTHUR M. FREEDMAN

Mental health organizations in the United States have been strong consumers of organizational development programs and allied planned change efforts. Mental health organizations have been primarily run under governmental auspices and are one of the few types of bureaucracies with an almost totally professional staff. With increasing involvement of government in other aspects of health care, organizational development projects in mental health systems represent an important and prototypic experience with *government-run professional human service and health care systems.*

I am of the opinion that OD, as practiced in such systems, can be quite different in many ways from enterprises with similar labels and objectives which are conducted in the private sector. In the vast majority of cases, OD efforts are engaged in by systems whose executives and managers are accountable to a board of directors whose members are generally concerned primarily with such issues that relate to dividends, profit margins, shares of the market, and public image. Further, most systems which employ internal and/or external OD consultants are those which produce tangible, consumable products rather than human services. Thus, managers tend to be concerned with issues like cost-per-unit-produced, efficient market research and sales methods, reducing service and maintenance costs, repeated consumption of items produced, etc. Governmental, nonprofit, human service delivery systems are more concerned with such issues as comprehensiveness of services provided, effectiveness, reduction or prevention of manifest need for service, etc. In a sense, one might, in a period of blind optimism and idealism, say that the human service delivery system might strive to work itself out of a job or function whereas a private, profitmaking, production-oriented system is more likely to try to make itself indispensable to its ever growing numbers of consumers. Although the "corporate" goals can be seen as antithetical both types of systems are concerned with similar internal dynamics: Maximum efficiency, effectiveness and appropriateness of the objectives, and operations of

Arthur M. Freedman is Assistant Region Administrator, Staff Training and Organizational Development, Region 2 for the Illinois Department of Mental Health. Previously he was a consultant in organization and community development in Houston, Texas. He holds a B.S. in Business Administration and an M.B.A. in Human Relations and Industrial Sociology from Boston University. The University of Chicago awarded him a Ph.D. in Clinical Psychology.

194

their subunits; the satisfaction of the members of their system; and the optimal integration of the efforts of their subunits in the service of their organizational objectives.

The material presented in this chapter should be shared with two kinds of readers:

- The organizational development professional called in from outside to unsnarl and facilitate mental health agency transactions, and

- The mental health professional in the system who has wittingly or otherwise become involved in management functions and/or organizational development and needs to become an intelligent *actor* in the situation or a knowledgeable *buyer* of services.

1. HOW DOES THE INTERNAL OD CONSULTANT FIND OUT WHAT IS GOING ON IN THE (MENTAL HEALTH) SYSTEM? FROM WHICH SOURCE (S)?

Since I have only recently returned to Chicago and employment in DMH after a three-year hiatus, I think I am in a good position to share some of my experiences on this issue. However, my experiences may be more relevant for the *new* internal consultant and only partially relevant to the more experienced OD practitioner.

Upon coming into the administrative offices of DMH's Region 2 (Chicago area), I found myself in need of information about what was going on in terms of the region's general goals and specific objectives so that I could begin to acquire a foundation of data to use to measure the current status of the staff development and organizational development function for which I was responsible . I soon discovered that such goals and objectives were not well spelled out; neither were they easily available. The DMH, in general, and the region, in particular, was in a state of flux. A move was in progress to eliminate the custodial functions previously performed by the department in favor of active involvement in residential, outpatient and "community mental health" programming. An exact operational definition for the latter type of programming did not exist and was "open" to ideas from anyone willing and able to make a contribution. This condition continues to a great extent; however, we now know more about what we *don't* want community mental health programming to be than we do about what we *do* want. And, the first two types of programming varied according to type of patient population (mentally retarded; acute or chronic, neurotic or psychotic; child, adolescent, adult or geriatric) and type and extent of treatment staff skills and willingness to innovate.

Thus, there was very little consistency in organizational structures and training needs—these varied according to the facility, treatment program, treatment unit and subregion (i.e., catchment area). Even the organizational structure of each facility's training staff groups (the staff development services or SDS) were set up differently: at one facility the SDS was primarily decentralized with most training taking place at the treatment program or subregional level rather than at the facility level; another facility's SDS group provided centralized "core" training at the facility level with specialized training taking place at lower levels; some

SDS training staffs set themselves up to handle all four tracts in our Mental Health Generalist series (the technicians, supervisors, specialists and administrators) interchangeably and simultaneously, whereas other training staffs differentiated themselves with subgroups of trainers specializing in each of the four generalist tracts.

This, then, constituted the work situation into which I had decided to place myself. I was not aware of all of this at the time. I had to find out about it. I did this through a fairly systematic series of interviews. I started with all of the assistant regional administrators — the business manager, the head of the community placement group, the head of the evaluation and staff utilization and allocation function, and my predecessor in my present position, the coordinator of training and development. From this, the second administrative level from the top in the region, I moved upward to talk with the regional administrator. In each case, I asked as few orienting questions as possible. Paraphrased, these were:

1. What kinds of functions do you perform? With whom, in particular?
2. What procedures and/or styles of operating do you employ in performing your functions? How have you structured or organized your staff?
3. What do you see as your own desired objectives?
4. What obstacles tend to interfere with your attempts to achieve these objectives?
5. What seems to facilitate your attempts to achieve your objectives?
6. What do you think should be taking place in the region, but is not?
7. What do you think is taking place, but should not?

The data I gathered from these interviews were temporarily sufficient to give me a global impression of the then-current state of the regional system from the perspective of the upper echelons. From there, I moved downward to the facility level and interviewed the SDS training staff members. The same seven questions were raised in relation both to the current condition of each facility's managerial and treatment functions as well as to the fit (degree of correspondence) between the training functions and the needs of the particular facility. Of course, at this time I was also quite interested in establishing a close, open, and trusting work relationship between myself and the facility-based training staff members. I felt that if we could learn to get along and work well together, and collaborate, the understanding would flow from that.

The interviews were discontinued for a couple of months during which I went through a period of orientation and consolidation — at this time my predecessor moved out from his staff position to assume a line position as the director of one of the larger subregions operating out of one of the largest facilities, and I took over his position as assistant region administrator responsible for training and development. When I resumed my interviews, I focused on a sampling of the region's six facility superintendents, their deputies and the fifteen subregion directors and their assistants. In this I was assisted by a very close friend, the recently deceased and very much missed Bob Grant.

There are at least four other formal structured means by which I am, at this time, able to keep in continuous contact with what was happening within the region, aside from my ongoing, informal contacts with regional office and facility-based personnel. One is the weekly, Thursday morning meetings which the region administrator held with the facility administrators and managers on a rotating basis — which I refer to as the "floating crap game". The primary function of these meetings is information exchange and consultation between the facilities' and the regional office staff members.

The *second* continuing means of obtaining information has been made available as a result of having organized monthly, all day regional training committee meetings. These meetings focus on two-way information sharing, creation and termination of functional and time-limited "task forces" and establishment of consistent but flexible operational policies and procedures to be applied throughout the region. Our primary concerns relate to problems encountered in developing custom-tailored training programs, their components and modules for the mental health generalist series for the various facilities, their treatment programs and subregions.

A *third* structural source of information is represented by the state-wide DMH training committee. This group meets monthly. The focus of attention primarily centers on identifying departmental issues which have training and development implications, e.g., overseeing the implementation of the mental health generalist career ladder series and examining and making recommendations on other professional treatment and institutional support (i.e., security, dietary, housekeeping) staff career series. The committee attends to the directions in which the department seems to be moving — for example, developing increasing interests in the area of community mental health programming — in order to prepare the state-wide training apparatus to acquire the skills and knowledge needed to cope with new, anticipated demands. The committee controls the activities of the learning media institute, an internal, multi-media resource and production operation which is intended to support the training and development enterprise. The committee also focuses on certain interdepartmental transactions which influence the training function on a state-wide basis — in particular, an ongoing liaison is facilitated through the committee with the department of personnel in order to insure a match exists between DP's criteria for initial employment, pay raises, and promotions for DMH personnel and the available training services required to meet those criteria. These criteria are amenable to being influenced by the DMH but are the prerogatives of the DP and are overseen by DP staff who are permanently assigned to the DMH. It has been through my formal associations with the state training committee and my informal, consultative relationship with the newly arrived director of the DMH division of training and development (the representative of the training function at the highest, DMH central office level) that have been providing me with a fairly adequate glimpse of the current and relevant (to my needs) system-wide perspectives.

Finally, I have been able to obtain a close look at what I have called "life in the trenches," (what life is like for the paraprofessionals and semiprofessionals who have direct treatment responsibilities on treatment programs and units). This perspective has been made available as a result of my responding to requests from such programs and units to have me conduct OD projects within their subsystems. Thus far, I have conducted three of these and have two more on my calendar. These activities have proven to be of invaluable assistance in helping me to see for myself the tasks for which the training enterprises in the various facilities have been attempting to prepare our treatment staff trainees. I have also been able to see, firsthand, the impact and implications of many of the organizational structures, procedures and policies which either facilitate or interfere with trainees' ability to apply their acquired skills and knowledge. Obviously, I can not hope to fill the demand for such consultative services if requests continue to come in to my office. I have, therefore, begun to use these consultations as opportunities to provide some of the facilities' training staff members some on-the-job training in OD. I have it in mind to train these selected people to the point where ultimately they are sufficiently proficient to conduct this type of project by themselves for subsystems within their own facilities with only consultative and planning assistance being required of me.

As an unintended example of how this can happen, I was recently asked to do an OD consultation with the thirty-person treatment, support and administrative staff of an adolescent treatment unit of one of our facilities. Two of the facility's training staff and I met with the two top administrators of the unit to do some preliminary objective setting and fact finding. At a later date, I made an on-site visit and conducted interviews with samples of the youngsters and staff. We decided to conduct a two-day workshop with all of the staff assigned to the unit (all three shifts). Arrangements for substitute staff coverage were made — not without considerable difficulty — dates were set, and a preliminary design for the workshop was developed by myself, one training staff member from the local facility and another training staff member from a second facility. Then, on the evening prior to the workshop, I was immobilized by a rather severe penicillin allergy reaction. The other two training staff men agreed to take over. Although I was home in bed, the trainer-consultants phoned me several times a day for both days of the workshop. We discussed what was happening, the impact of the design and proposed design modifications. The two training staff members got more of an opportunity to assume primary responsibility for conducting such a workshop than they might have had I been present. This gave them a basis for greater self-confidence and experience; I found out I was more dispensable than I sometimes like to believe; and the workshop seemed to be a resounding success — although we still have to evaluate its long-term impacts through follow-up consultations and other types of contacts for which I hope to be in better condition.

Thus, I believe (hope?) I have developed a functional and interrelated series of mechanisms which will provide me with access to sources of information about the system from a variety of perspectives — the first three or four levels of "front line" workers, program and subregional managers, facility-level management and SDS trainers, regional-level managers, department-wide training and development staff, central office and inter-departmental.

2. WHO IS THE OD CONSULTANT'S CLIENT?

OD jargon generally insists that there is a "consultant" or "change agent" and
there is a "client system" composed of a number of "clients." However, in my
OD consultation within the DMH system and as an external consultant with other
organizational systems, I have found myself unnecessarily constrained and occasionally misled by these labels. I have found it more realistic and, in the long run,
convenient in designing an OD strategy to think of client systems as divided
into *functional* subunits or subsystems. These are: (1) the change agent group;
(2) the target (sometimes called "consumer") group; (3) the sponsor group; (4)
the leverage group; and (5) the beneficiary group. (I no longer remember who
developed this set of terms or where I picked it up except that, as originally
used, it related to *community development* or CD rather than to OD and that I
first came across them when I was living and working in the "great" Southwest.
If I could remember his or her name I would gladly give credit here.) When the
client system is viewed in terms of these five functional subsystems, it becomes
obvious, to me at least, that is is *damned* important to differentiate and specify
when asking, "who is my client?"

The Change Agent Group in the case of my region within the DMH, from my
perspective, would be comprised of all the training and development staff members based in each of the six residential treatment facilities plus myself. We have
two general goals and one provisional. One of the general goals is implicit: to
demonstrate our value to the DMH system and, in return, to receive the respect,
rewards and cooperation due a valued and effective systemic function. The other
goal is quite specific: to facilitate the improvement of the performing level of the
mental health generalists to the extent that they are able to perform the functions
(paramedical and psychotherapeutic treatment, supervisory, managerial and administrative) required of them in accord with the DMH system's needs. The provisional goal is provisional only because the change agent group does not yet, as a
whole, possess all the knowledge and skill which is required to achieve it. This
goal is to enlist the collaboration of subsystems at each of the facilities in designing and mounting OD projects aimed at increasing the functional match between:
the subsystem's organizational goals, objectives, structure, procedures; the subsystem's members' personal needs, aspirations and desires; the subsystem's patient
populations' needs; and the needs of the communities from which the patients
originally came and to which it is intended they will return.

The Target Group for the change agents' activities in the DMH system embraces
all of the mental health generalists and other DMH employees who are required to
participate in in-service training programs as a precondition for either their initial
employment or for their promotion within the system; all staff at all levels of the
subsystems with whom OD projects are conducted; and key administrators whose
decisions influence or determine the region's policies and programs.

The Sponsoring Group for internal DMH change agents is, ultimately, composed
of the taxpaying citizens through the revenue collection apparatus (including the

federal governmental agencies, particularly HEW), then through the state government and its legislative and other relevant departmental bodies. One problem resulting from this intertwining series of relationships appears to be the high probability of divergent and, possibly, competitive vested interests being introduced by various special interest groups at each level in both the state and federal sequences. This introduces the probability that priorities will be changed and reordered along the way. It also necessitates a certain amount of negotiation and compromise between the state and federal groups. Nonetheless, the DMH system and its internal change agent group depend upon its sponsors for continued existence. It is, therefore, only pragmatic to satisfy whatever demands are made by the sponsoring group. It is similarly pragmatic to create as many degrees of freedom as possible with regard to the interpretation of those demands, the planning of means to satisfy those demands, the actual implementation of those plans and the interpretation of the evaluation of the effectiveness of the implemented plans.

Within the DMH system the identity of the *leverage groups* vary depending upon the identity of the particular target group in question at any given time. For example, let's say the target group for a change activity is the group of key administrators who manage a particular subsystem and those administrators are highly resistant to direct interventions in their business by the change agents. Assume the key administrators do not share the change agents' concern about the focus of the change agents' attempted intervention — perhaps the administrators do not believe that change is necessary, perhaps they feel they have reason to not trust the change agents' intentions or abilities to implement a change program effectively. Under such conditions, the change agent group might think it an expedient strategy to carry off what might be called a "billiard shot" attempt at influencing the target group by first identifying another group of persons (a leverage group) who are seen as highly credible by the target group. The ideal leverage group would be one whose members allowed themselves to be influenced by the change agent group. The change agents, then, would approach the prospective leverage group and would relate to them in such a manner as to influence the leverage group to act as *advocates* of the change agents and either intercede with the target group in the interest of the change agents or they might be encouraged to exert whatever pressure is necessary to sensitize the target group as to the legitimacy and validity of the change agents' concerns. In the case of the key administrators, it may be that they are more likely to listen to representatives of groups of their own subordinates than they are to the change agents. The strategy here would be for the change agents to address themselves to the subordinates rather than the administrators. Alternatively, the key administrators may allow themselves to be influenced only by their superiors in which case this group would become eligible to become the change agents' leverage group. In the event that the administrators' superiors close themselves off from the change agents but are open to influence exerted on them from yet another direction — for example, representatives from community groups — then, the change agent group must consider whether it is likely that a "double bank shot" might be effective. That is, the internal change agents might decide to address themselves to the community groups (the first leverage group) who would address themselves to the superiors (the second leverage group) who in turn would address themselves to the key administrators (the target group) who, assuming the double bank shot was successful, would then make themselves available to the efforts of the change agent group, the staff training and development trainers and consultants.

Finally, *the beneficiary group* is, simply, the group or groups which stand to benefit from the change agents' activities. The beneficiary group could be any one of the previously mentioned groups. It could be that more than just one group stands to benefit. For example, if, functioning as change agents, the facility-based training staff members are conducting a training program in treatment skills for a group of mental health generalists, the training process could be conceptualized in one or more of several different ways. This is important since the objectives of the training program would vary as a function of the conceptualization. If the generalist trainees are thought of as the target and as the beneficiary group, the training would probably be aimed at providing the trainees with an entertaining experience which would also provide the trainees with some basis for feeling good about themselves. If the trainees are the target group but the patients are seen as the beneficiaries, the training would be more likely to be designed to aid the generalists to provide the patients with experiences which are likely to assist them to function well in the communities from which they have come and to which they will probably return. If it is the communities which are identified as the beneficiaries, the training may focus on helping trainees to assist patients to learn how to live in their back-home settings without disturbing or upsetting other community residents. If the administrative staff members are thought of as beneficiaries, then training may focus on ways of helping trainees to work with patients in ways which are compatible with and do not disrupt existing organizational operations — regardless of what might be best for treatment staff, patients or community residents. If the beneficiaries are also the sponsors, the training may focus on ways of insuring that nothing takes place which might become a source for public embarrassment which could be used as a political issue. If all of these groups are identified as legitimate beneficiaries, then it is clear that some serious negotiations are in order around the questions of vested interests and priorities.

The same issues regarding relations and transactions between these types of groups evolve and should be dealt with when an OD project is being planned and designed. Too often, change agents allow themselves to believe there are no restraints (or that there are more restraints than there really are) being exerted by sponsor groups. Similarly, we frequently let ourselves pretend (conveniently) that the group which we are directly addressing is the only vested interest group or the only people who will be affected by the planned change effort when, in fact, this is *never* the case. Anytime something or someone changes in any part of a complex system there will be implications and consequences, albeit of different intensities, in every part of that system. I have found the use of this set of differentiating categories extremely useful in planning, designing, implementing, and evaluating the various training and OD enterprises in which I involve myself.

3. WHAT CHANGE AGENT INTERVENTION STYLES CAN AN INTERNAL OD CONSULTANT IN A (MENTAL HEALTH) SYSTEM ADOPT AND USE?

Some time ago, I guess when I was still trying to figure out just who I was and who I might be able to become, I found myself confronted by some undeniable feedback from a few people who were very significant for and well-respected by yours truly. The feedback was that my style of relating to others was generally too pedantic and repetitive. With their gentle but persistent assistance, I gradually allowed myself to become aware of my own fears of the possibility that, should I ever let go and fully reveal myself publicly as the person I really was (whoever or whatever that person might have turned out to be), I would probably be seen as inadequate, incapable, or undesirable. To protect myself from these anxieties — without ever testing out the validity of this basic premise — I adopted (stole, actually) a behavioral style which I had seen modeled and which *seemed* to be acceptable. The style was that of a professor who was lecturing *at* groups of students, many of whom were bored with and/or univolved in the monologue or subject matter.

That awareness, as it dawned upon me, led me to become conscious of the possibility that there may be more than just one functional and acceptable stylistic means of communicating something from one human being to another. Years later, *again,* oddly (?) enough, with the insightful guidance of my original mentor — Barry Oshry — during a workshop which we and several other staff members were conducting, I was helped to consciously recognize that there were quite a number of alternative, legitimate change agent styles, not all of which were equally effective under different conditions or for different specific functions. I also acquired greater conscious insight into the ways in which an individual might choose to respond to his feelings of anxiety regarding his functioning as a change agent. This response very often influences his selection of entry and intervention style.

Essentially, what Oshry was saying was that ". . . helpers are anxious people . . . anxious about whether they *really* have whatever it takes to be truly helpful . . . ." Many professional helpers (e.g., OD consultant, educators, or psychotherapists) can be considered "change agents." Although I used to believe that I was the only person trying to perform a helping function who *experienced* anxiety, I discovered, through this experience, that uncertainty and inner tension are virtually universal phenomena among helpers.

Oshry spelled out what he felt were some ramifications of this "basic " anxiety. These were centered around the issue of *how helpers reacted to their experienced anxiety.* There seems to be a continuum between two extremes. The *first extreme* being for the helper to find some theories and techniques, developed by others, for which the helper feels no responsibility (no ownership) and put all of that *between* himself and his client(s) or client system. In this way, the helper finds a means by which he can avoid feeling responsible for his impact on those clients he purports to be serving since he, his self, never interacts spontaneously or authentically with clients. It's always his self manipulating someone else's theory and techniques — if a failure occurs, it's obviously not *his* fault, it's the fault in the other person's theory or method.

At the *other extreme* is the helper who is willing to run the risk of exposing himself to the possibility of dealing with and relating to his client(s) or client systems on a direct basis. He may use others' theories and techniques, but he does not allow himself or others to find reason to believe that *they* are responsible for whatever does or does not result. It is clear to him that *he* is the functional agent, not his bag of tricks.

I suspect that, being human, all helpers probably move back and fourth along this continuum at different times when they are working with different client populations under varied circumstances.

Oshry continued to talk about various "styles" which he had observed among different helpers, each trying to be helpful in his own way. This idea intrigued me and I have thought about it quite a bit over the last four years. I have tried to write about it but have never really been able to get down to that something which I feel is basic but quite elusive. I'm going to give it another shot here in order to try to describe the various styles I use in my work in the DMH.

When I first joined the department, I employed part of a style which might be called, "the action researcher." Ideally, such a person would, as a part of his initial entry into a system, conduct a survey (through questionnaires and interviews), collate the obtained data, analyze it to some extent, and feed the results back into the system so that its members could decide what, if anything, the results meant to them and what they might choose to do about or with these conclusions. This seems to be a perfectly legitimate straightforward type of project. However, in terms of my needs at the time of my entry into the DMH system (finding out where I was, what kind of a system I was in and what I might have to offer which could be helpful), I wanted the results of the "data analysis" for myself and I was not about to share them. I used them to help me to orient myself and identify some general good, and short and long-term objectives for myself.

As I have mentioned elsewhere in this chapter, I recognized a need to establish a power base for myself. Thus, switching styles and becoming what might be called a "Nader's Raider advocate," I set out to enlist the cooperation of the existing training staff members based at each facility in my region. My approach was to plead the case of the patient and his community as the deserving but neglected "beneficiaries" of the DMH system's activities. I continued by saying that training staff members were in a critical position and could influence the system to function more fully in line with patients' and their communities' needs if we could act as a functional, regional group. I suggested that we organize ourselves in a grass-roots oriented structure — here I switched into a style which might be called, "the professor or educator" specializing in designing organizational structures and procedures. I presented a model structure which would have me, at the regional level, functioning as a "linking pin or servitor" between the "troops" and the "high command," both of whom would have means of controlling my actions to some degree with some slack left over to allow me some freedom. That is, training staff from the facilities would, after being influenced by their subordinate colleagues, tell me what nonnegotiable demands they wanted me to make when I transacted business, in their name, with the "high command." Similarly, when nonnegotiable mandates were handed down from above, I would function as the "high command's" servitor. In those instances where the demands (originating at any level) *were* negotiable, I would function as a "mediator or process consultant." When I had negotiable desires of my own, I could be expected to function as an "advocate" with myself or others as the beneficiaries.

When my desires were nonnegotiable, I would be the "big daddy or paterfamilias" who laid it out pretty straight as to what was going to have to happen.

Once the SDS, facility-based training staff members, and the members of the high command understood and, more or less, accepted the various change agent styles I was likely to assume (and vice versa) along with their contingencies, I felt pretty certain that we had established a reasonable set of mutual expectations. I was then able to proceed to enlarge the scope of my activities and exhibit additional or different aspects of these other, additional styles:

1. When involved in the process of training some of the facility-based SDS trainers in the theory, method and application of experience based learning, I employed several change agent styles. As a "professor-educator," I would hand out written, conceptual materials composed either by myself or by others with the intent of facilitating the trainers' acquisition of knowledge (and to increase my *credibility* based on providing them with valued and valuable information — I believe, by the way, that the issue of a change agent's credibility is one which is crucial and never ending). As a "model or exemplar" I would demonstrate different training methods or styles or techniques, their impacts on people and their products or outputs with the intent of enlarging the trainers' awareness of new (to them) or alternative but effective ways of implementing a training plan. As a "coach" I would guide them as they attempted to conduct a training event while using procedures which they had not yet fully mastered with the intent of facilitating their acquisition of skill competence or proficiency in using that procedure.

2. When chairing regional training committee meetings I usually assumed a "big daddy-paterfamilias" style in setting up an agenda or providing or obtaining needed information. In facilitating the management of any emerging staff differences, I switched to the "mediator-process consultant" style. In attempting to respond to requests for needed assistance I would employ either the "linking pin-servitor" style (when I didn't have the data but had to obtain and deliver it) or the "professor-educator" style (when I had it available in either written or oral form). I have also been simultaneously living out a "model-exemplar" style in these meetings by demonstrating the effectiveness of my style of conducting a planning or decision-making business meeting.

3. In conducting OD consultation projects at a treatment union or program, sub-regional planning group, etc., I again adopt a number of styles. In facilitating the trainers' acquisition of OD skills, I functioned in the "model-exemplar" mode while, simultaneously , functioning as either a "coach", "professor-educator" and/or "mediator-process consultant" with the intent of facilitating the participants' acquisition of the types and amounts of knowledge and skills which they require to be able to identify and manage their subsystems' treatment and managerial problems.

4. In preparing myself to function in these capacities, I guess I also assume the "action researcher" style — the intent being to continuously change myself in growthful ways.

5. I am also likely, at *any* time, to act out a "confronter-limit setter" style. The change agent styles are those which I believe are valuable and legitimate behavior patterns — at least they seem to work for me. I further believe that a change agent should be able to shift from one style to another (without being artificial) in a natural, authentic, and spontaneous manner. There are several additional change agent styles which seem to have either limited positive values or dysfunctional and negative values. Some of these are: the *John Birch Society-Conservative, Reactionary Advocate;* the *Jerry Rubin and the SDS Weatherman-Revolutionary, Nihilistic Advocates;* and the *Saboteur-Secret Agent.* I will not, however, take space or time here to describe these.

4. HOW IS A CONSULTANT TO KNOW WHETHER HIS ACTIVITIES HAVE BEEN EFFECTIVE?

This is one of the toughest issues I have ever tried to avoid. I frankly don't even like to talk about it. Not long ago I formed a task force from the ranks of my regional training staff members to develop a systematic means of evaluating our mental health generalist training series. We got so frustrated over the lack of information on methods, instrumentation, and analysis that we found a lot of other work to keep ourselves busy which — not intentionally, of course — somehow prevented us from coming up with a comprehensive proposal.

In responding to this question, I am hoping to gain some productive perspective by forcing myself to focus on two areas in which evaluation is crucial: training and consultation. Before I do, however, there are at least seven possible foci of any evaluation effort. In sequence these are: (1) the reaction of the participants (trainees or clients) to the training or consultative event — e.g., whether they liked the event, whether they understood the trainer or consultant; (2) whether the participants acquired an awareness of the existence and components of and contributions to "the problem situation" as well as of the impact of "the problem" on them, as people; (3) whether the participants acquired any conceptual or theoretical knowledge or information which the event was intended to convey to them — e.g., if the event was intended to facilitate the participants' acquisition of a certain amount of knowledge about administrative procedures involved in passing medication, the evaluation question would be, "To what extent did each participant acquire this information?"; (4) whether the participants have acquired a particular behavioral skill of an acceptable (functional) level of proficiency — e.g., is the individual person capable of performing a particular skill in an adequately effective and efficient manner; and (5) whether the participant is able to identify situations in and conditions under which it would be appropriate to apply his conceptual or behavioral learnings and to differentiate these from situations and conditions where such application would be inappropriate; (6) whether the participant is able to make the transition from the protected class or consultation setting and apply his learnings in an effective, appropriate manner; and (7) the extent to which the work situation is affected as a result of the participants' application of their acquired skills in that context — e.g., if participants experience an OD consultation program in increasing the efficiency of their problem-solving methods, the evaluation question might be, "Do the participants' on-the-job work groups function more efficiently after consultation than prior to that event?"

There are many problems related to obtaining valid and meaningful measures on each of these evaluative dimensions. In the *first area,* for example, the reactions of participants to an OD or a training event may or may not be significant. First of all, a person's *statement* about his reaction does not necessarily accurately reflect his inner cognative or emotional experience. Even if it does, a positive reaction may satisfy the consultant's need to be liked and to have his efforts appreciated but does not necessarily mean that the event facilitated the realization of the event's objectives and goals. Similarly, a negative reaction does not necessarily mean that learning has not occurred.

The *second area* comprises something of a problem. In general, an educational enterprise does not spend much time bothering with such questions as: Do the recipients really understand the problem at hand? Are they aware of the implications of the problem area and/or the objectives of the training or consultative event? Are participants or recipients aware that their attitudes, feelings, thoughts and behavior can not only be affected by problems and attempts to manage those problems but also that they can personally contribute to the cause, perpetuation and management of problems? In a mental health setting, in particular, such awareness issues are pivotal since many of us who work within such structures tend to be extraordinarily sensitive (perhaps too sensitive) to the relationship between "insight" and motivation. We think we know that people who are "motivated" are more likely to invest themselves or commit themselves to working on a project or problem than are those who are not so motivated. Thus we tend to try to help colleagues, supervisors, subordinates, clients, students, community representatives, etc., to become as aware as we need them to be of the issues with which we are preoccupied. It is as if we say, through our choice of behaviors, "Let us help you to see things accurately." Of course, we are actually trying to persuade people to accept our implicit judgment that their perspective is either erroneous or incomplete and that our point of view is accurate, appropriate, and complete. All or part or none of the above may be true and/or relevant. All that is important is that we *believe* that people should be aware, at a conscious and explicit (verbal) level, of *whatever* their experience of their personalized world happens to be at any given moment. Being clever, psychotherapeutically oriented people, most of us in the mental health "biz" have, over the years, acquired quite a repertoire of techniques for eliciting statements from other people which, we hope, reflect their thoughts and feelings. We then tend to interpret these statements and create conclusions as to the speaker's current state of, for example, awareness. What we do not, at present, know how to do very well is to determine just how accurate our "clinical" conclusions are for any given individual or, particularly, for a group of clients, recipients, or participants.

In the *third area,* the usual means of determining the extent to which a participant has acquired some substantive knowledge is a test of some sort. A positive result in a test may mean that the respondent has, in fact, assimilated and acquired mastery over the intended knowledge; or it may mean that he or she has retained the information and, by rote, is able to regurgitate it upon demand. A negative or inadequate result on a test, on the other hand, might mean that the test was more a measure of the person's limited ability to *express* himself at test-taking time rather than a confirmation if his inadequate comprehension. This is the problem of "false positives" and "false negatives."

Whether or not a person has developed proficiency in a behavioral skill (the *fourth area*) is a question which requires more than a test or a self-report for an answer. One way to hone in on the problem if the necessary skills and/or resources were available would be to conduct controlled, before and after studies of how well participants handle sample tasks which require the performance of the target behavior — if a relevant set of rating criteria was accessible along with a reliable panel of "judges" (who have been trained to the point where there is a high degree of interjudge reliability in *their* performance), and if there was enough time to go to this kind of trouble for evaluating the volume of participants to be processed through the OD or training program. Short of this, cooperative peers or supervisors of the participants might be directed to rate participants on the appropriateness and effectiveness of the target behavior as (and if) it occurs in the "real world." Short of *this*, if you can figure out a way of doing it, you might try setting up a sample task requiring the participant to exhibit whatever behavioral skills he might have acquired which has a built-in means of determining, in an objective and meaningful manner, the level of proficiency at which the person is performing the target behavioral skill.

The *fifth area* is the evaluation question as to whether a training or consultation recipient is capable of differentiating among situations and conditions in order to determine whether to attempt to apply his acquired learnings (and which particular acquisition is appropriate for what) is, basically, a question of the recipient's *diagnostic skill*. What is necessary, whether the recipient is consciously aware of it or not, is that he have a set of criteria available to him on the basis of which he can make some decisions about application. These criteria do not necessarily have to be explicitly formulated; some very effective diagnosticians describe themselves as operating according to a "sixth sense" (gut-level feelings, intuition, hunches). Some of the questions are: (1) Should I act or intervene at all? (2) Should I apply something that I know about at this particular time or should I defer to a more appropriate time? (3) What would have to be taking place in this setting, among these people, for me to conclude that conditions and this time is "appropriate"? (4) What would I have to see going on here that would tell me that this is the "wrong" time or place to act? (5) Whose needs or desires would I be satisfying (mine or theirs) if I attempted to intervene now or if I decided not to intervene? The training and consultative issue is to help recipients or participants to learn to ask these types of questions. The evaluation of training and consultation issue is to determine the extent to which people have acquired the demonstrated ability to ask these questions, receive accurate answers, come to appropriate and relevant conclusions and make effective plans which are contingent upon the conclusions. The best way I currently know of to deal with this issue is to set up role play, psychodramatic or simulated experiences for each of the recipients and participants and then examine and evaluate their performances. This is, however, a time consuming process and, therefore, costly and, therefore, frowned upon and judged "inefficient" by cost and coverage-conscious program and subregion directors and facility superintendents. What is needed is a less time-consuming method which lends itself to quantifiable evaluations of both individuals and groups of participants and recipients.

The *sixth area* is relatively straightforward. That is, what happens in the back-home, on-the-job, work setting in the presence of the fully trained or consulted person? Do conditions improve, remain unchanged or do they deteriorate? The assumption is that if the person has learned well, conditions will probably improve or, at least, not get worse (they will stabilize). If he has not, they will probably either deteriorate or will not improve (again, they will stabilize). If observable conditions either improve or deteriorate, the evaluator can come fairly close to a reasonable conclusion as to whether the person has acquired the ability to apply his learnings. When, however, conditions remain unchanged, the evaluator is confronted by a nightmarish dilemma. He has a 50-50 chance of making an accurate or erroneous judgment unless he spends a considerable amount of time tracking the condition of the work setting prior to the newly trained or consulted person(s) entry or reentry. He must find out if conditions had been stable, improving or deteriorating prior to entry or reentry. If they were improving and then stabilized then it's quite possible that the recipient misapplied his learnings. If they had been deteriorating and then stabilized, the application could be judged a success. If they had been and continued to be stable, the intervention must be called "ineffective". Thus, this evaluation question *is* answerable. However, whether the cost/benefit ratio which results is sufficient to justify the time and energy needed to come up with the answer eventually will determine whether this particular question is ever asked in the first place. My experience leads me to be highly sceptical on this issue.

Finally, in the *seventh area*, the effect which the participant has on the work situation as a function of applying his acquired skills and/or knowledge in that setting might just entail the least expenditure of effort of all. It may be possible to merely *observe* what, if any, changes occur in the work situation's emotional climate, norms and standards of behavior, procedures, objectives, policies and goals. If changes do occur subsequent to the OD or training event, the nature of those changes might be compared with the goals and the objectives of the event. If the result of the comparison seems to justify it, it may seem reasonable to conclude that there might have been a causal relationship between the event and the observable changes.

This may seem fairly straightforward. However, when I have tried to apply this approach to the training programs and OD consultations in which I am involved and I identify the multitude of variables which I feel the need to evaluate, I often experience a sense of being overwhelmed. Perhaps it's more of a fear of placing myself into a position in which I might find myself out of my depth, unable to successfully perform up to what, for me, would be an acceptable level of competence. I do not like to think of myself as inadequate. Yet, in this area, I do feel some of that. Thus, I have taken up a new course of study: I am currently engaged in the process of identifying some resources in this area, acquiring some expertise for myself and for other members of the region's facilities' training staffs.

Thus far, in terms of efficiency, we have been able easily to obtain only *gross* approximations of the impacts of our efforts. We are particularly adept in the first and seventh areas. We do know how to do the second through the sixth types of evaluation according to traditional "scientifically" approved methods — however, we have not been able to develop *inexpensive* and *quick* methods. In these areas, the methods with which we are familiar require an enormous and excessive amount of man-hours and scarce expertise in preparation, administration, compiling, analyzing and interpreting. In an operation such as the DMH, the use of our limited resources (time and expertise) for these evaluative purposes would be quite a luxury. We would, paradoxically, have to temporarily curtail our training and consulting activities — the demands for which are constantly increasing — in order to plan and implement an effective evaluation program to determine whether and the extent to which we are actually doing what we *say* (hope?) we are doing in those training and consulting efforts.

EPILOGUE

O.K., what payoffs can be expected as a result of having accompanied me on this tour of the wonderful world of OD in a mental health delivery system? I am hoping that my readers will have seen, as I was surprised to discover, that it can be *helpful* to allow oneself to engage in the process of asking oneself questions about one's work and then to respond to those questions. I mean to use the word "helpful," in the sense that, prior to engaging in question-response process myself, I had been feeling caught and struggling to stay afloat in a turbulent sea of buzzing confusion, being constantly confronted by apparently conflicting demands on my time and attention from parts of the system whose significance to the whole was unknown to me. Further, I was dependent upon other persons' perceptions of what had been (and was continuing to be) happening within the system. I was also dependent upon their often contradictory sense of priorities for problems on which I was expected to focus my attention. Initially, this "dependency" problem was not too much of an issue for me since, at least for the first several months, I was working under a colleague whose competence and judgement I valued highly. However, after he accepted a transfer, I was left (at my own choice) on my own without a buffer, interpreter, mentor, or sponsor to help me make sense out of my "world."

Thus for me, and, possibly, for my readers, the primary payoff which this question-response process can have is that it has some potential to constitute a viable alternative to the kind of consultative supervision needed to help an internal consultant *make sense out of the world* and to *orient the consultant toward and provide some perspective for the consultant's present and future work within the system.* To paraphrase Anna Freud, you don't have to be afraid; just pretend that *you* are the supervisor who can give you corrective, critical orientation and feedback.

SUGGESTED REFERENCES

1. Blake, Robert R., Jane S. Mouton, and Richard L. Sloma, "The union-management intergroup laboratory: Strategy for resolving intergroup conflict," *Journal of Applied Behavioral Science*, 1965. Vol. 1, No. 1.

2. Freedman, Arthur M., "Mental illness and interpersonal problem solving." *Mimeo*, 1968.

3. Hanson, Philip G., Paul Rothaus, Walter E. O'Connell, and George Wiggins, "Some basic concepts in human relations training for patients," *Hospital and Community Psychiatry*, 1970, Vol. 21, No. 5.

4. Hanson, Philip G., Richard Ermalinski, and Walter E. O'Connell, "Bridging the generation gap by utilization of human relations laboratory techniques." Paper read at the *79th Annual Convention of the American Psychological Association*, Washington, D.C., 1971.

5. Hanson, Philip G., and Walter E. O'Connell, "A program in community relations: Face-to-face confrontations." Paper read at the *76th Annual Convention of the American Psychological Association*, San Francisco, California, 1968.

6. Robertson, Richard, "The factory reject personality and human salvage operations," *Journal of Applied Behavioral Science*, 1966, Vol. 2, No. 3.

ORGANIZATION DEVELOPMENT IN A CITY GOVERNMENT SETTING

Like many others, the author began his intervention into his system using training-type methodologies. His client groups were trained in such things as (1) how to write a mission statement, (2) functional analysis, (3) structural analysis, (4) objective-setting, (5) planning, programming, budgeting, and scheduling, and (6) reviewing. Later these topics were reworded in order to diminish feelings of threat the terms gave to participants. Accordingly, the name of the OD function is no longer organization development unit but systems performance unit. The goal of the activity has not changed — to establish and maintain a problem-solving life-style within the agency. This systematic approach to defining the system and anticipating and solving problems is an example of how an OD program can increase the organization's effectiveness by creating a vehicle for them to use to make conscious changes in their operating methods for the betterment of the total system.

Organization Development in a City Government Setting

JOEL M. COHEN

PROGRAM ORIGINS AND DEVELOPMENT

The Human Resources Administration is the umbrella agency for six socially oriented agencies in New York City. It consists of the Community Development Agency (CDA) — Manpower and Career Development Agency (MCDA) — Addiction Services Agency (ASA) — Department of Social Services (DOSS) — Youth Services Agency (YSA) and Agency for Child Development (ACD). Central staff of HRA numbers about 500. The DOSS staff is the largest, about 25,000. The office of Staff and Organization Development has the responsibility for providing training to all agencies except DOSS. Our efforts then are aimed at about 15,000 people on all occupational levels.

Originally, our concern was in the areas of skills and concepts. We developed many programs designed to meet stated and actual operating needs. Executive and management development took precedence since many of the staff had limited managerial and supervisory experience. We were also involved with trainer development, clerical skills development, and specific skill areas such as finance, interviewing, counseling, etc. There was a need to get going, so evaluation of results tended to lag. When we did follow up research, we found that although in most cases new skills, concepts, and attitudes were acquired, many participants were complaining about the training. Interviews with trainees revealed high levels of frustration because of an inability to effectively utilize the new behaviors. Additional investigation surfaced the need for "training the system."

We began from a pure organization development approach. We scheduled meetings, seeking support and understanding of top staff. More often than not, meetings were canceled due to continual crises. We then attempted to assume a technical assistance stance in which we would serve as internal organization development consultants while training served as an adjunct to organization development. This made us feel righteous and well intentioned but results were limited

Joel M. Cohen is Director, Office of Staff and Organization Development, New York City Human Resources Administration. Prior to this he was with the New York State Employment Service and the Youth Opportunity Centers. He holds a B.A. in Personnel Economics from Brooklyn College and has done graduate work in group dynamics at Teachers College, Columbia University and in psychology at the New School for Social Research.

as individual units were reluctant to request our input. Further investigation revealed some of the reasons why. First was a hesitancy about revealing problems. It was considered by many a sign of failure to admit that problems existed in their own spheres of influence. Therefore, many problems were hidden rather than solved. Second, many units did not have a really clear idea of what their products were. Third, many individuals also being unaware of real responsibility created jobs for themselves which had little or no tie-in to their unit's needs. These and other reasons created an atmosphere in which training for daily activities was necessarily doomed to failure. We in the office of Staff and Organization Development held meeting after meeting trying to evaluate the data and arrive at a strategy which had some chance for making a successful impact on the system.

We saw as our prime challenge establishing a system in which it was legitimate to have problems as long as an attempt was made to solve those problems. In short, we had to introduce a problem solving life style. Concurrently, we also had to help individuals, units, divisions, and even whole agencies to become more precisely aware of their missions and functions.

After much internal debate, we realized that training rather than an adjunct must be our entree to organization development. We had previously developed, with an outside consulting firm (Education Systems and Design), a management development program which was now to be used as a stepping stone to organization development. The program consisted of two three-day workshops, one on communication skills and the other on planning skills. At the end of the second workshop participants were given a unit profile.* This profile was taken back to the operating unit, and the whole unit was involved in filling it out. The profile dealt with individual and unit job descriptions, functions and relationships. This data, then became the basis of a rough but effective functional analysis of the operating unit. This analysis was completed at the first of six one-day organization development workshops. These workshops were conducted once every other week with the data collection and individual unit relevance decided upon during the two week lapse. The workshops were conducted two ways. Where possible, we worked with the whole unit. This we found preferable. When a unit worked together the interpersonal interchange around work topics increased commitment. They went back to their own shops determined to put into practice the insights developed in the workshops. In other instances, we worked with groups of supervisors from diverse departments. The participants then became consultants for each other's units. Often this was not as effective as working with total units. The participants went back to their own units and then had to fill everyone in on what happened at the workshop and often sell them on trying out something new.

The step by step process is fairly simple but rather strenuous. First, each unit must arrive at a mission statement (what are we all about?). This mission statement was often, at first, so universal and unmeasureable that it was meaningless. Each unit tended to take on the burden of the whole world or at least the whole administration. We often had initial statements that read — "It is our job to abolish poverty in New York City." These units were on the side of virtue and their daily activities could not be questioned since they were "in the business of

* Appendix 11.1

doing good" and everything they did, in some way, contributed to their mission.
It usually was quite a job to get them down to such statements as "We are responsible for conducting narcotics workshops for teachers and disseminating information on Drug Abuse to Schools." We arrived at some informal guidelines for a mission statement. The statement must be realistic, take in the population to be touched, refer to strategy, and in some way be measureable. Methodology can often be
outlined briefly in an addendum. Once the mission statement is arrived at and
agreed to by the unit, we are on our way. Taking part in the creation of the
mission statement invariably results in commitment to it.

The next step is the functional analysis (what's happening now?). Worksheets
aid the unit in drawing a realistic picture of its own daily existence. Such factors
as lateness, internal strife, etc., are surfaced. It is often a great surprise when a unit
looks at its daily operation and becomes aware of what activities it is actually involved in.

Step three is the structural analysis (what is set up to make what is happening
happen?). This is the most difficult step. It is not easy to make clear what actually constitutes a structure. Participants often fall back on organization charts and
the fact of structures which exist as informal relationships between as few as two
workers is often overlooked. Much effort by staff is required during this phase.
In most cases the initial phases have led to a sense of purpose which results in the
necessary input being made to complete step three. Again, the results are often
surprising to the participants.

The next step deals with objectives (what do you want to happen?). Concur-
rent with this step an inventory of resources is taken in order to be sure the operating objectives are realistic. Usually at this stage units can arrive at a clear statement
of what they want to see happening on a daily as well as an ongoing basis. What
they actually do is create a model of activities. The interaction with other units is
a large consideration when this model is formulated.

Step five deals with planning, programming, budgeting, and scheduling. (How
do we get from where we are to where we want to be?) This includes timetables
and self-checking with recycling where necessary. It is a good idea to build definite
stops and take time to consider the probable effects of activities. Some units, once
having found the light, go barging straight ahead at full speed and end up no better
off for all their time, energy, and money expeditures. Not only is it necessary to do
continual unit soul searching but the soul searching should go back as far as step
one. The original mission statement is far from sacrosanct and goes through many
changes, most often during this step.

Reviewing — corrective action and recycling follow. Sometimes it is necessary
to change target dates, reschedule activities, reallocate resources, etc.

The process is fairly simple, as previously stated, but requires a severe amount
of self-discipline to follow through to a productive conclusion. When the effort is
made, we have found in every case that the conclusion is productive. Actually,
there is no conclusion as the process is ongoing and repetitive.

Our measure of productivity is this: The units that have gone through the
process as well as several of the units currently involved in the process have manifested lower turnover, increased production, and higher internal morale. We also
find a much greater utilization of skills acquired in other training sessions. We are

aware of the possibility of a Hawthorne effect being present with some of the gain being due to increased interest, but if nothing else has been accomplished, the willingness of staff to discuss and work on problems leads us to believe the approach is successful.

When we work with one unit we often become involved with one or more of the units that interface with it. They express curiosity and are impressed with increased effectiveness. This leads to new participants in our seminars and workshops and new clients for our organization development inputs. We obtain credibility and acceptance by doing, rather than by preaching the virtues of organization development.

In our workshops we no longer use terms like functional, structural, and systems analysis, or program planning budgeting systems, etc. We find that these terms tend to scare and turn off participants. Simple questions that can be answered involve participants and turn them on.

Our organization development effort has been very pragmatic. This has been necessary due to the day to day pressures of our operations. We have found that with a pragmatic approach organization development is a valuable tool to clarifying and achieving agency objectives.

When the individual, the unit, the department, etc., all are involved in the creation of mission and the methods of achieving that mission, commitment grows. Everybody has a "piece of the action" and contributes to meeting ongoing objectives.

To repeat: Our step by step process then is to answer these questions -

1. What are we all about? (Mission)

2. What's happening here? (Functional analysis)

3. What is set up to make what's happening happen? (Structural analysis)

4. What do we want to happen? (Objectives — model creation)

5. How do we get from where we are to where we want to be? (Program Planning budgeting systems)

6. Are we getting there? (Review)

We have found that top staff finds organization development a threat. They envision a covey of organization development consultants coming in and messing around with organization charts. In order to overcome the difficulties inherent in the term we have rechristened our organization development unit. It is now and will for the foreseeable future be the — systems performance unit.

Simply to state our approach to organization development I quote from the mission statement of our systems performance unit — "To establish and maintain a problem solving lifestyle in H. R. A. "

APPENDIX 11.1

Unit Profile

Prepared in Conjunction with the
HRA Office of Staff Development and Training
New York City

Unit _____

Location _____

Prepared By _____

Date _____

Suggested Procedure for Administering Unit Profile

1. Notify members of your unit as far in advance as possible. Include place, time and purpose of the unit meeting, i. e., to produce a unit profile.

2. Make preparations: Room –   Seating in a circle assists the purpose most. If your group needs to sit at tables, arrange the tables in a square.

    Materials –   Duplicated or newsprint copies of various parts of the unit profile instrument; scratch paper for notes, etc.; chalk boards, easels, etc.

3. Open the meeting and state the probable benefits of this meeting and suggest some guidelines that might include:

    a) Be honest – don't say what you think someone expects you to say
    b) Everyone's perception is important! Let us have yours and let us listen to everyone's
    c) Work for consensus. Do not vote (might be a cop-out to avoid locating the truth).
    d) _____
    e) _____
    f) _____

4. Organize two or more work groups of three members each if your unit has more than five members.
    Usually more is accomplished at more significant levels if work groups reach consensus first; then the whole unit builds its consensus utilizing the work group experiences and reports.

5. Initiate the unit's work on the profile* by displaying on newsprint an enlarged copy of the first page of the profile and instructing work groups on their tasks *or*
    moderating as the entire group reaches its conclusions. If no consensus is reached fairly quickly assign a committee to compile the information from manning tables, pay rolls . . .

6. Help the unit to continue by displaying the newsprint copy of the next page of the profile, instructing work groups or moderating.

7. Proceed through the remaining unit profile pages, one by one.

8. Unless it has already begun, help the unit to develop some of the implications of doing this activity together and promise that you will be developing suggestions for understanding and acting on what the unit profile reveals.

9. Put the results in a useable form for reporting to and working on in the next OD workshop

---

*See page 218

Alternate procedures could include:

a) Reproduce pages of the unit profile and distribute one by one in the meeting.

b) Reproduce the entire unit profile and distribute in the meeting, using it step by step.

c) Reproduce the entire unit profile and distribute to members individually before the meeting. Plan how you will use it during the meeting.

d) Reproduce the entire unit profile and distribute to members individually before the meeting asking that the profiles be filled in and returned to you (anonymously?) for collating. Promise to circulate a summary.

e) Do your own thing.

f) Help your unit to develop its own thing and do it.

Some Issues that may Surface or that You May Encourage to Surface During the Orientation to the OD Unit Profile Meeting

1. Do I really want to . . .

2. At a special or regular staff meeting?

3. What to do about possible blocking by my superior or other unit members?

4. What if doing the profile is seen as interference or meddling in the life of the unit — as creating more problems than it can solve?

5. What if it is seen as a waste or misuse of time?

6. What if it is seen as unproductive or useless?

7. What if it is seen as a threat to status, procedures, investments, etc.?

8. What if it is seen as something that simply helps me to accomplish an assignment for the OD workshop? *(Don't mention the OD workshop, if possible!)*

Census of Unit Members

Please give this information without signing your name. It is for use in your unit only.

What is your civil service job title?

_____

Are you professional _____ or support staff _____ ?

What is your gender? _____

Are you _____ 65 years of age or over?

_____ 45 to 64 years

_____ 25 to 44

_____ 21 to 24

_____ 20 or less years?

To what ethnic population do you belong?

_____

Name of Unit

1. General Description

   a) Population Characteristics

Professional		Support		Job Title
Male	Female	Male	Female	
			Sub Totals	

TOTALS ———— Total number of titles

Number				Age Group
				65 years or more
				45 to 64
				25 to 44
				21 to 24
				20 years or less

				Ethnic population

b) Functional Characteristics

1. Write a brief description of *what your unit must have* in order to do its
   work. What are the raw materials that you need to do your work?
   (In-Put)

2. Write a brief description of *what your unit does* to modify these "raw
   materials." (Thru-Put)

3. Write a brief description of *what your unit's products are.* Give your current production in numerical form if possible. What thing or service
   comes off your "assembly line"? (Out-Put)

4. How is the system different because your unit exists?

2. *Census of Concerns*

   a) List of Major Concerns

   List ten conditions in your unit that you are concerned about. Develop
   the list from your own knowledge and experience! Indicate your perceptions by a check mark (✓) in the appropriate column.

Concern	Intensity		Duration	
	Increasing	Decreasing	Recent	Longstanding
1.				
2.				
3.				
4.				
5.				
6.				
7.				
8.				
9.				
10.				

b) Most Critical Concern

Carefully consider the list. Select the most critical concern for your unit and write it below.

_____

_____

_____

_____

_____

_____

3. Manifestations of the Most Critical Concern

To get a fuller picture of the impact in the life of your unit, identify at least six manifestations of the most critical concern. *Avoid stating causes.*

Indicate "Intensity"
+ = Manifestation is increasing
− = Manifestation is decreasing

Indicate effect on "Productivity"
+ = "Productivity" is increasing
− = "Productivity" is decreasing

NB Before making a final determination of intensity and productivity check for data that show trends in concern area.

	Manifestation	Intensity	Productivity
1.	_____	_____	_____
2.	_____	_____	_____
3.	_____	_____	_____
4.	_____	_____	_____
5.	_____	_____	_____
6.	_____	_____	_____
7.	_____	_____	_____
8.	_____	_____	_____
9.	_____		

Totals

+	−	+	−

4. *Components Responsible to Serve Unit in Most Critical Concern Area*

Many organizational components have a policy, traditional and/or perceived responsibility to counteract and ameliorate the conditions which you described. Their mission and resources become significant factors in plans to improve your unit. Therefore, you are asked to list and briefly describe these components.

Component	*Description*

5. *Internal and External Resources Available to Work in Most Critical Concern Area*

Resources are defined as: individuals
    groups
    organizations

that by assets, interests, or competence can contribute to improvement in your area of concern. You are asked to select these resources in light of some defined capacity to produce action:

Purpose: Complete the section on purpose for organizations or groups with stated and *publicly known purposes only.*

Funds: Monies that are available to be applied to concern area.

Information: Facts, feelings, and opinions related to concern area.

Skills: Specialized capabilities that can be applied to the concern area.

Indicate kind of resource (s) by a check ($\checkmark$) mark only.

Concern _____

Resource	–ternal		Assets		Competence		Interest
	In	Ex	Purpose	Funds	Information	Skills	

12

ORGANIZATION DEVELOPMENT IN A PUBLIC SCHOOL SETTING

When one thinks of change in the public school one ordinarily thinks of curriculum changes, changes in the educational process, or changes in the administration. A recent innovation in the life of a few public schools is an OD approach to change. Adoptions of the OD approach have occurred only recently, largely since the late 1960's, but some significant efforts have been made in a few school districts. The authors identify differences in school systems and other organizations which often pose some unique problems for change agents. They describe in some detail their own approach to OD utilizing a number of instruments. Of particular interest is the Bonanza Game that was developed, which, when completed, provides data on nine different scales on areas of the school program the player (student, teacher, administrator, etc.) thinks needs changing or improving. The authors make extensive use of data-based interventions working with temporary teams established to implement changes based on the needs they identify. Although working with the public schools is unique, OD techniques have been found to be useful and valid as processes for change.

Organization Development in a Public School Setting

A. WALDEN ENDS AND DAVID J. MULLEN

THEORETICAL UNDERPINNINGS

One of the most basic concerns of organizational theory is the relationship between the individual and the organization which he serves. The classical organizational theorist viewed organizations, for the most part, as predesignated, omniscient machines concerned with products and production. He felt that any deviation from predicted achievement was caused either by man's unpredictability or by engineering and design failures. Bennis summarizes this classical approach to dealing with the inevitable conflict which is present in all man-made organizations as follows:

> In classical theory . . . the conflict between the man and the organization was neatly settled in favor of the organization. The only road to efficiency and productivity was to surrender man's needs to the service of the bloodless machine.[1]

In contrast, contemporary organization theorists continue to study the relationship between institutional conflict and organizational effectiveness but are now taking a significantly different approach than did the researchers of the classical theory. Argyris, for example, asks the question, "How is it possible to create an organization in which the individual may obtain optimum expression and, simultaneously, in which the organization itself may obtain optimum satisfaction of its demands.[2] In answer, Likert writes that he believes the most effective system of management for developing the human organization and increasing its productivity is the participative-supportive system.

A. Walden Ends is Associate Professor of Education at the University of Georgia. He was previously an elementary school principal and on the faculties of Michigan State University and the University of Iowa. He holds a B.A. in Education from San Jose State College, an M.A. in administration and supervision from San Francisco State College, and a Ph.D. in supervision and curriculum development from Michigan State University.

David J. Mullen is Professor of Education at the University of Georgia. Prior to this he was an elementary school principal, a school consultant, and on the faculties of Bloomsburg State College (Pennsylvania) and the George Peabody College for Teachers, Nashville, Tennessee. He holds a B.A. from Indiana University (Pa.) an M.Ed. from the University of Pittsburgh, and an Ed.D. from Teachers College, Columbia University, New York City.

Accordingly, the model presented below was developed upon the following assumptions which are developed at length by Beckhard in regard to the need for change and the need to develop a participative-supportive organizational structure:

1. The OD effort is a *planned change* effort.
2. The OD effort involves the total *system.*
3. The OD effort is *managed from the top.*
4. The OD effort is designed to *increase organization effectiveness and health.*
5. The OD effort achieves its goals through *planned interventions* using behavioral-science knowledge.[3]

In order to create a school organization which would operate in accord with the above assumptions, the following objectives are suggested to serve as guide posts in the project:

1. To develop a self-renewing, *viable* system that can organize in a variety of ways depending on the tasks.
2. To optimize the effectiveness of both the stable and the temporary systems by built-in, continuous *improvement mechanisms.*
3. To move toward *high collaboration* and *low competition* between the interdependent units in the system.
4. To create conditions where conflict is brought out and managed.
5. To reach the point where decisions are made on the basis of information source rather than organizational role.[4]

In operation, the overall strategy of the change model is to institute a new set of normative goals by which the organization can govern itself. The new goals are based upon the primary assumptions about the people and organizations which have been presented by Argyris and Likert. Essentially, the model is designed to accomplish the following things within the school setting:

1. Shift the basic value system of the school district so that human factors and feelings come to be considered legitimate.
2. Work toward the improvement of interpersonal competence.
3. Develop a more effective "team management," that is, the capacity for functional groups to work more competently together.
4. Develop an increased understanding between and within the working groups in the school district in order to reduce tensions.
5. Develop better methods of conflict utilization.
6. Develop "organic" rather than "mechanical" systems within the school district's organization.

   An organic system is characterized by the following:

   a) An environment in which the relationships between and within the organization's groups are emphasized.
   b) An environment in which there is mutual trust and confidence.

c) An environment in which there is interdependence and shared responsibility.

d) An environment in which there is multigroup membership and responsibility.

e) An environment in which there is a wide sharing of responsibility and control.

f) An environment in which there is a conscious effort to achieve conflict resolution through bargaining, compromise and problem solving.

In sum, the model utilizes the five elements listed in Beckhard's definition of organization development.

1. It is a cooperatively planned effort.

2. It is system wide: i.e., an entire school or, if small, an entire school district.

3. It is managed from the top.

4. It is concerned with improving the organization's health and effectiveness.

5. It is accomplished through planned interventions using the principles and practices of applied behavioral science.[5]

Item five, above, refers to *interventions* and the principles of *applied behavioral science.* As practiced in the implementation of this model, these interventions are not to be prescribed by "experts" from outside of the system but are to be identified through a collaborative effort between OD consultants and selected members of the school district. Together, the consultants and district personnel can then explore the operational difficulties of the system and participate actively in the reformulation of:

1. goals and objectives

2. new procedures for inter- and intra-group activities

3. new skills in understanding and interpreting the process of group behavior

4. the reconstitution of organizational structures and procedures for accomplishing the new goals

5. the altering of the norms and expectation in the working climate in the system, and

6. the identification of guidelines and procedures for assessing the results of the intervention strategy.

The interventions to be used in this model are drawn from the knowledge and technology of the applied aspects of the behavioral sciences. Although each application of the model should be unique and limited to the specific needs of the particular school district in which it is used, there are certain components of the model which are always present. Identified and defined below are those components which are typically present:

1. The Scope of the Project:

It is an organization-side effort to change the system.

2. The Method of Working:

The method of working is premised on the assumption that those who really know the system best and have a reason for wanting to change it are the members of the organizational change team. The OD consultants attempt to transfer their skills and knowledge to the client system through collaboration in order that they can independently assume responsibility for their own organization change program.

3. The Need for Legitimacy:

Organizational change efforts recognize the power of organizational authority as a force which can stop or destroy any effort to affect change within a system. Therefore, the OD consultants require that approval, support and active collaboration be obtained from those at the top of the organizational hierarchy; i.e., the superintendent and the board of education.

4. The Targets of Change:

The targets of change may be any elements within the system which are in need of being changed in order to achieve organizational effectiveness as defined in the criteria for effectiveness which is specified by the client system. It is appropriate to consider persons, the general organizational structure, the general culture of the organization, the attitudes, mores, and methods of working together, or any other element which seems to be hindering the potential efficiency and operational effectiveness of the organization.

5. The Client:

The person or persons in the organization who have the problem, the power to affect change and the desire to institute new methods of operating the system.

6. The Client System:

The organization in which the change is desired.

Conceptually, the model prepared for use with this change strategy was developed upon the "linking pin" design presented by Rensis Likert.[6] This design is an alternative to the traditional and more bureaucratic organizational structure which is commonly found in most school systems today. Bennis reports that the traditional bureaucratic organizational structure in all organizations is being threatened by the many rapid changes which are occurring in society today: i.e., by the increases in the size of organizations, by the greater complexity of modern technology, and by the changes which are coming in administrative and managerial behavior.[7] New managerial behavior, however, is not enough to cope with or eliminate the contemporary problems of modern organizations unless a new system of organization goes along with it.

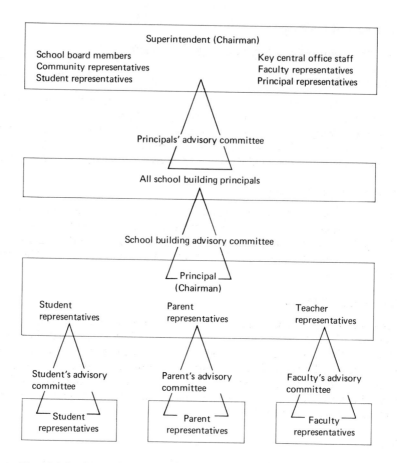

Fig. 12.1 System Level Advisory Committee

Figure 12.1 presents a diagrammatic representation of the change model showing the linking pin relationships within the organizational scheme. Essentially, each population element within the school system has access and representation in the organizational plan. Representatives from the student, parent and teacher groups work directly with the principal of their building on the "school building advisory committee." From this effort, the principal is better able to carry the needs and desires of his student body to a district-wide "principal's committee." Here the commonalties and differences in the needs of each particular school can be assessed and organized for presentation to the superintendent and the "system level advisory committee." The members of the system level committee are for the most part members-at-large and serve both the needs of the superintendent and the needs of their own particular interest group.

Beckhard[8] and Schmuck and Miles[9] both emphasize the need for establishing OD subsystems (i.e., the advisory/OD teams) within the organization in order to begin the change program as well as to provide a resident body of people who are committed to the project and feel responsible for seeing that questions, concerns and problems are cared for. The OD teams initially responsilbe for the change effort are the students' advisory committee, the parents' advisory committee, and the faculty advisory committee in each school. The selection of the members for each OD team will be done by members of the group which each is to represent. The criteria for the selection of the OD teams and the qualifications for each team membership should be collaboratively determined. For example, the following might serve as guidelines for selecting advisory committee representatives:

Students' Advisory Committee:

Three to four representatives from each grade level; to be selected by the students they represent.

Qualifications:

Possessing the ability to "tell it like it is"

Being open-minded

Being sensitive to the feelings and points of view of others

Having the trust and confidence of the students they represent

Parents' Advisory Committee:

Four to six parents selected by the principal and his staff to represent each of the elementary, middle and high school levels.

Qualifications:

Possessing the ability to "tell it like it is"

Being open-minded

Being sensitive to the feelings and points of view of others

Having the trust and confidence of the parents they represent

Considerations:

Selection should consider members from standing committees

Selection should consider choosing "at large" members without any standing committee affiliations

Parents who have demonstrated concern and interest in the school's program

Faculty Advisory Committee:

Four to six teachers or staff members to be selected by the faculty and staff members.

Qualifications:

Possessing the ability to "tell it like it is"

Being open-minded

Being sensitive to the feelings and points of view of others

Having the trust and confidence of the faculty they represent

Considerations:

Representative of a wide cross section of the faculty and staff

Sufficient tenure in the school which he represents to have a knowledgeable understanding of its problems

The role and responsibility for each OD team will be as follows:

1. To establish educational program priorities, using data obtained from the *Bonanza Game.*
2. To establish organizational problem priorities, using data obtained from the SODQ.
3. To assist in designing and planning interventions which will get at the problems diagnosed.

The chairman of the OD teams within each school (student, parent, and faculty) and one other committee member, to be selected by the committee, will represent his respective committee on the school building steering committee. The principal in each school will serve as chairman of the school building advisory committee within the school. The organization of the school building advisory committee is as shown:

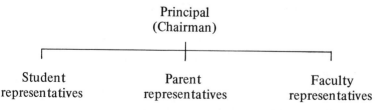

Principal
(Chairman)

Student representatives   Parent representatives   Faculty representatives

The school building advisory committee's responsibility will be:

1. To collaboratively establish educational program priorities, using data obtained from the *Bonanza Game*, from their school.

2. To collaboratively establish organizational problem priorities, using data obtained from the *SODQ* for their school.

3. To assist in designing and planning interventions for their school and the school system which will get at the problem priorities established.

The next level of the organizational model is the principals' advisory committee. This committee is made up of all the principals within the system and it serves the function of being the link between each individual school and the system level advisory committee. Each principal has the responsibility for representing the interests of his school and its OD teams. The responsibility of the principals' advisory committee itself is:

1. To serve as an interschool OD team communication link.

2. To negotiate disparaties among the educational program priorities of the schools.

3. To negotiate disparities among the organizational priorities of the schools.

4. To negotiate disparities among the interventions planned for getting at the organizational problems diagnosed and the educational program priorities identified.

5. To assist in maintaining the OD project.

The top level OD team, the system level advisory committee, represents the entire school system. Membership in this group will be drawn from selected schools at all levels within the system, as shown.

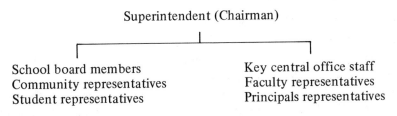

Superintendent (Chairman)

School board members   Key central office staff
Community representatives   Faculty representatives
Student representatives   Principals representatives

The suggested responsibilities of the system level advisory committee are:

1. To establish educational program priorities for the entire school system using data obtained from the *Bonanza Game* and reports from the school building steering committees.

2. To establish organizational problem priorities within the entire school system, using data obtained from the SODQ and reports from the school building steering committees.

3. To collaboratively design and plan interventions, with the assistance of the school building steering committees and the OD consultants, for getting at the educational program priorities and organizational problem priorities identified.

4. To maintain and support the OD project within the entire school system.

The structure for the OD teams presented in Fig. 1, is designed to meet four conditions which Likert feels are necessary if an organization is to successfully resolve its problems and efficiently coordinate its efforts for achieving the goals of the organization. Likert's conditions for the structure are these:

1. It must provide high levels of cooperative behavior between superiors and subordinates and especially among peers.

2. It must have the organizational structure and the interaction skills required to solve differences and conflicts to attain creative solutions.

3. It must possess the capacity to exert influence and to create motivation and coordination without traditional forms of line authority.

4. Its decision-making processes and superior subordinate relationship must be such as to enable a person to perform his job well and without hazard when he has two or more superiors.[10]

In order to assure that the conditions specified by Likert are met, training sessions should be conducted for all members who will be serving on the school building advisory committees, principals' advisory committee or system level advisory committee. The purpose of the training sessions is to instruct and assist the groups named above to understand and use of the following concepts, processes, and skills.

1. Organization development as a process for carrying out planned change within a school system.

2. Motivation and productivity.

3. Group processes and group behavior.

4. Communication processes and skills.

5. Leadership processes and skills.

A rationale for such training sessions is given by Bennis:

> The training process relies primarily and almost exclusively on the behavior experienced by the participants: i.e., the *group itself* becomes the focus of inquiry. Conditions are promoted whereby group members, by examining data generated by themselves, attempt to understand the dynamics of group behavior, e.g., decision processes, norms, roles, communication distortions, and effects of authority on a number of behavioral patterns, personality and coping mechanisms, etc. In short, the participants learn to analyze and become more sensitive to the processes of human interactions and acquire concepts to order and control these phenomena.[11]

Accordingly, the implicit purpose of the training sessions is to free up the members of the OD teams from as many constraints as possible and to create a climate in which the OD process can function effectively within the school system.

In order to facilitate the application of the above model, two data collection instruments were invented. The first, THE BONANZA GAME, was created in order to assess the degree to which a conflict was present between the educational value system held by those who were responsible for providing him with an instructional program. The basic assumption here is that often the educational value of the student are at odds with the educational values of his parents, teachers and principals at those places where they interface. As a consequence, the behavior of the members engaged in the learning transaction with the student may be somewhat less than productive or appropriate.

The *School Program Bonanza Game** was developed by Dr. David J. Mullen, and is designed to assess the attitudes and values of the player in nine areas which are related to the school's curriculum. When played, the *Bonanza Game* allows each player (respondent) to make weighted choices about the areas of the school program that *he* thinks need changing or improving. The areas of the school program which are open to choice in the *Bonanza Game* are the three R's, the social world, the physical world, the work world, the arts, health and physical development, making choices, relationships with others, and development of self. Under each category there are three illustrated choices. The first level choices cost nothing and typically involve a choice with little assurance that the subject area will receive a planned emphasis in the school program. The second level or middle choices cost a moderate amount of money (moderate in that the cost is usually half of the cost of the third level choice) and typically requires only a moderate degree of assurance that the subject area will be accomplished; very often a functional approach to school program. The third level or last choices cost the most and typically require a high degree of assurance that the subject area will be accomplished.

For example in the first category, "The 3 R's," the illustrated choices are:

a) Learn the 3 R's from need or interest (a cartoon drawing of a young man fixing a car while he is reading a "How to" book)
0 clips = $0

b) Learn enough of the 3 R's to do OK, to get along in the world (a cartoon drawing of a young man in the library reading books from the "How to Fix It, Get a Job, and Build" shelves)
3 clips = $300

c) Learn 3 R's well enough to be prepared to get into college (a cartoon drawing of a young man in a cap and gown reading a letter of acceptance from a college)
6 clips = $600

The instructions for the game are as follows:

Suppose that your school has just been given enough money to let each parent, student and teacher spend $2,000 for school program improvements. Also, suppose that the top row of pictures (the first picture in each area) is the way your school has been before you got the improvement money. In this game you have 20 paper clips and each clip is worth $100.

The idea is to decide where you will spend your $2,000. (Place your 20 paper clips.) The middle squares cost 2 or 3 paper clips ($200 or $300) and the bottom squares or choices cost 3, 4, 5, or 6 paper clips. ($300, $400, $500, or $600.)

Since you must put the *exact* number of paper clips or money called for in each square, you do not have enough clips (money) to make improvements in each area of the school program. Spend your money to improve those parts of the program you *value most.*

If you have any paper clips left over and do not have enough to put the *exact* number called for in a square, then clip the left-over ones to your answer sheet.

Follow These Steps

1. Fill out the information part of the answer sheet.

2. Start with the 3 R's — read and look at the pictures in each area from *top to bottom.*

3. Spend your $2,000 (20 clips).

4. Change your choices until you are satisfied that you are getting what you want.

5. Mark answers on the answer sheet.

The game forces the player to make preferences on the basis of their priorities. After several thousand administrations, the game was found to be simple to administer and easy to play. Any amount of help necessary can be given with the exception that the player himself must place the paper clips on the board unassisted. To date, there has not been one instance reported where there was anything but minor difficulty in playing or administering the *Bonanza Game.*

The second instrument to be developed for use with the model above is the School Organization Development Questionnaire (SODQ), presented in Appendix 12.2. The SODQ was developed by Mullen and Ends for the purpose of identifying particular problems related to the organizational processes and practices used within individual schools and within the entire school system. The variables assessed by the SODQ are as follows: 1) confidence and trust; 2) communication; 3) decision making; 4) control; and 5) organizational satisfaction.

A program for scoring has been developed which permits the entire system as well as an individual school to pinpoint and analyze the processes and practices which seem to be causing the most trouble. That is, subgroups can be analyzed by category: students, certified staff, noncertified staff, parents, by age, by race, by sex, or any other variable which is desired.

As is shown in the sample of the SODQ, the key factor in this instrument is the assessment of conditions *as they are* and *as they are desired to be.* Through a scoring formula, a factor is obtained which is an indication of the disparity between what *is* and what *ought to be*; in essence, a measure of organizational health.

The data which is gathered through the administration of the SODQ and the *Bonanza Game* is processed through the computer and then returned to the school district's OD teams for analysis. Ideally, the data is best returned to the OD teams just shortly after they have completed their training programs in order to sustain upon and build the interest, enthusiasm and energies which have been generated among the OD teams.

Following the establishment of the OD teams, completion of the training sessions and the data feedback session, the activities of the OD consultant becomes much less directive and much more collaborative when working with the school system. As collaborators, the OD consultant can then assist the OD teams in planning their interventions, and in continuing the work which was begun during the first phases of the OD Program. A few examples of the ways in which the OD consultant might assist the school district are as follows:

Problem solving:

Meeting with OD teams for the purpose of establishing their educational priorities

Meeting with OD teams for the purpose of diagnosing and identifying problems

Meeting with OD teams for the purpose of identifying and developing an intervention strategy for dealing with a specific problem

Plan making:

Meeting with OD teams for the purpose of making plans for getting at the educational priorities and problems which have been identified

Meeting with OD teams for the purpose of making plans for implementing the interventions and solutions to problems or plans they have invented

Confrontation:

Meeting with OD teams for the purpose of conducting meetings where OD teams can come together in order to negotiate their differences concerning the educational priorities, problems or plans they have identified.

Techo-structural change:

Meeting with OD teams for the purpose of designing changes in the school system's structure, work-flow, or procedures in order to implement the changes identified during the course of the OD Program.

In summary, the model presented here is an emerging management strategy which is essentially action research oriented. It is a process which can be used to alter almost any organizational problem(s) or processes found within contemporary schools. Today in the super-industrial society which is emerging, we are seeing many school systems that are under heavy attack because they have not been able to adapt themselves quickly enough to the growing list of demands which are being placed upon them. Instead of instituting needed changes, numerous school systems are suffering from the condition described by Toeffler as "future shock." Is there a solution? Perhaps, if school systems can adopt the change strategies of organizational development, they may yet be able to survive the impending crisis.

A Perspective on the Future of Organization Development in Schools

As reported by Schmuck and Miles the concept of organization development as applied to schools is brand new, being less than a decade old from the time of its first application.[12] It is best to describe OD in schools as being in its infancy. Although ten years is a long time, by some standards, in which to develop a body of knowledge regarding a particular endeavor, most OD practioners are not researchers! As such they do not systematically evaluate the outcomes of their intervention strategies, except in very informal ways, and thus little is known except through experience about the strategies and techniques for applying OD principles to school change programs. In a nutshell, "most OD projects in schools have been guided by a set of assumptions involving *trust* and *truth.*"[13]   Rarely, however, have the rigors of an empirical study been applied to the practice of OD in school environments. This situation has left a vacuum in the places where understanding should be abundant.

Being in the early stages of infancy, OD work in schools is very likely to go in one of two ways: it will either fade off into the sunset like so many other ideas and innovations which have been tried in the last twenty-five years or it will grow into maturity and adulthood as a method for creating and implementing meaningful and needed change into a system that has had few alternatives for making change during its past three or four hundred years of history. Perhaps *Future Shock* is the best thing that could happen to the American public school system, for now it has become a "do or die" proposition. Shall we "do" or shall we "die"? The choice belongs to the system.

APPENDIX 12.1 SCHOOL PROGRAM BONANZA GAME

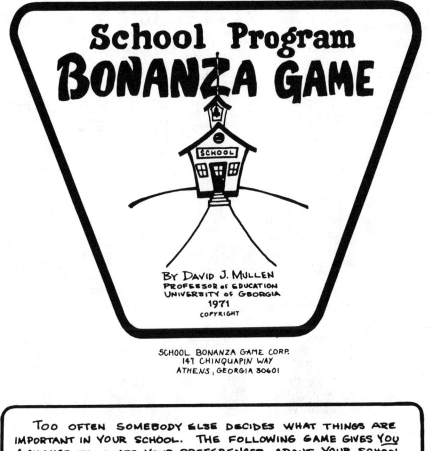

School Program
BONANZA GAME

$CHOOL

SCHOOL

BY DAVID J. MULLEN
PROFESSOR of EDUCATION
UNIVERSITY of GEORGIA
1971
COPYRIGHT

SCHOOL BONANZA GAME CORP.
147 CHINQUAPIN WAY
ATHENS, GEORGIA 30601

TOO OFTEN SOMEBODY ELSE DECIDES WHAT THINGS ARE IMPORTANT IN YOUR SCHOOL. THE FOLLOWING GAME GIVES YOU A CHANCE TO STATE YOUR PREFERENCES ABOUT YOUR SCHOOL PROGRAM. THERE ARE NO RIGHT OR WRONG ANSWERS. YOUR ANSWERS WILL BE USED TO HELP IMPROVE THE SCHOOL PROGRAM.

APPENDIX 12.1 SCHOOL PROGRAM BONANZA GAME

Copyright 1971 by David J. Mullen. Used by permission.

APPENDIX 12.1 SCHOOL PROGRAM BONANZA GAME (cont.)

APPENDIX 12.2 SCHOOL ORGANIZATIONAL DEVELOPMENT QUESTIONNAIRE*

Personal Data Sheet

Date _____ **School System** _____

Check one number in each of the categories below:

1. *School*   2. *Sex*   3. *Race*
   1. _____ East Coweta   1. _____ Female   1. _____ Black
   2. _____ Eastside   2. _____ Male   2. _____ White
   3. _____ Newnan-Central   3. _____ Other
   4. _____ Newnan Jr. High
   5. _____ Newnan Sr. High
   6. _____ Overall System

4. *Age*
   01. _____ Under 10   06. _____ 18 or 19
   02. _____ 10 or 11   07. _____ 20 - 29
   03. _____ 12 or 13   08. _____ 30 - 39
   04. _____ 14 or 15   09. _____ 40 - 49
   05. _____ 16 or 17   10. _____ 50 or over

5. *Position*
   01. _____ Pupil
   02. _____ Teacher
   03. _____ Other Certified Staff

- -

For Certified Staff Only

6. *Years of Experience in Education*
   01. _____ 0 - 9   03. _____ 20 - 29
   02. _____ 10 - 19   04. _____ 30 or over

7. *Years in this School System*
   01. _____ 0 - 4   03. _____ 10 - 19
   02. _____ 5 - 9   04. _____ 20 or over

Instructions

The questionnaire you are about to complete describes a number of behaviors, situations or conditions that occur to some degree in a typical school situation. When you read each item, do not think of it in terms of being either "good" or "bad" rather, answer the item in terms of *how often* the circumstance described takes place in your school situation and how often you think it should take place.

Marking Instructions

In the top corners of each page is printed the following scale for rating each of the items:

1. Almost Never
2. Sometimes
3. Often
4. Very Often
5. Almost Always

In the left column of the questionnaire you are asked to tell how it "*IS*" in your school in regard to each item listed. In the right column on the questionnaire, you are asked to tell how it "*SHOULD BE*" in your school in regard to each item listed.

IS means	- This is the way I think it really is in my school
	OR
	This is the way I believe it is handled here.
SHOULD BE means	- This is the way I think it *should be* in my school.
	OR
	This is the way I believe it *should be* handled in my school.

Below is an example of a typical item on the questionnaire:

IS	*ITEM*	*SHOULD BE*
1 2 ③ 4 5	You feel like you are an important person in your school.	1 2 3 ④ 5

In this example the item was answered by circling *3* in the left column to show that Often tells how it "*IS*" and by circling *4* in the right column to show that Very Often tells how it "*SHOULD BE*." Of course, any of the choices could have been selected, depending upon how the responder feels about his being an important person in his school at that time. Also, any choice to indicate how it "*SHOULD BE*" depending upon how the responder feels about it.

Please circle your responses clearly, as indicated in the example above!

PLEASE BE SURE TO MARK EACH ITEM IN BOTH THE LEFT AND RIGHT HAND COLUMNS!

Definition of Terms

Superiors - anyone who has power, authority or influence over you in your school situation.

Peers   - those people who are in the same type of position as you are in your school organization. If you are a student, then your peers are other students, etc.

(The following questionnaire has been based upon Likert's "Profile of Organizational Characteristics" from R. Likert, *The human organization: Its management and value.* New York: McGraw Hill, 1967, pp. 197-211.)

Questionnaire

1. Almost Never	1. Almost Never
2. Sometimes	2. Sometimes
3. Often	3. Often
4. Very Often	4. Very Often
5. Almost Always	5. Almost Always

IS	*ITEM*	*SHOULD BE*
1 2 3 4 5	1. Your superiors have confidence and trust in you	1 2 3 4 5
1 2 3 4 5	2. Team work is used in your school	1 2 3 4 5
1 2 3 4 5	3. You are able to take part in improving your school situation	1 2 3 4 5
1 2 3 4 5	4. Your superiors use information about how you are doing to help you do a better job in school	1 2 3 4 5
1 2 3 4 5	5. The way decisions are made helps you to feel that you are part of the team	1 2 3 4 5
1 2 3 4 5	6. Members of your school feel responsible for controlling their own behavior	1 2 3 4 5
1 2 3 4 5	7. You have confidence and trust in your superiors	1 2 3 4 5
1 2 3 4 5	8. You and your peers work to improve your school situation	1 2 3 4 5
1 2 3 4 5	9. You are concerned for and helpful to others in your school situation	1 2 3 4 5
1 2 3 4 5	10. Your superiors treat you in ways which make you feel important	1 2 3 4 5
1 2 3 4 5	11. Your superiors understand situations from your point of view	1 2 3 4 5

IS	ITEM	SHOULD BE
1 2 3 4 5	12. You take a part in making decisions which affect your school life and work	1 2 3 4 5
1 2 3 4 5	13. You accept the goals set for school life and work in your situation	1 2 3 4 5
1 2 3 4 5	14. You share in having control over your school life and work	1 2 3 4 5
1 2 3 4 5	15. You are able to bring about changes in the goals, methods, and activities in your school situation	1 2 3 4 5
1 2 3 4 5	16. You understand situations from your superiors' point of view	1 2 3 4 5
1 2 3 4 5	17. School life and work activities which affect you are developed by you or a group which represents you	1 2 3 4 5
1 2 3 4 5	18. You are satisfied to be in your school situation	1 2 3 4 5
1 2 3 4 5	19. Individuals and groups in your school communicate to improve school life and work	1 2 3 4 5
1 2 3 4 5	20. You try to reach high goals in your school situation	1 2 3 4 5
1 2 3 4 5	21. Decisions in your school are made by those people who are closest to the problem	1 2 3 4 5
1 2 3 4 5	22. You feel close to and friendly with your superiors	1 2 3 4 5
1 2 3 4 5	23. Students, teachers, parents, and administrators set high standards for school work in your situation	1 2 3 4 5
1 2 3 4 5	24. Your superiors work with you in such a way that you *willingly* do what they expect you to do	1 2 3 4 5

IS	ITEM	SHOULD BE
1 2 3 4 5	25. Information from those who "KNOW" is used in making decisions in your school situation	1 2 3 4 5
1 2 3 4 5	26. You feel free to share your feelings and problems with your superiors	1 2 3 4 5
1 2 3 4 5	27. Students, teachers, parents, and administrators take part in making decisions about school life and work in your situation	1 2 3 4 5
1 2 3 4 5	28. Your superiors share their feelings and problems with you	1 2 3 4 5
1 2 3 4 5	29. Information for improving your school situation comes from the students, teachers, parents, and administrators	1 2 3 4 5
1 2 3 4 5	30. When your superiors know your ideas about school life and work situations they try to use them	1 2 3 4 5
1 2 3 4 5	31. You treat your superiors in ways which make them feel that you trust them	1 2 3 4 5
1 2 3 4 5	32. You have chances to work with your peers in close and friendly ways	1 2 3 4 5
1 2 3 4 5	33. Others in your school situation are concerned for and helpful to you	1 2 3 4 5
1 2 3 4 5	34. Your superiors try to get your ideas about school life and work situations	1 2 3 4 5
1 2 3 4 5	35. Your school is organized in such a way that your ideas and views have a chance to influence the decisions which are made	1 2 3 4 5
1 2 3 4 5	36. The people who make decisions which affect you are aware of the situations faced by those in your peer group	1 2 3 4 5
1 2 3 4 5	37. Your superiors try to have you achieve high goals in your school situation	1 2 3 4 5

IS	ITEM	SHOULD BE
1 2 3 4 5	38. You give complete and *true* information about your work to your superiors	1 2 3 4 5
1 2 3 4 5	39. You take a part in evaluating your work	1 2 3 4 5

FOOTNOTES

1. Bennis, W., *Changing Organizations,* New York, McGraw-Hill, 1966, p. 67.

2. Argyris, C., "The Individual and the Organization: Some Problems of Mutual Adjustment," *Administrative Science Quarterly,* 2: 1-24, 1957, p. 24.

3. Beckhard, R., *Organization Development: Strategies and Models,* Reading, Mass., Addison-Wesley, 1969, pp. 9-13.

4. *Ibid.* pp. 13-14

5. *Ibid.* p. 9.

6. Likert, R., *New Patterns of Management,* New York, McGraw-Hill, 1961, pp. 104-115.

7. Bennis, W., *op. cit.,* pp. 18-27.

8. Beckhard, R., *op. cit.*

9. Schmuck, R. A. and M. B. Miles (eds.), *Organization Development in Schools,* Palo Alto, Calif., National Press Books, 1971.

10. Likert, R., *The Human Organization,* New York, McGraw-Hill, 1967, p. 158.

11. Bennis, W., *op. cit.,* p. 120.

12. Schmuck, R. A. and M. B. Miles, *op. cit.,* p. 231.

13. *Ibid.* p. 234.

ORGANIZATION DEVELOPMENT IN A STUDENT ORGANIZATION SETTING

Few organizations exist in such a dynamic environment as do student organizations. The students who belong to these organizations are themselves experiencing rapid internal changes. The author comments on some of the special problems encountered in working with students such as temporary membership, member roles and power, commitment, and the role of the advisor. In discussing an OD model he discusses development strategy, project length, and goal time-focus. The cases described are OD projects done with two fraternities and the governing board of a campus student organization. These projects are illustrative of what can be done to develop leadership in student organizations and help them to get organized in order to operate effectively within the constraints of the college environment.

Organization Development
in a Student Organization Setting

HENRY I. FEIR

Student organizations in higher education settings differ from other organizations — both volunteer and work — in a variety of ways. The consultant embarking on any sort of organization development intervention into these organizations needs to consider these differences as he prepares his strategies. In this chapter, I will try to highlight the considerations which I find important in preparing my strategies for intervention. I will also present three generalized cases of actual organization development interventions, including a brief critique of their effectiveness.

CONSIDERATIONS FOR VIEWING STUDENTS
AND STUDENT ORGANIZATIONS

I have found it useful to keep some personal observations about students and students organizations paramount when planning OD activities with students. Whenever I have problems with my interventions, I find they are frequently linked to a failure to consider one or more of these observations about the nature of my client system. I do not mean to imply that this list is complete, but I have found it useful.

First of all, students as individuals seem to be in transition, constantly changing. During their stay in college, students are concerned about adjusting to being on their own, seeking new friends, finding mates, beginning marriage, living for the first time with persons other than their families, deciding about career plans, or looking for jobs. Any individual student may be concerned about all or none of these things, and his concern most likely varies over time. The student may also find his basic religious, moral, and social values seriously questioned and threatened for the first time. All these individual changes coupled with the constantly changing campus climate combine to make the reasons for membership in a student organization and the commitment to that organization subject to continual re-evaluation (in terms of the student's needs). In other words, the needs upon which a student acts when he joins a campus organization may be changing so rapidly that the organization soon fails to provide the kinds of experiences which will satisfy his needs. The implications of these changing student concerns

Henry I. Feir is currently a graduate student pursuing a Ph.D. in counseling at the University of Iowa. He was previously with RCA as a training and organization development specialist. He holds a B.B.A. in marketing and an M.A. in communication from the University of Iowa.

for OD lie in providing a backdrop from which membership in, commitment to, and acceptable behavior norms in student organizations may be viewed.

Membership in student organizations may usefully be viewed as being *temporary.* In my experience, active membership in a student organization by an individual rarely lasts longer than two or three years. Frequently, active membership lasts only one academic year or less. This seems to be especially true for student governmental and policy-making groups. By active membership, I mean participation in the activities and maintenance of the organization on a frequent basis. In these terms, then, even more stable organizations such as fraternities, sororities, and professional interest groups seem to have large numbers of members whose interest and involvement wanes significantly after a couple of years membership.

Another aspect of membership revolves around the different roles that particular members assume. The formal leadership of campus organizations, the officers, usually are elected or appointed to their positions for either one semester or one year. Frequently, the top officers have held less formal positions or have informally been very active within the organization. Even in these situations, however, an individual student's leadership rarely lasts beyond two years. As officers move in and out of their positions, each may try to build on the work of his predecessor, try to reject his work and move in conflicting directions, or may simply ignore the former officer's impact. Similarly, as the formal leadership and power in the group changes, so does the informal leadership and power in the group change. The officers in any given student organization may or may not be seen by its members as having the most influence and power in the organization. The location of the informal power may shift often (three or four times a year) or it may remain as stable, or more stable, than the officer changes (one or two years). In my experience, most student organizations contain at least one small subgroup of the "opposition." Frequently, especially in the larger programming, governmental, and residential organizations, these subgroups consist of significant numbers of the total group, and in some instances the combined membership of the "opposition" subgroups in the organization form a majority of the members. A final observation about these subgroups that oppose, overtly or covertly, the formal leadership is that they are almost always a reaction to some dissatisfaction by certain members toward the behavior and decisions of the leadership. The fact that the dissatisfied members deal with these feelings by banding together in opposition is, I think, important in viewing the norms of participation in the decision making of the organization. Most likely, these "opposition" members feel that their viewpoint is not properly being taken into account.

Coupled with the issue of temporary membership and member roles in the student organization is the level of commitment by these members to the organization. Much as the active participation and the expressed needs of the student changes in relation to the organization, so does the student's commitment to the organization change. This commitment seems to depend largely on the student's reasons for joining the group and the nature of the needs that the group fulfills.

Some members of student organizations join the group almost solely for the purpose of having their membership on "their record." These members have little interest in the organization and will generally involve themselves only to the degree necessary to maintain their membership in good standing. Professional, honorary, and certain prestigious campus-wide programming groups seem especially to attract large numbers of members in this category. One step beyond this sort of commitment to the organization is the student who seeks an office in the organization for similar reasons. Unless his motivation changes after assuming office, he may be most hindering to the group because his lack of commitment may leave the members and other officers with the burden of doing that person's work as well as their own. In organizations with a large segment of the membership having low commitment to maintenance activities, this void may be especially hard to fill.

Among those members which seem to be concerned about the maintenance of the organization, differences also exist in terms of commitment. For all of the students in the group, membership is an extra-curricular activity. For many, if not most, of the members, their commitment to and participation in the organization reflects the secondary priority of the extra-curricular; however, some members will rank membership in the organization as their first priority. The students in the latter category frequently become frustrated at the lack of total commitment to the organization by other members. They either fail to recognize or to accept the secondary priority of the others' membership in the group. Likewise, the members who are not extreme in their commitment often consider those who are to be foolish "activity jocks."* Frequently these "activity jocks" become the officers of the organization.

As the individuals involvement in the organization increases, he frequently gains an increased sense of ownership in and loyalty to the organization. The organization becomes increasingly important to the satisfaction of his needs, especially those of affiliation and esteem.[1] The student may, in essence, act as though the organization were a part of himself, so much so that an attack against the organization becomes for him a personal one.

Taken together, these various reasons for joining an organization, the various levels of commitment to it, and the various amounts of participation in it, all may contribute to conflicts among different member groups who are operating at different levels of involvement in the organization. These conflicts may focus around unrealized expectations which members have for each other's involvement. I have found that helping an organization's members recognize this situation, when it exists, may allow the group to work toward relieving these tensions through acceptance of each member's involvement. This dissipates the wasted energy spent in reactions to these conflicts and allows the group to realistically plan its activities in a manner more consistent with the group's available member resources.

Before discussing a simple model for use in student organization OD efforts, I wish to present one final issue peculiar to student organizations — the advisor. I find it difficult to make many generalized statements about advisors to student organizations. Each campus and each group seems to have substantially different advisor-organization relationships in terms of the advisor's influence in, involve-

---

*"Activity jocks" refers to those students who seem to center their lives around participation in student activities, as distinguished from "jocks," those for whom athletics are central.

ment in, and goals for the organization. Some advisors are assigned by the school to the group; others are specifically chosen by the group. Some are involved in the daily functioning of the organization; others rarely participate in the group's activities. Some have goals for the organization consistent with the members' goals; others do not. And some advisors attempt to control the functioning of the group through subtle and covert guidance; others consider themselves to be consultants to the organization and act consistently with that role. In any event, the advisor's role must be taken into account in the change effort. He may be an important ally or a great hindrance or unimportant, but he should not be ignored.

AN OD MODEL FOR STUDENT ORGANIZATIONS

When I embark upon an OD project for a student organization, I find it useful to consider, explicitly, alternatives for action in three areas — development strategy, length of project, and goal time-focus. The *development strategy* concerns the relative emphasis on individual development versus organizational relationship development. The *length of the project* may vary from a one-time intervention to lengthy ongoing interventions. The *goal time-focus* may be on a shortrange objective to be completed in only a few days or weeks to a long-range one to be completed in several months or longer. Each one of these areas seems to involve some special considerations for the OD intervention when viewed in the student organization setting. Before proceeding, a word of caution: while I will discuss these three areas separately and sequentially, they are very much intertwined, and decisions in any one area may precede those in another area differently for each OD project. Further, the alternatives available to the consultant may be severely limited in any specific OD effort. In other words, because of factors out of his control the consultant may have to decide on actions less than desirable if these limits, or controls, did not exist.

When I enter a consulting relationship with a student organization, perhaps the most central issue in the planning and implementing of an overall OD strategy for the project is the one involving the basic *development strategy* which I will pursue. I can choose to focus primarily on the individual student in the organization concentrating on his developing skills and awareness in such leadership and membership processes as interpersonal communication, self-awareness, leadership styles, types of decision making, and power and authority. Or I can choose to focus primarily on the existing organizational relationships surrounding the above areas as well as others for the specific organization with which I am working. Or I can choose some combination of focus along this individual-organizational relationship continuum.* In other words, I can focus on a strategy which uses primarily Leadership Development technology (in the classic use of the term) or primarily Organization Development technology (again in the classic sense) or some combination. But no matter which set of development strategy technologies I employ, the focus of impact is on the particular issues surrounding organization life in the client organization.

---

* This dichotomy was succinctly presented in the context of major approaches to organizational change in a speech by Richard Beckhard before the New York OD Network, March, 1971.

An underlying philosophy which affects my choice of the development strategy mix which I employ in student organizations is the nature of their setting. The student groups with which I work are in an educational setting — the university. It seems to me then, that I have some responsibility to consider the primary function of individual learning when I make decisions regarding strategy. Further, the nature of the student's involvement in the student group magnifies my concern in this area. The student is very much a temporary member of the organization. One of his benefits from membership in the organization is, I believe, the learning which he can take away from that organizational experience and use in subsequent work and social organizations. This view tends to yield development strategies involving at least some time, if not the majority of time, focusing on individual development. In this way, the maximum effort in the OD project supports the individual's learning in ways that he can apply across various organizational settings. And the advantage of doing individual development activities in an organizational setting instead of a workshop setting with strangers is that the participants will be able to support each other's individual learning through their continued relationship in the group. This seems to increase the likelihood of the learning lasting over time. Thus the concern for improving the organization's effective functioning is tempered by a concern for improving the individual's functioning in organization settings other than the specific one involved in one particular OD effort. Even though OD efforts in nonstudent organization settings necessarily consider the individual's learning, I believe that his consideration is more important in the learning environment in which student groups exist.

Some additional observations seem to emphasize the desirability of focusing on the individual end of the development strategy continuum. Students seem to be much less sophisticated in their view of organizational functioning than are people in work settings such as industry. Students have primarily been exposed to the school model and the democratic-political model of organizational functioning. They are aware of only very limited factors affecting organizational behavior and are likely to choose within only a very narrow range of behaviors. Generally, I find the idea of looking at their own processes in their regular meetings and making decisions about the sort of organizational norms which they think will best achieve their group objectives, to be new for them and not regarded as useful for achieving these objectives. Frequently, when certain members of the group experience problems in the group's operation, the tendency is to blame someone's action or lack of action, and solutions tend to be of the nature which yields suggestions such as "Let's have a social function to fix things up." The outcome for me in terms of my intervention style is that I find it difficult to openly develop and share with the student client group anything but very simple approaches. Thus, while I try to look at the various aspects of the organization's situation, the alternative strategies for intervention, and the possible next steps, I rarely share them in any complete way with the students in the organization with which I am working. It seems only to confuse the process of the intervention, and, in some instances, scares the students away from agreement to any intervention at all.

A further outcome of the temporary and changing membership situation seems to be that the organization is constantly facing and re-facing problems concerning the integration of significant numbers of new members. This constant instability in the organization adds to the difficulty of focusing on the organization's culture in the more traditional OD sense. In other words, attempting to focus on intervention strategies which are designed specifically to change the acceptable norms of behavior in the organization (a common OD approach) is extremely difficult in the rapidly changing membership situation of student organizations. I have found that the lack of stability in the membership causes constant fluctuations in the norms of the members' interactions as they seek to become a part of that organization. Further, the lack of commitment and support of short-term members to long-range norm changes increases the difficulty of this sort of approach. It seems, then, that developing strategies focused on individual changes are more effective in this setting. The organization norms seem much too fluid and ambiguous to provide the primary target of an OD intervention.

A second issue for consideration in any OD project with a student organization is the length of the project. By *length of project,* I am referring to the length of the consultant's involvement as well as subsequent planned activities of some member of the organization as a result of the consultant's intervention.

Again, because of the rapid changes in student organizations, I find one-time efforts to be the norm. These range from short evening workshops or consultations to weekend off-campus workshop retreats. A slightly longer project may be spread over the course of a couple of weeks or months, but in my experience, more lengthy projects are rare.

An alternative to an ongoing integrated involvement with a group is a series of short one-meeting interventions. An organization may agree to an evening or weekend workshop and then decide afterwards that a further activity would be useful. Or an organization may invite you to help them with the integration of new members each year. But in most of these continued associations with a particular student group, no ongoing or extended commitment to continue this association is agreed to. One group of officers cannot effectively commit the next group to any sort of ongoing OD effort.

I do not intend to imply that I think that an ongoing OD project with a student organization is not possible given certain circumstances. In fact, longer involvement with the organization allows more change goals to be accomplished in a more thorough, lasting manner, but such an arrangement is very difficult to maintain, and I know of no such extended project.

The final issue which I will consider is the goal time-focus of the organization during the project. The *goal time-focus* may be on the immediate needs of the organization and its members or on some longer-range objective. For instance, the focus of the issues in an intervention may be on the current interpersonal relationships in the group or on organizing the membership for an upcoming event, or the focus may be on developing a plan for integrating new members into the group over the next few months.

I have found that various factors in student organizations seem to mitigate against a long-range goal focus in much the same way as against an ongoing OD project. Membership and officer roles change too frequently for any one group to commit the organization to a long-range problem. Furthermore, the very fact that the current leadership is only for a short time hinders the organization from considering long-range goals. I have seen many student groups attempt to develop long-range plans which are quickly lost in the fluidity of concerns and membership in the organization.

An implication accruing from the absense of long-range planning is "organizational amnesia." The organization lacks a very long *memory* and thus seems to repeat its errors and decrease its learning from experience. This is especially disconcerting to an OD consultant who may be associated with a particular organization longer than any of its members. The consultant finds himself having to redo and reconvince the members of the student group over and over again. This lack of organizational memory also inhibits attempts to focus on the longer process of cultural norm change in the organization. One approach which can provide longer lasting changes is structural interventions creating more permanent parameters for operation and guidance. Providing formalized structural changes has the effect of at least providing a jumping-off point for new officers. However, as the organization changes these new structures over time the group may very likely recycle through previously rejected alternatives.

Thus most OD in student organizations seems to focus on individual development in a one-meeting intervention concerned with near-range goals. In this way, working with student organizations seems to be markedly different from working with intact employee groups in industry or even from working with more permanent volunteer groups in the community. But within the framework of these special considerations, OD activities are carried on in ways very similar to the techniques used in other settings and in the field as a whole. These specifics are discussed in the next section.

SOME EXAMPLES OF SPECIFIC OD EFFORTS

I always find myself hesitating whenever I share specific workshop or OD designs with others. I think this hesitation stems from a very strong belief that the success of any design is largely dependent on those who lead it. I prefer to be adaptable enough in any situation so that I may change the design or the way in which I am conducting it in response to my perception of the ways the participants are experiencing it. Further, I try to develop specific designs appropriate to the specific group with which I am working. I, therefore, rarely use the exact design twice for different groups. This tends to be more true when I work with intact groups such as student organizations than when I work in an offered workshop setting where the participants will probably be from settings similar to previous participants. In any event, I want to make this caveat: None of the following designs may be appropriate to the specific groups with which you may be involved. They most likely will and should be adapted to the specific client organization.

In the examples described following, I try to present the preliminary steps prior to the actual OD meeting, the goals for the meeting, the design, and an evaluation of the meeting results with possible suggestions for further use. Some of the designs are more specific than others in order that you may understand the sort of format used in most of the meetings without my being redundant. All meetings use primarily experience-based techniques with didactic segments at a minimum. One final note: in order to present a wider range of student organizational OD efforts, I have drawn in the third example from the experience of colleagues with whom I have frequently worked. Therefore, since I have not experienced the third project presented following, I am relying on the descriptions presented me. I hope they are adequate for your understanding.

Fraternity 1 — An Evening Microlab*

This organization is a new social fraternity which was in the process of finalizing its initial organizing prior to moving to full active chapter status. At the time of the OD intervention the group was approximately one year old. The officers of the group were concerned that the initial enthusiasm and commitment to the organization seemed to be waning among many of the members. The group did not have a fraternity house at that time and lived in scattered locations around town.

I was asked by my co-consultant to work with him in developing a design which might help the fraternity reverse the trend mentioned above. The officers and members of the group agreed that they would be willing to devote an evening session to such an effort.

After some discussion my co-consultant (who acted also on behalf of the fraternity) and I agreed on goals for the session which focused on helping achieve cohesion and unity among the members and helping to recharge interest and commitment to the group by seeking to improve the interpersonal relationships of the members. At meetings prior to and following the evening session, the fraternity members discussed the problems of cohesion and commitment at their weekly meetings. Thus, the goals of the evening microlab seemed to be owned by the members.

In terms of the OD model presented previously, the approach adopted seems to fit into the three categories as follows: The development strategy moves during the course of the evening from an individual focus on interpersonal relationships to the implications for the organization. The length of the project is primarily a one-time effort with some preliminary and post session follow-through. The time goal is short-range, almost immediate, with an intent of maintaining any momentum gained at the microlab over a longer period of time; however, no formal method for maintenance was developed.

Fraternity 1 Microlab Design

Following is the design used for the evening microlab session (approximately thirty participants plus two staff members). The general flow of the design is from the intrapersonal to interpersonal in small groups to the total group:

---

*Gary L. Robbins and I acted as co-consultants for this project. Mr. Robbins was an officer in the group and a fellow staff member of the Leadership Development Program at the University of Iowa.

1. Expectations and Ground Rules

We began the experience with a short introduction suggesting that the participants should not set their expectations too high since this was only a two-to-three hour session. We also suggested that they would only get out of the experience what they put into it. These ground rules were explained: (1) Some exercises are non-verbal; (2) the focus in on the here-and-now feelings; (3) we will be interrupting the participants before they might be finished, and they will be switching groups so they can be with as many other members as possible during the experience.

2. Getting Acquainted and Loosening Up

The participants were led through the "introspection-fantasy experience," in which they were asked to relax and focus on various fantasies to increase their self-awareness.* Then they were asked to move without talking into an "eye contact chain," in which the participants greet each other by engaging in eye contact.[2]

3. Interpersonal Sharing (verbal)

The participants were instructed to form groups of six with those whom they knew least well. An "adjective construct" exercise was then used with them. This experience focuses on individual friendship values by asking the participants to list adjectives describing their friends.† At the conclusion of the construct the participants were told to share their adjectives in their small groups and discuss them in terms of their own values and their ideals for themselves and others. Following this, the members participated in "sharing and feedback," an interpersonal self-disclosure and feedback experience in which they were asked to disclose something about themselves and react to the disclosures of the other participants.**

4: Interpersonal Sharing (nonverbal)

The participants were asked to break up the existing small groups and form new groups of six. Then they were instructed to pick a partner from their group and do the "trust fall," in which they experience trust by falling backward with their partner catching them.[3] Then the participants discussed the experience in their small groups. Following that processing, they discussed who was the most and least open in the group. Then they were told to pick a partner from the small group whom they knew least well. The facilitators demonstrated four structured exercises: "pushing," "bring to knees," "arm wrestling," and "Indian wrestling," in which two participants physically wrestle each other in nonharmful ways.†† The pairs were then asked to do one or all of these nonverbal exercises. Following this, the participants discussed the experience in their small group in terms of feelings about their partner, about themselves, and any change in impression of the partner as a result of these nonverbals.

---

*   Appendix 13.1

†   Appendix 13.2

** Appendix 13.3

†† Appendix 13.4

5. *Community sharing*

The entire group was asked to form two lines of equal numbers facing each other. They then participated in a "line lift," a structured experience which gives all of the members of the group a chance to work together and support each other by passing each member of the group overhead.[4] Then the participants were asked to do a "pyramid," in which the group members kneel on each others' backs to form a human pyramid as a group cooperation task.* These two nonverbal exercises were physically exhausting to the members. This shared physical exertion seemed to heighten the intensity of the experience and increase the strength of feeling among the participants. Following the exercises, the entire group sat in one large circle and discussed "What happened to *me here*?" "What happened to the *group here*?" and, finally, "How does what happened here relate to the *fraternity*?"

The results of this microlab seemed to be very positive. The cohesion among the members and the commitment to the group seemed to increase substantially in subsequent verbal reports from officers and members of the group. Attendance and participation in the organization's activities increased. An unanticipated result seemed to be an increased sense of the potential for sharing among the members. They became aware of the possibility of a deeper interpersonal relationship with each other than they had yet experienced.

Of course, additional efforts with the fraternity would have helped maintain the gains made at the evening session, but this did not happen in this case. I have no information on the group beyond six months after the session.

In thinking back over the design of this effort, I consider it one of the most successful, given the time availability of the organization. The only part of the design for the microlab which I might change is to delete the "pyramid" from the design. It seemed to be anticlimactic after the "line lift."

Fraternity 2 — An Evening Microlab with Goal Setting [†]

This organization is a social fraternity which was in its second full year of existence as an active chapter on the campus. It had moved into its own house only three months before the OD effort began. Like the officers of Fraternity 1, the officers of Fraternity 2 were concerned about the apparent decrease in enthusiasm and commitment. Additionally, the membership seemed fragmented into various factions, thus impairing the overall cohesion and unity of the group.

My initial contact was with the president of the organization. He shared his view that a significant split existed between two segments of the group over the issue of pledge policy and other traditional rules. The group had initially developed an innovative posture toward traditional social fraternity living and membership rules. The core of this departure from tradition was a pledge policy which made minimal distinctions between pledges and actives. The president was part of the original group which wished to continue this progressive stance. The newer

---

*Appendix 13.5
†I acted as sole consultant during the preliminary and follow-up phases of the effort. The staff for the evening session also included James A. Robbins and Gary L. Robbins.

members and a few of the original ones wanted to develop a policy closer to that of the other fraternities on campus. Additionally, the president indicated confusion among the members about the goals of the group now that the initial goals of organizing and finding a house had been achieved.

After a couple of information gathering interviews with the president, I met with the entire executive committee of the fraternity. It appeared to me during that meeting that the president was much more interested in outside help for the fraternity's problems than were some of the other officers. It also seemed that the split among the members of the house previously described was present among the officers also. After gaining a little better understanding of the concerns of the executive committee, I suggested possible alternative ways to proceed. We agreed to a proposal which would involve the membership as a whole for an evening. This would be held instead of their proposed "leadership evening." Throughout the meeting I felt a great hesitation on the part of two or three of the officers to discuss openly with me the problems of the fraternity.

After a subsequent meeting between the president and myself, we agreed to goals similar to those for the Fraternity 1 situation, with the addition of a goal setting activity at the end of the microlab. We hoped that the microlab part of the evening might generate sufficient openness in the group to allow an honest exchange during the goal setting portion.

The goals and design of the intervention for this OD project were more oriented toward a development strategy focusing on organization issues than was the previous one. The length of the project was also longer than that of the first fraternity. The time goal was still focused on short-range solutions to the present situation.

Fraternity 2 Evening Design

This design was for approximately forty members of the group and lasted over four hours. The general flow was from intrapersonal awareness to interpersonal sharing to organization issues.

Sections 1 through 4 of this design are identical to the same sections in the design for Fraternity 1.

5. Goal Setting — Phase 1

The members of the fraternity were asked to individually list on paper what they personally wanted from the fraternity and what they saw as the overall goals of the organization. Then new groups of 5-6 members were formed. The participants were instructed to share their individual lists, discuss them, and develop one group list of goals for the fraternity which took into account both their own personal goals and the larger goals of the group. Each small group chose one of its members to act as recorder/spokesman of the group. Finally the spokesman for each group shared his list with the entire membership. These reports were recorded by a staff member on newsprint and posted for the whole group.

Following this activity, the spokesmen were asked to rank the goals reported in order of priority from most to least important. This activity was conducted using a "fishbowl" technique, in which participants form a subgroup which is observed by the remainder of the larger group.[5]

6. *Goal Setting – Phase 2*

Following the priority ranking, general reactions to the list of goals were solicited from the members. Initially reactions were to be in the form of suggestions for action in moving toward fulfillment of these goals. But as members began sharing their views, significant interpersonal concerns started emerging. Various individuals claimed certain of the goals and then shared their feeling about others in the group who had behaved in ways which prevented them from attaining their goals. After about one-half hour the agreed-upon ending time was past. The other staff members and myself tried to tie together some of the general threads of the goals with the expressed interpersonal concerns of the members. We also raised some alternatives for dealing with issues raised during the meeting. Two courses of action were agreed upon: The membership would continue the evening's discussion at its next chapter meeting; the president of the fraternity would meet with me to pull together some additional alternatives.

7. *Follow-up*

During the two-week period following the evening workshop described previously, I met the president of Fraternity 2 on three separate occasions. We discussed various alternatives such as working with the executive committee, a small group of influential members, the entire chapter at its weekly meetings. He also summarized the discussion which took place at the membership meeting following the evening session. From his reports, it appeared as though a great deal of discussion, both at formal meetings and at informal gatherings, had been generated among the members as a result of the workshop.

By the beginning of the third meeting between the fraternity president and myself, I was receiving very strong signals from him on the reluctance of the fraternity to continue the effort with any outside consultant help. I opened this issue with the president and he agreed that he could find only minimal support for additional sessions, although he maintained that he would like to continue. Following some further discussion about his alternatives, we agreed to terminate our OD relationship.

In looking back at the intervention I have described with Fraternity 2, I feel that this effort was a less satisfying one for both the client and me. I was unable to gain satisfactory commitment and cooperation from the members. The agreed-upon goals and tactics toward the goals seemed consistently to be in dispute or misunderstood. On the client's side, I feel that a significant amount of negative data was opened up and then left incompletely resolved at the end of the evening session. Even though I was told that the data generated did create substantial informal discussion among members in the weeks immediately following the session, I have an insufficient sense of the results of these informal discussions.

Although any statements as to the factors which led to the results outlined above would be merely conjecture on my part, I have, nevertheless, come to some tentative notions about some of the hindering factors in the situation and the behaviors of all involved. First of all, I chose, mistakenly it would now seem, to negotiate and plan primarily with the president. The only contact with the other officers was at a meeting of the executive committee. Since the president had been describing various splits in the group, I should not have expected the officers to be candid at this meeting. Second, I tried to explain and develop an extended-time, long-range effort with the group from the beginning. Throughout the entire OD effort it was apparent that the fraternity members did not understand such a broad, sweeping program as I was describing. In other words, the goals and nature of the program were confusing for the clients. They were, in retrospect, interested in a one-shot program focused on gaining unity in the group. Considering the multitude of disunifying, conflicting goals and interpersonal relationships which existed, this goal of unity was ambitious for a one evening program. My own failure to clarify this perception with the officers of the organization hindered the effectiveness of the intervention.

Looking back at the situation from my current perspective, over three years removed, I would approach the project differently. I would rely much less on the agreements with the president and instead work with the entire executive committee, thus gaining some semblance of commitment to the intervention from members of more than one of the various subgroups in the fraternity. Second, without developing this broader-based commitment, I would probably not work with the group, or work with it on a narrower range of leadership and group member skills.

Even with the hindering factors mentioned previously, the evening session was, on the whole, a positive experience for many of the members. Some of the sought-for openness was achieved, and useful issues were raised. Further, the organization did not suffer any negative effects on its functioning or the interpersonal relationships of its members. In large part, the project was probably less satisfying for me than for the organization. I had developed expectations for the possibilities available by using OD technology. This unmet potential frustrated me. In other words, I developed goals and expectations for the intervention which were far more ambitious than those of the client. My inability to communicate these and to achieve these was unsatisfying to me.

Executive Committee — A Weekend Teambuilding Retreat[*]

This group was the governing board of a large (over 400 members) student organization engaged in campus-wide programming including a wide range of social, cultural, and educational activities and entertainment. The organization was well established and well financed. At the time of this retreat, the university provided the group with several full and part-time professional programming and advising staff members.

As part of the organization's internal leadership development activities, it had evolved a weekend retreat in the spring shortly after the selection of the new executive committee. The goals of this retreat included providing the new executive board information about the functioning of the organization and building a positive working team relationship among the new board members prior to their selection of officers of their board. The former goal was achieved through presentations during the first part of the retreat by former board members and the advisors of the organization. The later team building goal was achieved through use of a series of structured experiences and some facilitated planning meetings.

---

[*]The staff of the OD part of the project consisted of Linda St.Clair, who was an advisor to the group, and John E. Jones, who acted as consultant for both the design and the conduct of the retreat.

The idea of the retreat had strong support from all of the 12-14 board members who participated in this specific one. This support had been built from previous retreats and continues in ones subsequent to this one described. The group used different external consultants in different years.

With reference to the OD model presented, the retreat used a development strategy focusing on the relationships among the members of the team. It was designed as a one-time effort with the exception that the advisor-consultant had an ongoing relationship with the executive committee such that the learnings gained in the retreat would be reinforced over the year by her actions. The time-focus was on building a team immediately but with implications for a continued working relationship for almost one year.

Executive Committee Retreat Design

1. Information Sharing

Approximately the first third of the workshop consisted of informal presentations by the outgoing executive committee and the advisors on the past functioning and policy of the organization and the board.

2. Rapport Building and Leadership Development

This phase of the retreat began with "getting acquainted" exercises, such as those described in Pfeiffer and Jones, Vols. 1-3, to introduce further the members to one another and to begin developing openness among the board members. During the remainder of the weekend we focused upon other leadership and interpersonal issues centering on communications, decision-making, and interpersonal relationships. This was accomplished through the use of such structured experiences as: "one-way, two-way communication," in which participants are asked to draw a diagram by relying only on verbal instructions, first without being able to ask questions and then with questions;[6] "consensus-seeking," in which the participants are given a group task that requires them to come to a consensus on several points;[7] and "giving and receiving coins," in which participants experience the feelings of giving and receiving as they share themselves with another member of the group through the use of a coin.[8] In the concluding discussion of these experiences we focused on the leadership and group functioning issues raised rather than on the feelings generated during the experiences. This lack of attention to feeling was carried throughout the retreat as the emphasis on task accomplishment was reinforced. In other words, "T-grouping" was discouraged, while a work or task norm was encouraged.

3. Committee Functioning Decisions

The executive committee spent a large segment of time during the OD phase of the retreat focusing on explicitly deciding how they wished to operate as a board during the coming year with special emphasis on communication. One technique used was having the participants divide into pairs and interview each other on specific issues and goals of the group. For instance, how should decisions be made? By whom? Who is responsible for sharing information? What types do people want to share? The results of these interviews then served as a basis for discussion of these issues by the total group.

During these work meetings, the consultants acted as facilitators of the meetings by trying to keep the group focused on explicit agreements on the various issues and agenda items mentioned previously.

In both discussions with the participants in the retreat and with the consultants, there was common enthusiasm about the positive value of the weekend. Subsequent similar retreats have, for the most part, yielded similar positive feelings on the part of both participants and staff. My own observation in working with this group and other groups is that this board does seem to function consistently in an effective manner. The various boards have taken the organization through some major changes with a minimum of confusion and an ability to maintain a strong programming thrust. Compared to other campus organizations undergoing major changes, this group seems to be managing their changes in a superior manner. Overall, I would rate these retreats as some of the most successful OD efforts in a student organization setting.

SOME FINAL COMMENTS

In choosing the previous examples of specific OD efforts in student organizations, it would seem obvious that these three do not emcompass the wide range of such efforts. Similar considerations to those presented above carry over into work with students or youth in a variety of organizations (e.g., student governments, dormitory living units, recreation clubs, professional interest groups, service organizations) and organizational settings (e.g., universities, schools, churches, communities). Further, I and others have been involved in various OD type activities involving faculty and staff with students as well as community leaders with students and mixed student-adult community volunteer efforts.

All of these various settings in which students operate demand some considerations special to this particular group of clients. And within this client setting each organization demands specific attention to its own particular ways of functioning. This is no less true for student organizations than for any other category of organizations.

And finally, I have intended to provide one perspective in approaching OD in student groups. The purpose of the designs, considerations, and comments presented is more to give you a feel for this area of OD rather than any specific prescription for OD. I believe that any OD effort is inseparably tied to the consultant's individual style and approach. Although the basis for any OD effort is founded on current behavioral science knowledge, the outcome is dependent on a multitude of factors which are neither clearly definable nor necessarily apparent.

No design or approach can stand on its own, apart from the persons who are facilitating it. Designs are merely tools which the consultant uses. Much as a fine paintbrush does not insure a fine painting, a good OD design does not insure an effective OD effort. The skill of the consultant in applying this design is the crucial difference. Perhaps I have belabored this point, but I *do not* want you to leave your reading of this chapter with the idea that the designs presented *is* OD in student organizations. Rather they are reports of some of the results of an OD approach to specific student organizations. I think this distinction is critical.

APPENDIX 13.1 INTROSPECTION-FANTASY

1. The participants are asked to lie down on the floor in a comfortable position. If possible they should not be able to reach those around them.

2. Everyone is told to close his eyes and remain quiet during the rest of the experience. (At this point the facilitator may wish to play some appropriate relaxing music.)

3. The participants are told to concentrate on any noises that they might be able to hear in the room. Then, concentrate on the floor. Can each one feel the places where his body is touching the floor?

4. Now the participants are asked (without moving) to be aware of different parts of their body. Can they feel the skin on their scalps and foreheads. Can they hear their heartbeats and feel their pulses. "Feel the abdomen and chest expand and contract as you breathe. Feel the blood flowing in your legs. Can you feel the soles of your feet?"

5. Next everyone is told to tense his body. "Make it rigid. Then relax." This is repeated once or twice.

6. The facilitator instructs everyone to imagine some pleasant experience. "Try to experience it in your mind. Enjoy it and relax."

Following this last set of instructions participants may move into some other type of activity, either verbal or nonverbal. But some transition is usually made rather than abruptly switching to some completely different type of activity.

Suggestions for Administering:

A warm floor, preferably carpeted, is desirable so that the participants can get comfortable. A soft, smooth, soothing voice is helpful to facilitate relaxation. I have found that timing between instructions is critical to an effective experience. Only practice leading this type of experience with feedback from participants or other staff will probably build good timing. With the importance of timing, I think it is useful to rehearse the "Introspection-Fantasy" and try following the instructions yourself before leading it for the first time.

APPENDIX 13.2 ADJECTIVE CONSTRUCT

1. Participants are asked to write down on a sheet of paper the names of two friends.

2. The participants then list one descriptive adjective for each.

3. A second adjective is listed for each name.

4. Finally, a third adjective describing a physical appearance is listed.

5. The participants share their adjectives verbally and discuss their implications in terms of the traits the participant values for himself and others and the implications of the values for the participant's interpersonal relationships.

APPENDIX 13.3 SHARING AND FEEDBACK

1.   The participants are asked to share something about themselves which will help the others in the group get to know them better. Each participant shares in turn around the group.

2.   After all members of the group have shared, they are asked to react to what has been shared.

3.   Then the participants discuss their feelings in undertaking this exercise with their group.

4.   Next the facilitator instructs each participant to pick one person in his group and share his impressions of that person. This is also done one at a time around the group.

5.   After the participants have sufficient time to clarify and understand each other's impressions, they are asked to discuss their feelings both in giving and receiving the impressions. "Did you accept it? Reject it? Were you anxious? Relaxed? Receptive to the feedback? Defensive?"

6.   Finally the participants are asked to share and discuss why each one chose the person he did to give his impressions of.

APPENDIX 13.4 STRUCTURED EXERCISES

Pushing

1.   Two participants stand facing each other with arms outstretched in front of them as if to shove someone. With each participant's palms facing his partner, they touch their palms (right hand on one with left hand of the other and vice versa) and interlock fingers.

2.   When both participants are ready, they try to push each other across the room. The pushing continues until one partner overpowers the other or until they agree to stop.

3.   The participants then share their reactions to their partners during the pushing.

Bring to Knees

1.   This structured experience begins the same way as "Pushing" (Instruction 1).

2.   When both partners are ready, each one tries to bring the other one to his knees by bending back his partner's hands and wrists towards the partner's arms. This continues until one partner is brought to his knees, one yields, or until they agree to stop.

3.   The participants then share their reactions to their partners during the exercise.

Arm Wrestling

This structured experience is a common activity which most people have participated in or watched at some time.

1. Two participants lie on the floor, on their stomachs, facing each other (or they may sit at a table facing each other). Each partner puts his elbow on the floor with his lower arm extended vertically. The partners then grip each other's hands while keeping their arms vertical.

2. When both are ready, each one tries to force the other one's arm to the floor without lifting or moving his elbow. The wrestling continues until one succeeds, one yields, or they agree to stop.

3. The participants then share their reactions to their partners during the wrestling.

Indian Wrestling

1. Two participants stand facing each other such that the outside right foot of one participant is next to the outside right foot of the other participant. The partners then clasp right hands as if to shake hands.

2. When both are ready, each one tries to pull and push and twist the other without moving his right foot. The exercise continues until one partner succeeds in throwing the other off balance enough so that he moves his right foot, or until one yields, or they agree to stop.

3. The participants then share their reactions to their partners during the wrestling.

APPENDIX 13.5 PYRAMID

1. One-third plus one of the participants are asked to kneel on the floor on their hands and knees. Then a second one-third of the participants climb on top of the bottom row on their hands and knees such that each person on this second tier has his right hand and knee on one participants back and his left hand and knee on another participants back. Finally the remaining one-third less one participants climb up on the backs of the second tier similarly to the second tier participants.

2. When all three tiers are in position, a signal is given and everyone in the pyramid thrusts his arms and legs straight out and crashes to the floor.

3. This experience is used merely as a group activity to achieve a sense of being and working together in conjunction with other structured experiences. No discussion specific to this exercise follows.

    Please note: Before beginning, the facilitator should make certain that none of the participants has back trouble or any other ailment which this exercise might aggravate.

FOOTNOTES

1. Affiliation needs include a person's needs for love, affection, and belonging. Esteem needs include one's needs for praise, recognition, and status. These notions of need satisfaction are consistent with Maslow's Hierarchy of Needs. See Maslow, Abraham H., *Motivation and Personality,* 2nd ed., New York, Harper and Row, 1970.

2. For a complete description see Pfeiffer, J. William, and John E. Jones, *A Handbook of Structured Experiences for Human Relations Training,* Vols. I-III, University Associates, Iowa City, Iowa, 1969, 1970, 1971, Vol. I, p. 110.

3. Pfeifer and Jones, Vol. I, p. 109

4. "Live lift" was developed for this workshop by Henry I. Feir and Gary L. Robbins. For a complete description see "Elevated" in Pfeifer and Jones, Vol. II, p. 110.

5. For a complete description see Fordyce, Jack K., and Raymond Weil, *Managing With People,* Reading, Mass., Addison-Wesley, 1971, p. 165 ff.

6. Pfeiffer and Jones, Vol. I, p. 13 ff.

7. Pfeiffer and Jones, Vol. II, p. 22 ff.

8. Pfeiffer and Jones, Vol. I, p. 113 ff.

14

ORGANIZATION DEVELOPMENT:
SOME EMERGING PERSPECTIVES

Organization Development: Some Emerging Perspectives

J. JENNINGS PARTIN

CHARACTERISTICS OF THE PRECEDING CASES

The history of OD is a story of evolution. It had its roots in the laboratory environment of the behavioral scientist and has since transcended that setting into the world of organizational life. OD practitioners operate according to a conceptual model derived from behavioral science disciplines but they are also opportunistic. Every OD program is shaped by the nature of the situation in which it is to be implemented. Consequently, OD programs vary from organization to organization. But if there are observable characteristics of OD activities, there are bases for comparing and contrasting them. In comparing the preceding case studies with the seven characteristics of OD activities, some interesting perspectives emerge which may be indicative of where OD is headed in the near future.

1. The target is the total organization.

I'm sure that the OD practitioners reporting their activities here would agree that their target was always the total organization. But the rest of the organization rarely sees that. In reality, OD functions have difficulty in establishing charters giving them legitimate rights of entry into any organization at any level.

In practice, the role of OD in an organization evolves as a function of available opportunities (e.g., crises, problems) and the skill of the practitioner in influencing the system before a crisis develops. In many, if not most, of the cases, OD came in via the backdoor as a result of some felt need the client organization had. The OD practitioner in these cases works with the client group whoever they are and wherever they are located. Once his credibility is established, he can then develop strategies to get involved with strategic organizations that can influence the total system. Initial efforts in OD seldom begin at the top of the organization. This happens in spite of the theory which says that the most effective changes begin at the top and move down throughout the rest of the organization.

The cases described did, however, consistently work with the top management of the client group. In only one case (Faltot) did the OD practitioner work with the company president at any length. It is often difficult for OD practitioners to work at levels higher than the reporting level of their boss or the next level boss (usually the top executive of the function in which the OD group is found). In practice, OD activities are focused on middle management or managers of operating divisions. In the cases described, the projects were often an offshoot of a management development program (Carrigan, Faltot, Hill, and Wakefield) in which the participants were exposed to behavioral science applications to management and to the practitioners themselves. In these instances, training and development programs provided the necessary seeding which later developed into OD projects with some of the participants. Very often successes at lower levels of the organization provide a basis for taking on system-wide problems with the support, if not direct involvement, of top management. To the practitioner the target is the total organization but this is usually negotiated after there have been demonstrated successes at lower levels of the organization.

2. The goal is improved organizational effectiveness.

The client organization must have some felt need to improve itself. Books could be written about program failures in which the OD practitioner sold himself and his program to his client without the client really owning the program. The charisma of the OD practitioner rarely is sufficient to obtain behavioral changes in clients who are not committed to changing.

In the cases described here, the client group had problems which they wanted to solve. Scott reported an example in which an operating manager wanted to improve accountablility and control procedures. Another of his examples was an investment group which wanted to explore new market ideas based on customer needs. Carrigan described a program which dealt with the problem of how to decrease a sales force by thirteen regional managers. Wampler worked with a stewardess college to train instructors, recommend curriculum changes, and improve the overall learning climate.

Generally speaking, it is better for an OD practitioner to be invited in to assist in solving a felt problem than to gain entry by convincing the prospective client that he has a problem he may not recognize. The latter has been done successfully but this is a high risk situation and the credibility of the OD practitioner is usually severely damaged if he is wrong or can't achieve the desired results. In helping people help themselves, OD is established as a helping function and lends itself to the consultative approach on which much OD theory is based.

3. Strategies, Methodologies, and Interventions are based on the Behavioral Sciences and other Socio-technical Disciplines.

The programs outlined by the contributors typically emphasized such interventions as data gathering, team building, job enrichment, and management by objectives. All of the cases used client data as a basis for determining any course of action. Most of the practitioners gathered data by interviewing the client group. Some used questionnaires and other instruments. Once the data were gathered, the most frequent type of intervention was an action-research team building design. Carrigan and Koppes described variations of typical designs. Hill, Wakefield and Ends/Mullen described similar projects which were focused on back-home applications following an initial effort designed for other purposes. Job enrichment programs were more prominent in the work of Scott and Wakefield, representing banking and utilities, than the other organizations represented here.

It is interesting to note that a large majority of the interventions were focused primarily on task. Interpersonal issues were typically dealt with only as they became major obstacles in solving task problems. Only one case (Carrigan), described a typical free-flowing T-group design. This appears to represent a trend. Many organizations are skeptical of anything resembling "sensitivity training" but they do recognize the need to resolve interpersonal issues that are barriers to accomplishing the organization's objectives.

Most of the interventions were "soft" (i.e., dealing with process issues centered around work tasks). Scott and Wakefield dealt with "hard" interventions which led to changes in organization structure, job design, and extensive changes in work flow. The relative emphasis on "soft" rather than "hard" interventions is probably typical of OD as it is practiced today. Both are needed if the goals of organization improvement and increased effectiveness are to be realized. Scott and Wampler both referred to the needs that go unmet if OD is predominantly concentrated on group process issues.

4. Examines the relationships of management practices, individual feelings, and behavior in relationship to outcomes.

All of the OD projects described here were in one form or another attempting to redistribute power and influence throughout the client organizations. The data gathering, problem identification, problem solving, and action-planning activities had a high involvement of the client groups. The Koppes article in particular was concerned with the management style of the general manager, comparing it with the style of the previous general manager and the transitional problems that had been evident. The problem of management styles is often a threatening issue which many organizations and managers would prefer not to deal with openly. "Soft" interventions typically deal with this if it becomes an issue in solving task problems. It is probably characteristic of many OD programs today that they do not deal with management styles implicitly. It would more often come up in management development programs or team building programs where there was sufficient trust or safety to allow it to be discussed openly.

The relationship between individual motivations (e.g., feeling) and job performance is becoming increasingly apparent to the management of many organizations. It is probably indicative of the degree of openness in most organizations doing OD that these issues are often dealt with while discussing task issues rather than confronting the issue directly. It is frequently a major task of the OD practitioner to help his organization develop insight into the effects of attitudes and feelings on performance.

5. A continuing, long-term effort.

The nature of organization change is such that it usually takes months and years to accomplish. Behavioral change of the type that OD typically deals with usually requires a two or three year effort to accomplish. Since the OD movement is relatively recent itself, there aren't many OD programs that have existed more than five years continuously with a single client organization.

It is a highly subjective judgment that determines when OD began in many organizations since they usually had some form of management development, systems analysis, or organization planning effort previously. However, in the behavioral science terms used here, the earliest programs reported began in the early 60's. Carrigan reports that the SK & F Management Course began about 1960 and in 1967 contained its first T-group. Wakefield reports that Mountain Bell's initial OD efforts began in 1962 and from there became increasingly behavioral science based. Wampler marked the introduction of OD to American Airlines as being 1966 with a substantial shift occurring in the next three years in their concept of the management process which was reflected in their management training program. The longest OD project reported by Hill at Boeing-Vertol was three years.

It is difficult to compare and contrast OD projects on the basis of time involved. They usually consist of phases with varying degrees of involvement over time. In some cases OD began in a management development program beginning with an initial program of perhaps one week's length. This often was followed by (1) a later request for assistance from a participant regarding one of his concerns or (2) an outgrowth of the back-home application part of the training program.

In either case, the OD project was the result of an initial contact between the OD practitioner and the manager, usually during a training program. The OD project came later. In most cases, one thing leads to another and the length of the OD project is a function of such things as (1) the needs of the organization, (2) the amount of time available for OD projects, (3) the severity of the problem, and (4) the availability of the OD consultant.

One of the major tasks of OD practitioners is to develop long-term objectives and develop strategies for attaining them. This involves closely working with the organization's top management to integrate operational objectives with behavioral ones. Only as OD programs are viewed as relevant to the organization's needs will the OD program be given sufficient management support to enable it to exist long enough to realize some of its potential in the long run. The inability of some OD practitioners to do this accounts for some of the reasons why OD staffs are eliminated for "budgetary" reasons. I'm confident that OD is a worthwhile enterprise and given enough time and support and if properly done, can make unique contributions to the organization. Measurement of results is one thing; learning how to maintain OD efforts is another. Both of these are major tasks for the OD movement to accomplish if it is to be a long-term, continuing effort.

6. Based on Explicit Human Values.

All of the OD projects described here were participative in nature. In effect they all dealt with power, attempting to redistribute it in the client organizations. Carrigan described one project in which one group of managers decided how they could reorganize with thirteen fewer managers. Wakefield and Scott mentioned some efforts to redesign and enrich jobs to make some jobs more meaningful and effective. In these cases, the configuration of power within a hierarchical organization was changed through OD interventions. The value here being that individuals should have increasing measures of self-control over things that affect them. Successfully done, this takes into account individual motivators and the role they play in influencing how work gets done. The OD ideal might then be a fully functioning person working in concert with every other member of the organization. When significant differences occur there can be a problem-solving mechanism built into the system such as the one described by Koppes.

OD practitioners frequently find themselves "in the middle." Typically, they know what management wants and what changes the rank and file would like to see. Faltot described a situation in which middle management identified problem areas that certain executives didn't particularly want to deal with. Any OD program, no matter how uncreative or poorly done, will result in some changes — often not the ones anticipated. Every change is related to some organizational value. It is the role of the OD practitioner to identify the value norms or assumptions of the client organization and make them explicit. Otherwise, his programs could fail because prevailing norms will deny the change or unanticipated issues will emerge which may create greater problems than before.

It is probably safe to say that human values are probably one of the most delicate issues OD practitioners deal with. This is true for a number of reasons: (1) Values are often difficult to identify, (2) it is hard to measure their strength and extent of influence, and (3) the practitioner himself may lack sufficient knowledge or skill to deal with them even if known.

OD theory says that openness, trust, collaboration, confronting conflict, and self-realization (where they exist to a large degree) make an organization healthy. OD strategies, interventions, and methodologies touch on these issues. However, it seems clear from the cases reported here that much more needs to be done if genuine systems change is to become reality and not mere behavioral science jargon.

7. The Assigned Task of One or More Persons in the Organization.

The OD program of any organization needs an "architect." A total organization change strategy must be developed and coordinated according to some unified plan. This is particularly difficult to accomplish in multidivisional organizations. If the central staff or corporate OD staff are too controlling, it makes it difficult for the divisional OD group to develop programs to meet unique divisional needs. Depending on the degree of divisional autonomy, there may be little need to closely coordinate divisional and corporate OD programs other than on an exception basis.

But for one exception (Feir) the OD group was a part of the organization's personnel function. Feir's group reported into an administrative function outside of personnel but still reporting to the chief operating officer. There is insufficient data to indicate where an OD function should report structurally but there is much to indicate that many OD efforts will fail if they are not coordinated by someone who is able to integrate them with the operating objectives of the organization. Most personnel organizations report in at high levels in the organization but are often viewed as being too control-oriented or too insulated from the "business" of the enterprise to have much of an influence on the sources of power in the organization.

Where the OD group is located in the hierarchy doesn't seem to be too important. The main thing is that the OD group members have access to key decision-makers. The ability to gain access to powerful people appears to be a function of the competence of the OD practitioner. But a program's relevance to the needs of the organization is just as important as the OD person's competence.

In many ways, the OD practitioner must live by his wits, taking advantage of opportunities as they come. He must, however, be competent to do whatever projects he takes on. The OD program will be relevant to the extent that one has access to knowledge of the plans and problems of the organization. This is too important to the success of OD in an organization to (1) allow anyone to implement a change program whose knowledge may be too limited, (2) allow programs to exist which are in conflict with the total organization's objectives, or (3) allow incompetents to implement organizational change programs.

The nature of the change process is such that it requires a concentrated, coordinated effort. This can be done when change is mutually reinforced by other elements in the system; otherwise, the change dissipates. It appears then that two strategies should be employed to ensure the success of the OD philosophy in an organization: (1) Train operating managers to be skillful in the use of OD techniques relevant to their needs and (2) coordinate OD efforts with a "chief" OD practitioner with sufficient knowledge and skill to manage OD efforts that will integrate the objectives of the organization and the OD program. In small organizations (approximately 1000 members) this might be the role of a person who has other responsibilities as well. In larger organizations it should probably be the responsibility of someone reporting to the chief executive of the corporate organization (or the division).

Conclusions

There is still much to be done to accurately define OD, what it is and what it is not. Its concepts require much more testing to determine their validity in every application. Some things are apparent, however, regarding the few cases reported here.

1. OD is comparatively new to the organizations represented.

   Antiquity occurred in the early 60's, significant changes in the mid 60's. Three to five years with a client is a relatively long time in OD history.

2. Most OD projects evolved from training programs.

   Unfortunately, many OD people regard training activities as being too limiting to deal with significant organization issues. This has often led to "family feuds" between the OD group and the training group in organizations where they are separate. The experience here seems to be that training can be a valuable OD intervention provided it is designed and developed properly. If nothing else it often provides a good springboard for getting into OD. It provides a seedbed for planting the seeds of behavioral science applications to management.

3. OD skills are unique.

The practitioners who reported here were formerly trainers; they designed and conducted training programs. At some point in their development they acquired group facilitation skills, skill in using instruments, and interviewing. These skills enabled them to make interventions based on data the group provided and which was used as a basis for problem solving and decision making by the group. These skills, coupled with a consultative approach, tend to distinguish the work of an OD practitioner from other functions. They are applicable to developing human resources and helping solve problems of the human system which makes them unique in the organization.

4. Limited use was made of outside consultants.

Only a few cases reported here made extensive use of private consultants. Most organizations represented here relied on its internal OD group to design and implement the projects described. This has some advantages: (1) It builds a power base for the internal person, (2) who is readily available for consultation, and (3) who knows the organization and can integrate the OD program into the culture of the organization. Some of the disadvantages are: (1) Some projects greatly benefit from "expert" skills which more than pay for the cost of a private consultant, (2) often the internal OD consultant needs a consultant, and (3) the outside consultant can bring fresh ideas into the organization.

In these days of cost reduction, outside consulting funds often become scarce. It is often more economical to develop the internal resources than to purchase them from outside. Consequently, the broader the range of skills an OD practitioner has the more useful he can be to his organization.

A Final Word

The path OD has taken in the cases presented here shows an attempt to be relevant and responsive to emerging needs that tended to fall outside the scope of the more traditional organization functions. Life in the gray areas of organizational ambiguity is for hearty souls. The cases described here were attempts to achieve clarity, common understanding, resolution, and action — where they were needed and when it appeared to be an OD function. Such efforts as these, documented and based on sound theoretical foundations, will do much to contribute to making OD values, theories, and concepts become realities and not the dreams of visionaries only.

GENERAL OD BIBLIOGRAPHY

Argyris, C., *Integrating the Individual and the Organization*, New York, Wiley, 1964.

Argyris, C., *Intervention Theory and Method: A Behavioral Science View,* Reading, Mass., Addison-Wesley, 1970.

Beckhard, R., *Organization Development: Strategies and Models,* Reading, Mass., Addison-Wesley, 1969.

Bennis, W. G., *Changing Organizations,* New York, McGraw-Hill, 1966.

Bennis, W. G., *Organization Development: Its Nature, Origins and Prospects,* Reading, Mass., Addison-Wesley, 1969.

Bennis, W. G., K. D. Benne, and R. Chin, (eds.), *The Planning of Change* (2nd. Edition), New York, Holt, Rinehart, and Winston, 1969.

Bennis, W. G., and P. E. Slater, *The Temporary Society,* New York, Harper and Row, 1968.

Blake, R. R., and J. S. Mouton, *Building a Dynamic Corporation through Grid Organization Development,* Reading, Mass., Addison-Wesley, 1969.

Blake, R. R., and J. S. Mouton, *Corporate Excellence through Grid Organization Development,* Houston, Gulf Publishing, 1968.

Blake, R. R., and J. S. Mouton, *The Managerial Grid,* Houston, Gulf Publishing, 1964.

Blake, R. R., and H. G. Shepherd, and J. S. Mouton, *Managing Intergroup Conflict in Industry,* Houston, Gulf Publishing, 1964.

Bradford, L. P., J. D. Gibb, and K. R. Benne, *T-Group Theory and Laboratory Method,* New York, Wiley, 1964.

Cummings, L. L. and W. E. Scott, (eds.), *Organizational Behavior and Human Performance,* Homewood, Ill., Irwin-Dorsey, 1969.

Etzioni, A. (ed.), *Complex Organizations: A Sociological Reader*, New York, Holt, Rinehart, and Winston, 1961.

Etzioni, A., *Modern Organizations*, Englewood Cliffs, N. J., Prentice-Hall, 1964.

Etzioni, A. (ed.), *A Sociological Reader on Complex Organizations* (2nd ed.), New York, Holt, Rinehart, and Winston, 1969.

Etzioni, A. and E. Etzioni, (eds.), *Social Change: Sources, Patterns, and Consequences*, New York, Basic Books, 1964.

Evan, W. M. (ed.), *Handbook of Organizations*, Chicago, Rand McNally, 1965.

Fordyce, J. and R. Weil, *Managing With People: A Manager's Handbook of Organization Development Methods*, Reading, Mass., Addison-Wesley, 1971.

French, W. L., and C. H. Bell, Jr., *Organization Development: Behavioral Science Interventions for Organization Improvement*, Englewood Cliffs, N. J., Prentice-Hall, 1973.

Gardner, J. W., *Self-renewal: The Individual and the Innovative Society*, New York, Harper and Row, 1963.

Golembiewski, R. T., and F. Gibson, *Managerial Behavior and Organization Demands*, Chicago, Rand McNally, 1967.

Haire, M. (ed.), *Modern Organization Theory*, New York, Wiley, 1959.

Hornstein, H. A., B. B. Bunker, W. W. Burke, M. Gindes, and R. J. Lewicki, (eds.), *Social Intervention: A Behavioral Science Approach*, New York, The Free Press, 1971.

Kahn, R. L., D. M. Wolfe, R. P., Quinn, J. D. Smoek, and R. A. Rosenthal, *Organizational Stress: Studies in Role Conflict and Ambiguity*, New York, Wiley, 1964.

Katz, D., and R. L. Kahn, *The Social Psychology of Organizations*, New York, Wiley, 1966.

Kelman, H., *A Time to Speak*, San Francisco, Jorsey-Bass, 1968.

Korman, A. K., *Industrial and Organizational Psychology*, Englewood Cliffs, N. J., Prentice-Hall, 1971.

Kuriloff, A. H., *Organization Development for Survival*, New York, American Management Association, Inc., 1972.

Lawrence, P. R., *The Changing of Organizational Behavior Patterns*, Cambridge, Mass., Howard University Press, 1958.

Lawrence, P. R., and J. W. Lorsch, *Developing Organizations: Diagnosis and Action*, Reading, Mass., Addison-Wesley, 1969.

Lawrence, P. R., and J. W. Lorsch, *Organization and Environment–Managing Differentiation and Integration*, Cambridge, Mass., Division Research, Harvard Business School, 1967.

Leavitt, H. (ed.), *The Social Science of Organizations*, Englewood Cliffs, N. J., Prentice-Hall, 1963.

Likert, R., *The Human Organization*, New York, McGraw-Hill, 1967.

Likert, R., *New Patterns of Management*, New York, McGraw-Hill, 1961.

Lippitt, G. L., *Organization Renewal: Achieving Viability in a Changing World*, New York, Appleton-Century-Crofts, 1969.

Lippitt, R., J. Watson, and B. Westley, *The Dynamics of Planned Change*, New York, Holt, Rinehart, and Winston, 1958.

Litwin, G. H., and R. A. Stringer, Jr., *Motivation and Organization Climate,* Cambridge, Mass., Division of Research, Harvard Business School, 1968.

McGregor, D., *The Human Side of Enterprise,* New York, McGraw-Hill, 1960.

McGregor, D., *Leadership and Motivation,* Cambridge, Mass., The M.I.T. Press, 1966.

March, J. G. (ed.), *Handbook of Organizations,* Chicago, Rand McNally, 1965.

March, J. G., and H. A. Simon, *Organizations,* New York, Wiley, 1958.

Marrow, A. J., D. G. Bowers, and S. E. Seashore, *Management by Participation,* New York, Harper and Row, 1967.

Maslow, A. H., *Eupsychian Management: A Journal,* Homewood, Ill., Irwin-Dorsey, 1965.

Schein, E. H., and W. G. Bennis, *Personal and Organizational Change Through Group Methods: The Laboratory Approach,* New York, Wiley, 1965.

Schein, E. H., *Process Consultation: Its role in Organization Development,* Reading, Mass., Addison-Wesley, 1969.

Schein, E. H., *Organizational Psychology,* Englewood Cliffs, N. J., Prentice-Hall, 1965.

Seiler, J. A. (ed.), *Systems Analysis in Organizational Behavior,* Homewood, Ill., Irwin-Dorsey, 1967.

Skinner, B. F., *Beyond Freedom and Dignity,* New York, Alfred A. Knopf, 1971.

Tannenbaum, A. S. (ed.), *Control in Organization,* New York, McGraw-Hill, 1968.

Tannenbaum, R., I. R. Weschler, and F. Massarik, *Leadership and Organization: A Behavioral Science Approach,* New York, McGraw-Hill, 1961.

Trist, E. L., *Socio-technical Systems,* London, Tavistock, 1960.

Walton, R. E., *Interpersonal Peacemaking: Conformation and Third Party Consultation,* Reading, Mass., Addison-Wesley, 1969.

Weber, M., *The Theory of Social and Economic Organization,* New York, The Free Press, 1947.

Whyte, W. F., *Organization Behavior: Theory and Application,* Homewood, Ill., Irwin-Dorsey, 1969.

Yukl, G. A., and K. N. Wexley, *Readings in Organizational and Industrial Psychology,* New York, Oxford University Press, 1971.

DATE DUE

SEP 9 75			
APR 12 77			
NOV 30 77			
MAR 15 '89			
			PRINTED IN U.S.A.